THE CENTER OF BUOYANCY

THE LIFE OF A SHIPWRIGHT SAILOR GUURL

DIANA TALLEY

Photograph copyrights for - Front cover: Elizabeth Thomson Becker. Aft cover: Sandy Lam

Cover design: Marion Roh, RohGraphics

Editing: Jenn Hager and Robin Dudley

Library of Congress Control Number: 2024916019

ISBN: 979-8-9912649-0-7 (paperback) - ISBN: 979-8-9912649-1-4 (EPUB)

Printed by IngramSpark in the United States of America

First Printing

"A rowdy tale of a woman finding solace, meaning, and buoyancy after the devastating loss of her father by suicide, working side by side with world-class tradesmen, building and repairing wooden boats, a profession of specific old-world skill, craft, and vocabulary concentrated in Port Townsend, Washington, a Victorian-era seaport that was once the port of entry for three-masted sailing ships."
—Jan Halliday

"I have known Diana Talley as a treasured friend for forty years. Her book brings alive some shared history of the Wild West when it seemed anything was possible, through gifted story telling from ground zero in the sailing, fishing, and boatbuilding communities. I was deeply moved by her stories, laughing and weeping along the way. Thanks, Diana, for a well-crafted and tender read."
—Tim Nolan

"Diana is a storyteller and a role model for women in the marine trades. She tells it like she sees it. Reading her book is like when you end up elbow-to-elbow with one of those barstool raconteurs who actually does have a ton of awesome stories. Belly up and enjoy."
—Robin Dudley, PhD

"Gut-honest storytelling, deep belly laughs, and some salty boatyard shockers. I learned about America in an era of profound transition. A timely reminder of how far women have come in the maritime trades. But what sticks with me most is Diana's loyalty, grit, and love--for a few good men and all the salty hearts that built our beloved community."
—Kaci Cronkhite

THERE IS A GLOSSARY OF MY TERMS AT THE BACK OF THIS BOOK

For my Dad.

Who likely would have been so proud of me.

CONTENTS

The center of buoyancy of a floating body

is the point about which all the body parts

exactly buoy each other

—Encyclopedia Britannica

PREFACE

My lovely man died after many years of living with every possible indignity Alzheimer's could throw at him. We faced it together, made a partnership pact, clear-eyed up front to live this time well. We did just that.

Finding joy was the purpose for writing when the entire rest of my day was devoted to the grave solemnity of caring for Rick. It started out as a daily meditation but quickly changed to so much more. Unexpected bonuses followed. As I searched for happy stories, the hard and sad ones also asked to be looked at. By writing them down, a heft of pain was excised from my heart. A weight I hadn't even noticed.

CHAPTER 1
LAUNCHING A LIFE
1975-1978

"Think positive and the rest will follow."
— Rick Petrykowski

BORED AND BEAUTIFUL

A t 22, I thought it was love that brought me to San Francisco, but it was just a man who I had been chasing, who couldn't run quite fast enough yet.

My mother had firm plans for her post-war baby girl. Sizing up my good looks, she believed that with training I could capitalize on my thick dark hair, bright blue eyes and full lips to snag a man with money and prestige, as she had done.

Like many other mothers of her generation, she taught me several skills that would ensure that once I had him, I'd keep him. Through her tutelage, I learned to excel in the role I was expected to play: proper cosmetic application, the importance of foundation garments, good manners, how to keep a house, polish silver, and sew.

After a year of accommodating myself to what I perceived as his every need, it was clear these skills weren't enough to interest him, let alone keep him. The last of many scraps of paper I would find in his pants pocket with another woman's name and phone number on it, encouraged me to finally quit doing his laundry and sharing his home. Needing to support myself, I found work in a garment shop on Union Street.

Ostensibly hired to sew alterations on fabulously expensive leather coats, my skills as a world-class flirt segued into boosting their sales department too. My dad had been a first-class flirt as well and could sell anything to anyone.

I found a modest house on San Francisco's Potrero Hill for $65/month to move to by myself, and would commute by bus to Union Street. I filled it with whatever furniture I could acquire for free. Rent was cheap but I paid for it every time I got up in the middle of the night to use the loo and stepped barefoot on the banana slugs that were my uninvited roommates.

Vintage clothing was popular during this time; clothes from the 40's were everywhere, especially in my closet. The cut and style was most favorable to my full-figured young body. Working in this clothing shop, I'd take care to dress my "single" best, covering the important parts; my choices always pushed the envelope of appropriate.

While I was waiting for a bus one morning, a middle-aged housewife walked quickly up behind me. My low-cut, pale blue cotton, sleeveless jump-suit was form-fitting. She grabbed the back of my garment, unzipped it and took a look inside. "She's not wearing any underwear; she's not wearing any underwear," she kept screaming as she ran down the street. "Hahahahaha." Abandoning the lesson for proper foundation garments was the first of my mom's teachings I let go.

San Francisco was not like the small-town Seattle I had come from. My Washingtonians were far less aggressive than what the crowded Bay Area population flouted. But even though my new city could be rough and wild, it offered so many more opportunities for entertainment, and my social life was full.

I went dancing most nights with my best friend Kurt, a beautiful German gay man; but I could never find a "date." After my heartfelt attempts at a romantic relationship, this platonic friendship was refreshing and easy to understand. Kurt introduced me to his family of friends who would come to the house on Potrero Hill for long, sumptuous dinner parties. It was here that I discovered my love of entertaining.

At work after a night of dancing, I'd pretend to know worldly things in conversations with the upper crust customers visiting the shop. So young and enthusiastic, I'd say things like "bonsoir" in the middle of the day with my sexiest French accent. Customers would look embarrassed for me. Clearly, I was struggling to fit in.

Something big was missing, though I couldn't know what. Just being beautiful wasn't cutting it, my life didn't feel whole, and I was bored. San Francisco quickly lost its luster, even with the flower in my hair.

Since I was looking for something different, my friend Annie suggested I move to Sausalito where she lived, a place called Gate 3.

Different doesn't begin to express how different it was. It was my first true culture shock.

Annie Hallet and Me on the shore of Gate 3

RAY

The door was open and it felt so inviting, I popped my head in. No one was there, but what was there, drew me inside. It was a boat. This place I came to understand later was a wooden boat building shop. The idea that people actually built boats had never crossed my mind. They were always just floating structures on the water, and nothing more.

The smell of the room was delicious, spicy and pungent. Fresh wood shavings and sawdust littered the wood planked floor all messy-like, and weird looking hand tools lay on a long workbench. The warm afternoon light filtered through a bank of windows and stacks of lumber were here and there, extra long pieces leaning up against the wall.

Not just any boat; this was a Sid Skiff, a 16 footer in frame, which is arguably the most dramatic aspect of a boat under construction. The finished shape is recognizable, but only the ribs and backbone have been built. It's like looking inside a body still being formed and seeing the future it will become. Or so I thought. I'd never really looked at a boat up close before.

Alone, I stood in awe and understood for the first time what a boat really is: tradition, commerce, industry, art, history, beauty, community, voyaging, fluidity, adventure and a connection to the sea and everything that lives in it, on it or by it. The possibilities were endless, and my worldview instantly got very big. It truly felt like a bolt of lightning struck me, humbled, where I stood. I knew this was something I had to learn to do.

Ray, John and Janice Speck - 1977

I soon met Ray Speck: soft-spoken, funny, and articulate. A joie de vivre emanated from this wicked good boat builder of my brand new piece of personal inspiration. Overwhelmed with emotion and knowing nothing save an unexpected purpose to my life, I begged him for a job. I would gladly sweep the shop – about my only potential skill – and of course I'd work for free, just for a chance to start my dream by working with this talented boat builder.

Ray couldn't have been kinder as he let me down, explaining a small one-man shop had no room for what he knew then (as I know now) that a young, unskilled, inexperienced, clueless anybody, such as myself, would only be a distraction and never a help. He wished me well as I left to seek an "in" elsewhere.

A MAJOR TOOL

I've heard it said that some women from my generation have had to bring extra skills into the workplace in order to secure a position in the professional sailing or commercial fishing industry. Oft times it would be cooking, the hardest job on a boat. I found this to be true in the boat building industry also, though cooking wasn't it for me.

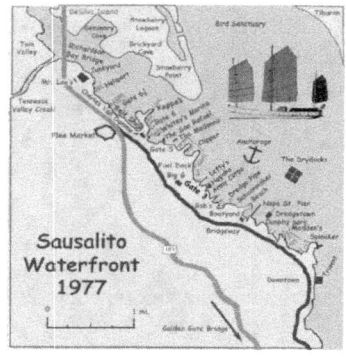

The Gates in Sausalito were originally the working part of the waterfront. Many ships had been built here during World War II. This was a hidden world from the wealth and tourism close by. Accessed by a potholed dirt road, the short distance from Sausalito's thoroughfare to the Gate 3 parking lot didn't inspire. It felt like entering into a time warp as almost nothing about it seemed 20th century. Mounds of dirt covered with native scrub plants helped hide the hidey-hole. Dead cars were parked where they'd died, and boats pulled ashore, the same. Children ran about, dirty and happy with every kind of dog as their sidekicks. The women were outstandingly beautiful and carried themselves with immense grace and style and the men were rough and tumble. Everyone seemed amenable and welcoming to new residents. Dirt lanes led to sub-neighborhoods where shacks and sheds housed tools and maritime commerce along with several families.

Every manner of floating home was tied chockablock to the original work dock from the ship-building days. The pier was holding tough. Skiffs and rowboats and small sailing craft were too numerous to count. Floating homes unable to tie up had built a series of walkways extending from the beach, connecting another sub-neighborhood. Wooden gangplanks were their access.

The tide would come and go and the smell was decidedly high

volume humanity and low tide. Miles and miles of extension cords were strung about, their source of power stolen from the paying customers on the Sausalito hills that lauded over this mystical place. Humanity beyond the shore-side floating homes were living in dozens of anchor-out boats. The anchorage was loaded. Curiously inviting and massively challenging, it was a lively, colorful, accepting community.

Housing was nonexistent since I didn't have a boat. A flatbed truck of unknown ownership with a plywood box on the back sat empty. With no windows and only a crawl-through door and sitting headroom, it looked like home to me. I moved right in. This truck was parked on the Sausalito Shipwright's Co-op property. According to their bylaws, anyone using said property must be a member. The Co-op owners held a meeting to decide what to do about me. I was invited to attend.

Stating their position and legal requirements, they offered me a membership. Already craving an opportunity to "get into boats," I didn't need to mull it over. YES, please! There was a minor hitch. Dues would be six dollars per month and every new member was required to bring in a major tool. "Hmmm. A major tool. What's a major tool? All I have is an orange screwdriver." "Oh you know, something like a bandsaw." "What's a bandsaw?"

They couldn't have been kinder to me. Every one of them just sat silently and no one laughed, waiting for my response. After a moment of mulling, I offered that I had one other tool I could bring to the boatyard: a massage table. I don't remember any kind of open discussion, just knowing looks amongst themselves. A vote was taken and unanimously I was accepted as their new dues paying member. My table and massage expertise would be traded for rudimentary instruction in boat building. A very good trade.

"Diana! I wrecked my back," was often heard at the end of most days. With their help, I learned some valuable skills and made my beginning. My major boatyard tool was one of the most used at the Co-op while I was there.

MY FIRST BOAT RESTORATION

Still knowing only that I wanted to start, my first boat restoration was pulled off entirely by committee. My community committee at Gate 3 put together everything I needed for the lessons I would get from the boys at the co-op.

Someone knew of a retired flat-bottomed cedar skiff, currently serving as a planter box outside a realtor's office in Sausalito. It magically showed up. The shipwrights took turns teaching me some basics: how to sharpen tools, scraping and sanding, elemental metalwork, how to make oarlock pads, how to seal a dried-up old wooden boat bottom. They lent me tools. All kinds of paints, goos, fasteners, oars and accoutrements were freely and generously given. (Someone offered to paint the name on her stern.)

Locally, there was a famous wooden boat named the *Diana Dollar*. Tongue in cheek, I decided to name her the *Diana Dime*.

Launch day came and a good amount of neighbors and friends treated it like a momentous occasion. Finally in the water, friends on the docks threw dimes at me, as blessings.

Without fully understanding what I'd taken on, I realized only then that I now owned my first wooden "yacht." I had access to the water beyond a shoreline and I had better learn how to row, what with the fierce afternoon winds common to the bay.

The *Diana Dime*

This was my first real step to becoming a waterman.

THE MARIN CITY FLEA MARKET

Every Saturday, rain or shine, we all went to the Marin City Flea Market located in a large dirt field about a mile from the Gates. We went to buy, sell or just perambulate. With acres of space, it was one of the largest flea markets in the Bay area.

Marin City was deeply connected historically to the Gates and also was a stark presence that differed visually from the wealth of downtown and the hills. A former dairy farm, in 1941 an enormous housing development was built for the shipyard workers who came for the defense jobs of World War II. Working at Marinship, the Sausalito waterfront shipyard, they had launched 93 liberty ships in less than three years at what we now called simply the Gates.

Lindsey Cage had moved here from Louisiana to work at Marinship during the war, and said Louisiana was a good place to be away from. He was a close friend of Don Arques, the patriarch of the Gate 3, 5 and 6 scene, who enabled that community to flourish on the Marinship property he had bought surplus after the war. Lindsey had a vast scrap pile that was a treasure trove to all who appreciated the "Bank of Lindsey." You could barter or buy useful "repurposing" stuff needed for your project. Known as Black Santa, he gave all the children at Gate 3 a big Christmas present every year. He founded and ran the flea market.

New to the waterfront, I'd become acquainted with the middy blouse, an historical naval uniform of midshipmen. Square cut with a full collar, they were built of quality wool and meant to last. Most of the sailor-boys on the waterfront wore them, and longing to be a sailor-guurl too, I imagined wearing one would help me be just that.

Walking through the flea, I found a guy selling a pile of middies along with 13-button Navy sailor bell bottom pants. I found my size in the stack of middy blouses and put it on. The fit was perfect. "I'll buy it!"

Being a hot summer day I wanted to take it off. There is a

protocol on how to do that. Being ignorant, I created a scene instead. Treating it was like a sweater and pulling it up from the front bottom, I got stuck mid-removal. So tight was the tension on my body, I was frozen and couldn't make it or my arms move another inch, up or down. My tank top had ridden up with the weight of the wool and I wasn't wearing a brassiere. Half naked now, I yelled a muffled cry through the thick navy blue wool, "Help!" The poor guy had to pull it down for me and then instruct me how to do it right. I was laughing so hard, tears streamed down my face. Everyone else around me was too.

Me n my Middy

"I suppose you don't want it now?" he asked.

"No! I definitely want to buy it now!"

CALLOUSED HANDS

I couldn't find a "date" living in Sausalito, so after a year or so I decided to move home to the Great Pacific Northwest where it had never been a problem. And yet I still craved the lifestyle I'd been introduced to at Gate 3, living on a houseboat and pursuing a career in boatbuilding.

I investigated the houseboat community of Lake Union in Seattle to find it was a completely different universe than what I expected, and beyond my financial or cultural reach. I re-grouped. Still hungry for a life of boat building, I was unable to put myself into a place where I could start. My dreams seemed hopeless. In the professional world, experience mattered and no one would hire me without experience. Catch 22. I enrolled in college instead.

Friends from Bainbridge Island invited me over one weekend. They introduced me to Al Davenport, an older man who lived anchored out on a small houseboat in Eagle Harbor. He was a kind of self-appointed "fleet admiral" who maintained a shadowy control over any and all boats anchored in the bay that weren't occupied. He represented himself as their caretaker. I told him of my hope to find a liveaboard situation and he pointed to a large steel-hulled retired commercial fishing boat named Ruby, anchored across the bay. "You can move right in," he said. So I did.

It was heaven for several months until the owner appeared and found me living on it. After some tense negotiations, I agreed to purchase the beast. All those months, I was rowing ashore every day and then by foot, ferry and bus, commuted to the University of Washington.

Poor, always poor, I applied for a job through the work-study program to help with my finances. I was still able to find something that paralleled boat building.

I had heard a story told, maybe a Jack London story, where a young green fellow walked the docks at Fisherman's Terminal in Ballard, looking for a chance as a deckhand on a fish boat. Because he was asking for a job, the captain looked at his hands. They were soft, smooth and unsullied by hard work, and a bellwether of inexperience.

I remembered this story when I applied for my first paid job as a carpenter through the work-study program in the drama set department at the UW. I looked my employer in the eyes and said, "I'm a carpenter. See my hands?" Rowing ashore daily, my hands were calloused. He hired me on the spot. Suddenly, I had to learn how to use a tape rule, square, even a pencil properly!

It was obvious I was unskilled at the very best. But everyone in the department showed me the way, never openly judged and helped me to become a beginner carpenter.

MY BUG

We were a couple for 26 years, together longer than any other romantic relationship in my life. We helped each other, went places and got better together. She was a 1961 Volkswagen Bug and I loved her. She taught me how to use mechanical tools when I couldn't afford a mechanic, which led to my becoming proficient. I could jack her up and drop the engine in a few heartbeats. Elegant in her simplicity, she guided me. I bought her in San Francisco only because I could afford her price of $350, cheap due to her life-long recurring illness of "mal de transmission." The stick shift had to be forcibly held in the first gear position. I learned to love second.

The manual *"How to Keep Your Volkswagen Alive For the Complete Idiot"* became my bible. Since she had so few moving parts, tearing into her engine to repair or maintain became wildly fun. We went everywhere and I learned more than a modicum of patience because of it.

Being German, she let me know that driving through a hot desert was horribly uncomfortable for her. Often, her engine would just stop and I'd ease her to the side of the highway. And since she was even more stubborn than myself, I learned not to fret about her occasional strikes. I would simply roll myself another cigarette, light it up and enjoy the moment. Afterwards, she would always start right up and down the road we'd go. Over the decades, I came to see these temporary uncontrollable stops as something spiritual, her way of saving me from an accident that might be waiting ahead, maybe around the next corner.

I never saw her as the rest of the world might have. I leaned on her for all modes of transportation. When moving back to Washington State from San Francisco, I had a flat- bottomed skiff I wanted to take with me; my first restoration. With the help of friends, I tied her transom to my back bumper, led the bowline over the top of the car to be tied off to the front bumper and fashioned side-ties to the car handles; my first pick-up truck. We drove slow those 900 miles all the way up I-5, but I always drove slow.

While living in Seattle and commuting to college, her transmission screamed, "I quit." This time she was stuck in second gear. I, along with most college students, lacked money for anything other than bare necessities. Seattle is a town of many hills. I learned that if you were to choose a gear to get stuck in, second was King. Avoiding major arterials and steep road grades, we navigated very well for months.

One early morning, coffee cup in hand, I left my house and went to get in the car. The car wasn't there. I even turned around to make sure I'd left my house. Yup, she was gone. Beyond distraught, I called the Coppers and anyone else I could think of to report a theft. My beloved car! After school that day and hitchhiking both ways, I came home to a note that read, "I found it!" A friend had taken it upon himself to cruise the neighborhood and found her just two blocks from my home. Apparently, the thieves had hot wired her and tried to drive away. Two blocks stuck in second gear was too much. They had abandoned her.

Though deeply offended that they were blind to her gifts, I was giddy to get her back.

NILS - THE NORWEGIAN BACHELOR

Ruby Jean with angel wings

"The ugliest boat in the bay" was the affectionate title given to

Ruby, my new home. I was the fifth person to live anchored out in Eagle Harbor. Purchased for $1,000, it broke my bank, but like the rest who chose this lifestyle, the privacy and simplicity fed my soul, as did the unfettered view of downtown Seattle and the Cascade mountain range.

New to this kind of living, my learning curve was steep. So ignorant, in fact, I never thought to ask reasonable questions of my more experienced neighbors. "Am I doing this right?" I just "did it" without much thought. Later, my middle name would become "Comfort" but for now it was, "D'oh!"

I'd acquired a serviceable rowboat, learned a few knots to secure her and a bailing bucket for the rain. Every morning I'd jump in, cast off and row ashore. Returning at night, I'd tie her up and "step" aboard. Ruby's freeboard was substantial, so this step was always athletic. Living at anchor, I was a TV show for anyone with eyes: a kind of slap-stick comedy.

Nils was a retired merchant seaman in his 80s. A lifelong Norwegian bachelor, he was taciturn and kept to himself. His modest 26 foot cabin cruiser was anchored strategically to blend in with the shoreline. I never even knew he was there until he rowed over one day to abruptly make my acquaintance.

Coming alongside, I heard his gruff directive, "Build yourself a ladder!" He loudly threw some short two by fours into my rowboat and quickly rowed away. "D'oh!"

Nils Johnson

UNCLE BRUCE

A professional diver, Bruce retrieved the wallet I foolishly lost overboard and wouldn't accept pay. We became consequential friends and he, a chosen brother I could always count on.

Bruce had a million dollar smile and a compassionate ear, and was genuinely interested in everyone he met. You always knew how he felt about anything, especially you. We would often run into each other on Winslow Way, lean against Sandy's Barber Shop wall and talk until the world was put right. He was the guy you'd want to see when you were in a pickle. I desperately needed money once. Without hesitation he gave me a thousand bucks and blessed me with his selflessness, affection and trust. I always called him Uncle Bruce.

Bruce MacLay

He approached me with an idea he was developing, a roughly 6 mile rowing event from Alki Beach in West Seattle to Eagle Harbor on Bainbridge Island. There would be hundreds of human powered vessels, crossing shipping lanes to gather on the lawn at Winslow Wharf for a salmon feast and awards ceremony. He was going to call it The Cross Sound Rowing Race. What did I think? Still lacking an understanding of the joys of rowing, I told him it was the stupidest thing I'd ever heard of. He went ahead with it anyway. Still wildly popular, it is widely known as the premier rowing event of the Pacific Northwest.

BATHING ON A BOAT

Living anchored out, I didn't have electricity, water or a septic system. But I did have a skiff, privacy and a wonderful view. Early on, I started my maritime trades career as a finisher. It can be a dirty, dirty line of work. Bathing could be an issue. Carrying buckets of water out, standing naked and sort of washing oneself, was almost funny.

I had some shore-side friends who cared for me. "If you ever want to take a bath, please feel free to come out. Anytime, you're welcome." I'm proud and autonomous. "Oh, no thanks. I'm positive I'll never want to do that."

Later, after a particularly dirty, dirty day, I longed for a bath. I remembered my friends and drove to their place. Expecting them to be there expecting me, they were gone. Damn, I'd brought my towel and shampoo.

Of course the house was locked except for the window to the bathroom. They had said anytime. Finding something to stand upon, I fell forward through the tiny opening and collected myself, right next to the claw foot tub.

I had the presence of mind to lock the bathroom door before I stripped down and delivered myself to a perfect tub of hot soothing water to soak my working bones. Soon enough my friends arrived home. They saw my car, so didn't call the Coppers, when they found themselves locked out of their bathroom. They let me finish my tub. We laughed a lot when I was dry. But I never did that again.

LORI AND I

We ate at Mac's Tavern, with our elbows on the bar. It was the local eatery on the dock by Winslow Wharf. Every working day it was burgers and fries. We were immensely prosperous at $5 an hour and highly sought after.

We are new to the industry. It never occurred to us that anyone with opposing thumbs could do it. Boat owners didn't enjoy finish work. Sanding was tedious, repetitive and hard on a body. Who knew? We sure didn't.

Our shoot-from-the-hip business plan meant we never read instructions on the cans of product. Just open and go, go, go. Something other than throw-away brushes and dust in the varnish or even knowing there were different grits of sandpaper: this information wasn't important to us and no one told us. And yet, everyone wanted Lori and me because we had opposing thumbs.

A BUSINESS PLAN

Entering the yacht finishing service industry, I also had to come to grips with my attitude about American capitalism. I never fully embraced the money part of business. There was something unkind about the drive for it.

My first customers were all people I knew and I was having trouble justifying charging my rate of pay to my friends. Seeking counsel, I put this dilemma to Mark, a successful large-business owner.

"Diana, if you don't become friends with every one of your customers, you're doing something wrong," he told me.

This business plan has served me well ever since.

DAD

As a child in the 1950s, I lived with my family in the suburbs of West Vancouver, B.C. Mom kept herself and the house in tip-top shape while Dad was the provider. Family roles were defined and conventional.

Dad came home from work, wearing his dark suit and tie, white starched shirt and hard-soled polished shoes. His full head of hair combed straight back; the natural curl fell into a rhythm and, being prematurely white, looked like wavelets on a shoreline. His neatly trimmed mustache, sparkling blue eyes and knowing look rivaled the Hollywood leading men of his era. I adored him.

Mom's mother, my Nana, adored him as well. She gifted him yearly with crazy wild underwear in leopard, zebra and tiger prints. They would hang on the clothesline like flags of my grandmother's self-confidence. It was their happy private link.

Mom and Dad threw cocktail parties in our spacious living room. Music played on the record player while husbands and wives danced convivially. Children were allowed a brief appearance. Dad would ask me to dance; let me stand on his shoes while he led, doing the waltz or the "One-Two-Three, Cha Cha Cha." Then off to bed I'd go.

I was sick one year. So sick in fact I missed a good deal of second grade. Eventually my tonsils were removed, but not before being bed-ridden took its toll on my hygiene. High fevers produced headaches that were so fierce, my long braid never saw shampoo or a hairbrush for weeks. It became a tangled nest of hardened snarls. Mom and Dad had a long talk and decided my hair would have to be cut off at the nape of my neck.

I had never had a haircut; it was a kind of symbol of non-compliance. The standard Canadian "do" at that time was short, neat hair. We were definitely outlier Americans who knew how to drink tea with milk and sugar but laughed just a notch too loudly.

Dad took on the deed. Still in his business suit, he grabbed a pair of scissors. We sat together on the edge of the bathtub and both began to cry. He couldn't do it. He just couldn't do it. Instead he found a bottle of baby oil and lovingly and patiently slathered my snarls with it and combed out the braid until it was tame. It took hours but we kept my flag of individuality.

Something went between Mom and Dad when I was born. I never got the story. They chose my first and middle name together, but Dad would not conform. He never in my life called me by my first name, only by my second. No one else carried that placard; it was his alone to display, our private link that I honor still.

Dad was an outdoorsman. A child himself of the teens and 1920s who came of age in the hills of Idaho, he loved to fish for steelhead in the wild British Columbia rivers. He and my brothers would drive north in the Pontiac, loaded with camping and fishing gear for our family vacations. They always went somewhere so remote, access was limited but also close to a tiny train depot. Mom and I would catch the Canadian Pacific Railway out of Vancouver town, and travel in style and comfort, in those heavy powerful cars, to wherever the boys were camped. So happy to be reunited, I would jump into his waiting arms from the top step of the passenger car. These were almost the only times I would see Dad without his suit and tie.

He did have a workshop out back behind the house where he did Dad things. The boys might go and work alongside him there, but I was never invited. Whenever I would pop in to see what he was doing, we never worked together. Rather, he would put his tools down and tell me a story and I would become "rapt" around his little finger.

He adored me too. This was our defined role, to be the two members in good standing of the Mutual Admiration Society.

I slept in a four-poster, dark, rich bed made of cherry, with my black and white mustachioed cat, Boots. My bedroom floor was figured linoleum, littered with images of brightly colored animals, circus tight-rope walkers, lion tamers, fairy princesses, and Paul Bunyan and his blue ox Babe.

Every night my Dad would put me to bed. He'd sit on the side in his dark suit and tie and ask me what the story should be about. I'd lean over the edge and peruse the options, so many characters to choose from on my linoleum floor. Once I decided, he'd launch into a tale of depth and magic, taking me to faraway places and filling me with wonder.

These evening moments did far more than just deepen my admiration for him. His gift of storytelling served as a spiritual guide of sorts which I've called upon throughout my life to evoke warmth and humor while building my own private links through relationships. Along with his sincerity and kindness and pure and open heart, I wanted to be just like him. Dad will always inform my daily life.

CHAPTER 2
DAMN THE TORPEDOES
1979-1980

"Risk your life. Do something that will let you know how close death is and how amazing life is."
—Brion Toss

FALLING OFF

There's something horribly dangerous about the assumptions we make when it might be better to ask a timely question.

I was already living, anchored out on my own boat in Eagle Harbor. My first wooden sailboat was tied alongside. A 26 foot sloop named *Larksong*, it had been a gift from a bad boyfriend, in lieu of the bouquet of roses I surely did deserve. By all appearances, I was quite likely a sailor-guurl, but had yet to learn a stitch about it. Owning a boat doesn't distill down to knowledge. I still thought that when you put the sails up, wind always came from behind.

A young sailor boy owned a luscious Danish racing sloop named *Sabina*, and asked me to accompany him for a day sail. I was interested in this sailor boy and so said yes. I wore my best sailing togs, a crisp new ball cap, rubber boots and mascara.

Sailing south out of the bay in a fair north breeze, he decided to put up the spinnaker. Handing me the helm, he ran forward and told me to fall off as soon as the chute was set.

A spinnaker, or chute, is a large, light, billowy sail that is only set when the wind is coming from behind. Very powerful, it demands focus to keep it filled, and can become an untamed kind of beast within seconds if the helmsman blows it. Falling off changes the direction of the boat to sail more downwind.

"OK!" sez I. Too ignorant to know what he was talking about and embarrassed by that, I figured there's only two ways to turn to probably fall off, whatever falling off might mean, so I never thought to state my position.

Standing on the very bow, he raised the sail all manly-like and yelled to fall off. Smiling broadly, I turned the tiller smartly so the boat went directly into the wind instead of off the wind. I had blown it.

The massive spinnaker almost pushed Paul overboard and only

luck and great strength kept him aboard. He screamed with a tone of voice I think I never heard again, "Fall off, Fall off! The other way."

Like all lessons learned the hard way, I'll forget no more how to fall off.

ROMANCE AND PAIN

Taking a chance on building a deeper friendship, Paul and I set off on his father's Columbia 21 (a 21' fiberglass daysailer without a cabin or any kind of shelter) for a three week cruise of the San Juan archipelago. The friendship took, so after returning, we went the next step and moved in together on his anchored out houseboat. This began my maritime education in earnest.

Paul emulated everything I thought I wanted to be. He had a well-equipped shore-side wood shop and generously invited me to use it. Here is where I could design, lay out and build things on my own, with tremendous help from him. I jumped into learning about boat building. Reading everything available, I walked the docks, spoke to anyone with a willing ear or opinion, stepped aboard whenever I could and paid attention.

My first design and build - *Rose* - named for my Nana

Paul's 32' Danish racing sloop, *Sabina*, introduced me to inshore sailing, reading the wind, currents and tides. Engineless, it sharpened my skills. We sailed together often. I also learned patience.

Paul was a third generation Yugoslav purse seiner. His grandparents met after immigrating to the United States, they settled on the south shore of Eagle Harbor, Bainbridge Island, close to where his houseboat was anchored. His father and uncles grew the family business, each owning several boats and becoming highliners of the fleet. Paul and his brothers grew up fishing salmon with the large crews. I was invited to join his dad's boat as a deckhand. I loved catching fish. It made sense to me.

Wanting to stand on his own away from the family business, Paul looked for alternative fishing opportunities, something autonomous. He leased a Puget Sound gill netter one season. I was his deckhand but it never felt right to either of us. So he re-invented a traditional fishery from "the old country" he'd learned about from his grandfather: Pot fishing for bottom fish. Trial and error and design alterations produced a smart collapsible fish-catching machine that could neatly stack on deck. Concurrently, we also tried our luck at beach seining.

We were soon commercially fishing for bottom fish out of his 14-foot wooden rowboat, *Codfish*. Money wasn't important to us. It was all about romance and pain.

One January evening, our beach seine payed out in frozen clumps over the stern of our rowboat at the mouth of Eagle Harbor. It was the coldest winter on record at that time and we had yet to discover gloves. Pulling by hand and looking at each other, we both said, "We need a vacation."

The cover of the 1979 January/February *Wooden Boat* magazine had a breathtaking photo of Bahamian sloops. This, we decided, was what we needed to graduate ourselves from the rowboat into a proper smack boat. We immediately booked a flight.

THE BAHAMAS

On February first, we left for a three-week vacation. First order of business was to find the sun, but tucked away in the recesses of our minds was the search for a boat. Not just any boat, lord knows we could have bought several half-rotten yachts back home. Our boat would have to be sound first, pretty next, and suitable for our purposes as a sailing fish boat.

We planned our itinerary. The effect of the cover photo of two Bahamian sloops side-by-side was fabulous, but their narrative was missing. We set out to discover those boat's stories. First stop, Nassau, Bahamas.

Bursting with anticipation, we struck gold on our first day. Within hours we'd seen every fishing smack or racing sloop in Nassau, all the shipyard piers and ways, and even the lonely beaches where an occasional boat was blocked up above the water's edge. Everywhere an owner could slap a new coat of paint on the bottom or topsides, we saw it.

Our first and lasting impressions of this fleet were that a great deal of pride went into designing, building and maintaining. Never before or since have we seen the same care and love applied together to produce such a population of enviable watercraft.

Every boat looked similar and yet each was unique in a subtle way. We found ourselves walking over and over past one particular boat anchored out beyond reach. Her lines and grace really caught our eye. We yelled from the beach to the men on board, who concerned themselves more with the business of cooking over a Dutch oven than with acknowledging hooting tourists. We tried renting a dinghy, but none were to be found. The last recourse was to dive in and swim for it.

Seeing our plight, a local sport fisherman offered to take us out to the boat of our dreams. "How much will it cost?"

"That's not the Bahamian way. We like to help people out."

As we paddled up to her, she seemed unmistakably familiar, like a friend from a past life. "Is the owner on board?"

"No. He's over at the fish market, but I'll take you to him."

We said goodbye to our new Bahamian friend and hello to a newer one as we transferred our loads and bodies from one boat to the next.

The scene at the market was a carnival of conch shells and laughter; young boys hatcheting filets of the day and women cooking up conch fritters, selling them for 10 cents apiece, and old men sharing stories in between singing out today's best prices. All this laced together with smiles the size of turtle shells. The warmest smile of all came from Alfred Bain, owner of our favorite boat.

As names and handshakes shared all around, we learned that Alfred had built her some 25 years prior. He lived on Andros Island, Mangrove Cay, and only came to Nassau occasionally to sell his live catch. But right then he was preparing for one of the legendary springtime regattas with his sleek racing sloop, the *Avenger*. We'd seen it earlier that day in the shipyard, along with his racing competitors, all having their spectacular party dresses painted on. We'd also seen it on the magazine cover that had called us to the Bahamas, where Alfred's fishing sloop had been helping step the mast of his racing sloop. Providence, our great friend, had brought us together.

"Would you ever consider selling your smack boat?"

There was another broad smile. "Every time I come to Nassau, someone wants to buy my boat." Little wonder, when it's about the prettiest one around. But it serves him well and to replace it with a new one would take six months' work and twice as much money as she's worth.

"Well, would you show it to us then?" A broader smile yet. Every man loves to show off his sweetheart.

Back on his boat in the two short hours that followed, we learned how he'd designed and constructed her with hand tools. *Horseflesh* was his favorite choice of building lumber. (*Horseflesh* or *Lysiloma Sabicu* is a kind of Bahamian mahogany wood.)

Paul and Alfred talked fishing shop and exchanged ideas on fish pots. As we had guessed, each boat was equipped with a live well for the purpose of transporting fish to the market. We had seen such affairs in Canadian trollers, but never as sophisticated and well designed as these. Holes in the midships planking allowed the free flow of salt water into and out of the boat and kept fish alive and swimming for days; solid bulkheads fore and aft of the live well, along with interior pyramidal walls side to side, answered every inshore sailing fisherman's need. When the boat heeled over, the weight of the water in the live well stayed in the center of the boat and never compromised its displacement or stability.

Even though Alfred wouldn't sell us his boat, we learned from him about simplicity of construction and lifestyle. When it was time to go, he talked of his home on Andros Island. "Could you come visit me there?" he asked.

By the time he would be home we had to be on our way, but we vowed to come back. And if we did, Alfred promised to help us build our own Bahamian sloop under his direction in his own backyard.

VELCRO

Our next stop was in San Juan, Puerto Rico, where our 13-seater airplane was grounded due to weather. We were stuck until the wind laid down. The airline put us up in a swanky hotel, and after checking in, we went to the bar. Three sailors shared our table. All of us were naturally drawn to each other: a Bahamian merchant seaman heading out on his next voyage; an American delivery captain, carrying a wooden sextant box, just finishing a trip; and a west-coast American wearing a Mickey Mouse t-shirt and jean jacket who asked where we were from. "We're from Seattle," Paul said.

Our new friend replied, "I don't know much about Seattle, but I live in Eagle Harbor on Bainbridge Island."

"Whoa!" said Paul. "We're not really from Seattle. We live in Eagle Harbor too. It's not that big. How could we not know you?"

The conversation was lively, deep into the night.

Wanting to travel with minimal luggage, I had made most of my clothes for this trip. My "uniform" was a pair of ankle-length, wrap-around culottes. They were lightweight, attractive and comfortable, and provided me with a modicum of dignity and "cover up" as I navigated the foreign culture of the Caribbean and Central America. They fastened with Velcro, a new technology to me.

Mid-evening I rose to use the bathroom. The sound was deafening to me alone, as I inadvertently stepped on my hem. Ripppppp went the Velcro as the aft half of my britches peeled away. Traveling light, I wasn't wearing any little pants.

With as much grace as I could muster and slowly so as not to give away my predicament, I reached down to the seat where half of my pants laid and re-secured them. No one at my table seemed to notice.

Feeling like I'd dodged a big one, I turned to face the table behind me. A family of five from Des Moines, Iowa: parents, children, the whole catastrophe, sat with faces of shock and joy.

What do you do when your pants fail you? I engaged the family in a conversation. Also stuck to weather but on their way home after a long vacation, they unanimously declared that this moment was the best part of their trip. I guess the moon over Old San Juan never shone so bright.

CHAPTER 3
HARDTACK
1980

"I have often marveled at the thin line which separates success from failure." —Ernest Shackleton

IZZY

A conversation in Puerto Rico providentially led to a Caribbean country we had never heard of. Coming from our world of privilege, Belize was a complete culture shock.

At that time about 95% of all commercial fishing in Belize was done with working sailboats. The country and its waters were abundant with colorful, attractive, and simple boats that were hand-hewn with a machete. We immediately knew that one would meet our needs.

All these boats were almost exactly the same, built of local hardwoods and pitch pine. Each had a large fish hold mid-ships, varying only in size, possibly craftsmanship and of course the type of recycled materials used to rig them. By traveling on buses, outboard skiffs, and hitchhiking in cars and sailboats, we were soon able to see almost every boat in the small country.

The boat we chose and were able to purchase was one of the largest of the fleet and built fairly well. It was 32 feet on deck, 9 feet wide and drew 3 1/2 feet. With no standing headroom below deck, it was a "get down on your knees and crawl." The rig consisted of a mast 35 feet high, the boom was 26 feet long and the jib carried a 13 foot club that was secured with a lashing through a hole in the stem. About 600 square feet of sail all together.

The western-rig sailboats we were familiar with generally had a forestay, shrouds and back or running backstays that support the mast from all angles, and keep it from tumbling down. In contrast, Belize's simply designed rigs boasted "bigger isn't always better," and worked well. The polypropylene bolt rope sewn to the luff of the jib served as the forestay we were used to sailing with. Without the jib up, the mast was only supported by the shrouds, so we were inclined to always carry that jib. Our shrouds were heavy-gauge twisted copper wire, connected to ceramic electrical insulator dead-eyes that likely served together earlier in an on-shore capacity.

Every boat was equipped with a dual-purpose depth sounder/river-anchor in the form of a 16 foot pole that lay on deck. When it looked like you might be getting into shallow water, someone would run forward, pick up the pole and stab the bottom. Pulling it up, they would yell out the depth. That same pole could be used to push deep into the Belize river mud and then tie off a bowline and you had a perfect river anchor. Internal ballast always consisted of a huge pile of dirty rocks and hundreds of large, demonstrative cockroaches.

This boat was to be our charming new home for a long time. Her name was *Isela #72* and was from San Pedro town on Ambergris Caye, an hour and a half ride north in a water taxi from Belize city. We called her *Izzy*.

We sailed her to Belize City, hauled her and did some repairs: built bunks and storage bins where the fish hold had been, and painted the bottom. Then we proceeded to buy anything we could find that was needed to assure we would be able to safely sail her the 6,000+ miles through the Panama Canal, out halfway to Hawaii and north to the Strait of Juan de Fuca and eventually home to Bainbridge Island.

You couldn't really buy much of anything in Belize. There were no charts of the area, because every year or so a hurricane would blow through and re-arrange any channels there might have been. We did manage to find a small-scale chart of the Caribbean Sea, a used sextant, a short-wave radio for time-keeping, one well-used life jacket, a leaky rubber life raft, sail needles, palm and twine, and some flashlights. Paul's brother Tom and his wife, Cheryl, visiting from the Northwest, brought down a proper compass, some HO249 tables, pilot charts, a book on sailing directions and *Bowditch*.

Just before we left, a Swiss woman named Anna, sailing her way around the world, came aboard as an extra hand for the leg to Panama. We were ready to go, but shared one last cup of coffee at Mom's Café with a sailor who had actually been to Panama. He drew a map of the opening to Limon Bay, or the eastern entrance to the Panama Canal, on a napkin as a final aid to navigation.

Away we went, ostensibly heading southeast, but in order to get there we first had to sail northeast to avoid the Barrier Islands and coastline farther south. Once we left the islands behind and with no shelter from the fetch, the Caribbean was kicking up a helluva storm, with strong winds from the Northeast and huge waves.

I had never sailed in the ocean before. This introduction during a proper storm reinforced my belief that the ocean was always rough and never calm. That false belief loaned a kind of strength and confidence to me and kept me from being afraid.

We pinched it best we could, making northing until we felt safe to tack south towards Panama. There was only one island to avoid on this stretch – Lighthouse Reef. So beautiful! Just as we passed it, it to our lee, the jib blew out. We couldn't steer away from this reef under mainsail alone. Paul looked at me and said, "You're the guy with the sewing experience." And he was right. So I ran forward, dropped the jib, held on to the toe rails with my naked toes, and quickly sewed it back together with a Homeward Bounder stitch. Up went the jib and we clawed ourselves away from the reef and continued on.

The Caribbean Sea is a body of water unlike the Pacific and Atlantic in that she has a lot of fetch but is very shallow. With any kind of wind, the waves get really big. I remember being on deck, admiring the Sea in all her majesty, and watching these huge waves moving towards us. They looked as tall as our 35-foot mast, and with every wave set, *Izzy* sailed up to the top, peaked and sailed down into the next trough. Over and over, just like a duck.

I was never frightened, partly because this was before Momdom. No one on the planet depended on my existence to keep them alive. But also my generation was taught – and I fully believed – that we would never live past the age of 30. I was still pushing 30, so I was living the dream.

Having said that, I will share a confidence. This part of the trip, my sleeping attire consisted of a tank top, no pants and no little pants.   One of my jobs was to handle the sails at night. Almost every night I'd be down below in my dry bunk and hear, "DROP THE MAIN!" After dark, the wind would rise and overpower our mains'l. I'd run on deck, creep forward, hang onto the mast and shrouds, undo the main halyard, and yell, "READY!"   Then Paul, the helmsman, would have to turn the boat into the howling-wind which was always the worst part of the procedure. And always, every time, as we came into the wind with the boat violently bucking and the waves crashing on deck, usually up to my waist, I'd pee my pants. But I had neither pants, nor little pants and the waves always swept the deck anyway. Additionally, whilst dropping the mainsail, as we're hobby-horsing and I'm pulling the lacing around the mast down, gathering up the sail best I could, the headboard (the hardwood triangular pieces of wood bolted to the peak of the sail) would come down like a wild thing alive.   It was always a gamble who would win, the head-board or my head.

After many days, we reached the point of land we had been pinching the sails to avoid: Cabo Gracias A Dios! or Cape Thanks To God! Christopher Columbus, who named it, probably had the same kind of sailing experience we were having. We were finally able to ease the sheets and tend to other matters, like the multiple salt sores on our bums.

Sailing southeast for several more days, we again approached land. It had been overcast the entire time, so we'd been unable to get a sun shot with our sextant to locate our position. It looked to be a very rich coast, or likely Costa Rica. Not a sign of humanity or ships had we seen. Panama was bound to be left, and so we turned that way: intuitional navigation.

Eventually, we came upon the first lights we'd seen in 3 weeks and realized that this probably was the eastern side of the Panama Canal. The winds were light as we ghosted along in the early evening. Pulling out our Mom's Café napkin aid to navigation, it was clearly the entrance to Limon Bay. We basked in the pleasure of our success, feeling fairly smug.

Our deckhand Anna said, "Look at all the large container ships anchored in the bay." Moments later Paul chimed in, "Oh my god, they aren't anchored, they are moving and they are moving directly at us! We don't have any running lights!"

We grabbed a flashlight, shone it on our mainsail and hoped for the best. Definitely feeling at full attention, we watched each massive wall of steel barely miss us, and skirted disaster.

Sailing to the quarantine anchorage, our shakedown had left us feeling triumphant and possibly a bit over-confident for what must come next.

PROVISIONING IN PANAMA

After clearing customs, we made our way to the Cristobal Yacht Club, where we discovered every kind of international sailor and boat. This would be our haven as we prepared not only for the Panama Canal, but for the Pacific passage home.

The community of world class sailors embraced us wholeheartedly. Our boat was by far the smallest and most humble, yet we were treated as equal adventurers. Feeling a part of this family of like-minded souls helped build our confidence in our endeavor. *Izzy* was affectionately known as the "coconut boat."

Here we began the re-fit and provisioning which was a mighty responsibility. The 3-week passage from Belize had shown us some weaknesses in the sails and rig, which became the first order of business, right after buying cigarettes. We'd run out on that trip, along with many foodstuffs. I was determined to do a better job this time.

The yacht club was within walking distance of downtown Colon. Our jib was in tatters so a sailmaker was our first search. Locals showed us the way to the best, on that side of the country. A big man, possibly in his 70s or 80s, he wore coke-bottle glasses and used a measuring stick with 3 inch numbers, "So to be able to read it," he said. A lifelong sailmaker, he had a few more left in him to build. We acquired some heavy sailcloth and poly line for the boltrope, and left him with the materials. He was excited to be building traditional sails for a working Caribbean sailboat.

Next we searched for heavy line to rig up running backstays to reduce the working (the damaging movement) of the mast in a heavy seaway. We also needed hardwood for deck cleats and bolts to fasten them down. Simply built, this boat had no cleats to tie the lines we would need to transit the Panama Canal.

We decided to build and install lazy jacks as well, as an extra hand or two on the forward deck. Those lazy jacks later taught us that when the main needed to be dropped in high seas and winds, instead of turning the bow into the wind – our usual sphincter-awakening experience – we merely needed to wing out the main boom until it was in line with the wind and then just drop the sail. No white knuckles or extra pain for the boat or ourselves.

Colon was a small sleepy town. The world of sail and commerce passed through it but it had not commercialized itself yet with shops like Fisheries Supply or West Marine. At the time we faced the truism that if Colon didn't have it, you likely didn't need it. Thankfully many boat owners at the yacht club generously gave us spare items we would need later.

Shopping for groceries to last a 2-month voyage took some research and thought. What kind of foods would be nutritious, palatable and last? How would we store them and how much water should we carry? I made these decisions and shopped at the local markets, and brought it all back by taxi.

Transiting the canal was the last item to navigate, and many rules needed to be followed. The boat was required to have four line handlers on board as well as the captain, to handle the four points of attachment from the boat to the locks. A canal transit advisor or a pilot was assigned to each vessel. You were required to maintain a speed equal to every other kind of boat transiting during your appointment, at least 5 knots. Locks would never wait for a straggler to catch up. And, an appointment must be made.

Hillel, Knud, Paul and Anna sailing Gatun Lake

We carried an 18 hp 2-cylinder Johnson outboard that only ran on one cylinder. It was nothing we could rely on, but it was all we had. Our community of sailors stepped up to help. Three foreign sailing hitchhikers, waiting for the next boat going their way, offered to be deckhands. Knud was from Denmark, Hillel was from Israel and Anna, who had been our deckhand from Belize, was from Switzerland. Boat owners on the dock lent us the four extra lines that needed to be very long, as well as offering local knowledge as to protocols. Appropriate food and drink must be provided, not only for the line handlers but specifically for the canal transit advisor. We were told that all advisors expected a bottle of spirits to help savor the day. Wanting to comply – we weren't ourselves any kind of drinkers -- we bought a cheap pint of rum, thinking it would suffice. Hats off to this pilot! Coincidentally, he came from Belize. There was no place to relax down below and no head or bathroom of any kind for our 10-hour transit.

We paid our $35, filled out the paperwork, and made our appointment. Everyone assembled early on our appointed day, but on our way to the locks, the outboard died 200 feet from our slip. Forced to cancel, we were never charged extra for our delay. The next day went better. Keeping up with the procession was our main concern. Whenever we could, we raised sails and moved along at a generous pace. I'm sure I saw the pilot smiling every time we did.

Late in the day entering the Miraflores – our last set of locks – a huge ocean-going tug boat offered to tow us the rest of the way side-tied. Plenty tired by now and fighting the outboard, we accepted their kind invitation. As the locks finally opened, the tug reversed hard without notice. Paul grabbed the tiller but the rudder slammed heavily to the side. Only later would we discover that the pintle, a bronze part of the rudder attachment assembly, was lethally weakened in that maneuver.

We tied up at the Balboa Yacht Club on the Pacific side in Panama City to drop off our crew and pilot. Since we had no sleeping accommodations to offer, they, along with our borrowed gear, took the train back to Colon with our deep thanks.

We spent the next few days wrapping up legal requirements, purchasing things and taking long walks in the historic city. We called our families, upbeat and over-confident, before our next step.

LEAVE – RETURN – LEAVE AGAIN

Without fanfare, we cast off and headed south from Balboa, confident in our vessel, crew and decision. We had strapped the outboard motor on deck and were dependent only on the winds and currents now. We soon discovered that the Bay of Panama had almost no wind and only the currents were moving us slowly south. After three days of mostly drifting, we gained Cape Mala, 110 miles from where we had started. Looking over the side, the bottom of our boat was already fouled with a tremendous amount of growth. We decided to turn back north to get the bottom cleaned and repainted. Shortly after turning, the lower pintle on the rudder broke in very light airs. This was, no doubt, from our being side-tied to the tug in the Panama Canal. After nursing our way to Balboa, we bought some bottom paint and eyebolts to repair the rudder.

The island of Taboga was 12 miles from Panama City. It had a perfect sandy beach to careen on where we could scrape and repaint the bottom. At least, that is what we were told. Contrary to the average tides on the Caribbean side which were at most 3 feet, the Pacific side tides were huge, averaging 13 feet but, depending on the season, as much as 23 feet. Knowing the tides would serve and low on cash, we decided to do our own bottom job there.

Taboga was strictly protected by the local community. Tourism was allowed, but only in certain areas and under the watchful eyes of the police. Unaware of the rules, we blithely set our sails at the convenient high tide and aimed our boat for shore. While sailing in, a uniformed guard with a gun was running down the beach yelling at us in Spanish. It was crystal clear what he was trying to tell us but we kept our heading anyway. Standing on the bow and wearing next to nothing, I was shameless. "Uno momento por favor. Uno momento," I said, hoping my gender and attire would keep him from shooting me. He did not shoot, and in fact, was very kind and understanding. After the keel hit the sand, we took the time to have a different conversation with him. "Lo siento mucho. No estaremos aquí mucho tiempo." (I'm very sorry. We won't be here long.) And we weren't. After fixing the rudder we roughly scraped the hull and globbed on as much bottom paint as we could between squalls.

On the following high tide, we floated off and set our sails to head south again. With a boatload of food and $11 in our pockets, we asked for a safe passage from the huge cross on the hill overlooking the bay and Village of Taboga.

FIXING THE RADIO

A week after leaving Panama, we took a wave that deposited about 2 drops of saltwater on our shortwave radio. It quit working. This instrument was more than just an avenue to radio plays on the

BBC; it was our only sure-fire relationship to time. And time is a necessary ingredient to navigating with a sextant. Our progress west became charted now with dead reckoning instead of intersecting known lines of position.

We continued on into the southeast trades and ran down the 2-3 degree north latitude line out to about west 112 degrees longitude, where we turned northwest into the doldrums. It was in the doldrums one day that I was on deck singing some 1940's show tunes at the top of my lungs. Paul decided there must be better music than this available and tried the radio, as I had so many times. A few snap, crackle, pops and it worked. Paul searched for WWV, (a high frequency shortwave radio station that continuously broadcasts a time signal. It is vital for navigation without a chronometer.) It turned out we were only 55 miles east of our dead reckoning position after 28 days without time until the radio fixed itself. Not only were spirits raised with our discovered longitude, but also because of an alternative to my singing.

THE LEAK

"If you can keep a boat afloat for 24 hours, you can do it forever!" Tristan Jones had said. I bought into that myth because I didn't know any better. But after three days of bailing 800 gallons per day, or 5-7 minutes every hour, it seemed clear the boat was sinking.

"What do you want to do?" Paul asked.

"The second to the last thing I want to do is drown at sea. The last thing I want to do is go back to Panama." Right then and there, he decided I was a keeper.

We were maybe 3 weeks out from the canal and had already returned once for a broken pintle on our rudder. Pride goeth before a fall (or a sinking).

Exhausted, I took to my bunk. Just before sleep overtook me, I heard a high-pitched, low-decibel sound like a whistle, directly under my ear. Further investigation showed this was the location of our leak.

When we had hauled our boat in Belize City, we'd hired the local shipyard to spot-cork, putty and paint the bottom. In their zeal, one of "the boys" had puttied the seam before cotton had been driven in. All these weeks of hard sailing had swept the seam clean of the putty. This was why the boat leaked so heavily.

Paul dove overboard, armed with a butter knife and some cotton to jam into the seam. In no short order, the leak was fixed. And he got to keep me after all.

ALBATROSS

It was a stunning trade wind day, the kind of day that made you pay attention. Bright sunlight shone on the large wavelets of the force 3 Beaufort scale gentle breeze. The only sound was the soft whoosh of our bow wave. We had the ocean all to ourselves.

Albatross by Nancy Zydler

Not another living thing was visible to us, save a lone albatross miles away on our stern. Moving faster than our sailboat, he gained on our position. No flap of a wing, just a constant hover about 20 feet above the water. We were riveted to his condition.

BOOM! He could not have hit our mast more perfectly if he'd tried, but we were pretty sure he was sound asleep when he did it. It scared the crap out of us and he looked completely embarrassed as he flapped a few times and headed west again.

LESSONS LEARNED LATE

When preparing for the next passage in Panama, I had done research on how to provision. My provisioning for our three week trip from Belize had been seriously insufficient. This time though well intentioned, several decisions fell dangerously flat. Things like plastic. Didja know there's such a thing as food grade plastic? I did not. So storing food in anything else ruined it. And on a trip where there would be no ports to resupply when provisions ran short, it was a terrible mistake.

In my defense, I assumed our passage would take roughly six weeks. Wishful thinking had prevailed, but there were so many calms we didn't anticipate; it took 2 months longer than that to reach our destination. We had not enough food or water.

Our "equipment" was far less than minimal. Even saying it was minimal is bragging. We had almost no clothes, one lifejacket, a flashlight and some batteries, navigational equipment, a short-wave radio, a suspect inflatable life raft, and a few cooking utensils: a pressure cooker and two-burner propane cook stove, stick matches and two propane bottles. A length of plastic tubing was also aboard.

Most of our staples were things like rice and beans. In retrospect, those foodstuffs required substantial amounts of water to turn them into edible meals. We heavily rationed our supply and Paul designed the original water maker, building a still to turn saltwater into fresh. Providence as in all aspects of our life provided us with the tubing we needed for the process, as well as enough propane and matches to light the stove daily for months.

We would fill the pressure cooker with saltwater and attach the plastic tube to the vent on top. As the water boiled, steam went through the tubing that we circled in a large bucket of cold salt water. The temperature change then condensed the steam into drops of priceless distilled water. We could make three cups per hour.

We had bought several flats of fresh eggs and stored them in the coolest part of the boat, the lazarette. I'd read that the trick to longevity was to first coat each egg with Vaseline but to also turn them often, to keep the innards from sticking to the shell and spoiling. Of this, I was committed. Eggs were a tasty source of protein onboard.

With prudence, I always cracked an egg outside of the cabin on the stern deck. They proved usable a good long time until one sad day I cracked an egg into the aluminum pot and the smell was so spectacularly foul-smelling and noxious, that without thinking, I immediately threw the pot and egg into the ocean. Losing the pot, half of our galley gear, was better to me than losing my reason to live by spending another second in proximity to that stench.

We caught fish when we could but came to understand that fish aren't everywhere in the ocean. Our canned goods weren't stored properly either. Lying against the hull, the saltwater intruded into them and spoiled several cans. Being short on provisions, we stretched out our use of them. Pineapple was a special treat, saved for Fridays. Opening a can one Friday, it had been spoiled and was unusable. Bereft, we decided to open the last can, because it was, after all, Pineapple Friday.

CHANNEL FEVER

Our trip was filled with disappointments. Whenever we'd expected this or that, we were surprised with some added hardship. Most demoralizing was our drifting: three weeks in the Gulf of Panama, three weeks in the Equatorial Doldrums and another four weeks in the North Pacific High. It seemed like the wind would never blow for more than a day, inching us along, and those days were few and far between.

The North Pacific High that year had captured us about 900

miles west of the Washington coast. Then one evening we got a little southwest breeze. We began to gather hope as we entered into the second night of it. By the next morning it switched to a westerly and began to howl. At noon, the wind was a force nine nor'wester and we had to fall off on a broad reach with the jib still flying. After so many weeks of drifting we couldn't bear the thought of heaving to when we were doing 5 to 6 knots.

The storm lasted three days and was, at times, truly frightening. Often a wave would break just at the right time to carry us down the face of it on our beam ends, actually surfing broadside. Three days of hanging on by our toenails, sailing so fast we had no chance to beat into the 15- to 20-foot swells the last hundred miles north, so as to be on the right latitude for Cape Flattery, the last ocean cape close to home.

Everything was wet down below, and now in the northern latitudes it was damn cold. We really expected to lose the boat, and were scared but also surprisingly serene. The intense fury of this storm tested every plank and fastener holding *Izzy* together. It seemed a funny twist of fate to come so far without dying, only to sink on the front porch of home.

The second day of the storm was the worst. Unable to sleep or prepare food, and sore from the battering of our cavitating vessel, optimism had plummeted. We were scared.

The third day, when the wind eased, saw us with our main up, close hauled and heading northeast towards our intended latitude. By the fourth morning, the water had shifted from deep blue to the dark green that indicated we were close to the North American continent. Even knowing how desperately we needed to step ashore, there was a note of sadness seeing the color change.

We sighted land the following dawn outside of Grays Harbor, a mere 80 to 90 miles south of Neah Bay. We were drifting amongst anchored commercial fishermen, trollers off the Washington coast. With no wind, the currents pushed us north about 13 miles per day. It took another week to reach the Strait of Juan de Fuca.

The last few weeks were especially hard on me as I had come down with a colossal case of "channel fever," the angst you can't help but experience, being so close to home but unable to get there. Hearing Seattle weather and news on the radio, I was past ready!

We gave a letter to a sport fisherman who motored by, addressed to our parents since we were several weeks overdue. He insisted on calling them as soon as he got in to let them know we were alive. This was a great kindness to us but especially to our parents, who had worn worry furrows in their carpets, pacing and waiting.

As we entered the Strait of Juan de Fuca, sailing between the island of Tatoosh and the shoreside wash rocks, wrapped in our damp Guatemalan blankets, water sloshed in the bilge. The lush scent of the evergreen rain forest, kelp beds and moist land overpowered our senses. The experience was otherworldly after months of only gray and blue and the smell of the ocean.

Everything changed. Everything was good again. All of a sudden, I felt at home and happy, like now all the hardships of the trip were over and everything from now on would be easy.

As the wind faded and we drifted to an anchorage right next to Seal Rock, just east of Neah Bay, we hauled in two red snapper for dinner. Our first night home and our local fish jump onboard. Our pantry held only some rice, a can of tomato paste and a small onion. I fixed the best dinner in months and we guzzled water judiciously.

In celebration of our homecoming, we ate the onion raw. It was so much better than Champagne.

STEPPING ASHORE

After clearing customs in Port Townsend, we rowed to Union Wharf and went ashore to stretch our legs. I walked like a drunken sailor. The ground felt fluid, like the waves in the ocean we had just been sailing on. With tattered clothes and no shoes, I weighed 30 pounds less than when I had left the Northwest seven months earlier. Confidentially I was 3 months pregnant.

I took my first hot shower in 3 ½ months at the Port Townsend Boat Haven.

Twas a spiritual experience, that shower.

Hungry, always hungry, we took our 11 bucks and went looking for a meal. Instead, we bumped into Ron Keys. Our good friend from Bainbridge Island happened to be in town, cruising on his boat. One look at us and he insisted on taking us to dinner at the Sea Galley downtown. It had a salad bar! A salad bar! It also had fresh brewed coffee, which I longed for but decided it was too late in the day. The three of us talked for hours, savoring the fresh food and good company. We took the time to tell Ron everything about our trip.

Photo by Cathy Nickum

Waking aboard at anchor the next morning, I found a thermos of fresh, hot, dreamy coffee on the stern deck. Ron had delivered it, stealthily hush-hush. I'm still smiling about that.

Anxious to get home to Eagle Harbor, we filled up our water "tank" and blew the whole handful of one dollar bills on some food at Safeway by the Sea. We phoned home to hear the combined exhales of all our people. That too, was a kind of spiritual experience.

I believe sailors have short memories because they keep going out there, forgetting what it's like. Once again, there was no wind. We drifted in and out of Admiralty Inlet, passing Marrowstone Point several times with the tides, never finding ground to anchor. It took another 3 days to drift/sail the 37 miles to Eagle Harbor. We ran out of food again!

On our last day sailing south, our friend George Buehler passed us in his cutter *Juno*, heading north. We yelled to him and told him of our plight. Motoring alongside, he threw over a large bag of fresh-baked chocolate chip cookies and some lifeboat food ration biscuits which were surprisingly delicious. As we ghosted along the eastern side of Bainbridge Island, we spotted Linda Golden standing on the bluff with her children. They all let out a boisterous, "We love you!" She'd been watching for us.

We arrived at our houseboat well after dark to the smell of creosote that hung in the still September air. Paul said, "Smells like home." Wyckoff, our local creosoted log industry and future Super-fund Site, stood silent sentinel as we drifted by.

My mom and Paul's parents had both fixed up spare bedrooms, just in case we walked off the boat hating each other. But you know, nobody seemed surprised that the exact opposite seemed true.

CHAPTER 4
GUNG HO
1980 – 1983

Photo by Cathy Nickum

"Things are never quite as scary
when you've got a best friend"
—Calvin and Hobbes

WORMS

Home now, we dealt with re-entry into daily life and the promise of a baby. Walking to build muscle strength and stamina and eating fresh fruits and vegetables were key. Our privacy and solitude offshore changed, like a flip of a switch. The new explosive social life was challenging. People sought us out, but living on a houseboat anchored in the bay provided a bubble of anonymity we craved. We chose not to go public with my pregnancy until I was far enough along that we couldn't hide it anymore.

What with a baby coming, money and the need for it also radically changed. All of a sudden, money seemed important. We had a fish pot fishery to develop, a solid business plan in our minds and a boat to make it all happen. She did need a complete overhaul first, though.

Paul built a tidal grid on his father's waterfront beach where we could work on her hull without going to a proper boatyard. At a large high tide we brought Izzy in for what we hoped would be a "shampoo and set" haul out. Of course we found she needed so much more.

The to-do list included things like rebuilding a proper fish hold amidships like the one we had removed in Belize to make room for our modest living accommodations on our passage. We wanted to install a wood stove for heat and rebuild the galley and living space so it would be large enough for three.

The boat looked a mess and wanted a complete refinish of topsides, bottom paint, deck, houses and interior. Possibly 20 years old by now, no one had ever done more than slap on thick enamel down below, probably without sanding. But that thick enamel paint proved to have been a life-saver.

A close inspection found that teredos (shipworms) had digested most of the entire portside waterline. At our last commercial haulout in Belize, the young "boys" (as they were called by the shipyard boss) who had painted and puttied our bottom, had neglected to paint the pencil-width scribe line of the boot top (the painted stripe that separated the white topside hull from the red bottom). Our months of sailing on a starboard tack offshore had put the entire port side under water constantly. The baby worms had entered this tiny naked piece of wood, which then invited the ubiquitous "termites of the sea" to a feast of longleaf yellow pine.

They grew quite large leaving long tunnels in the wood and it was a miracle that the boat didn't sink from their damage. But as they traveled towards the inside of the planking, they ate wood right up to the 20 years of thick enamel paint. "Nope! We ain't gonna eat that," they said. It was those years of neglectful maintenance that had kept us afloat.

THE JONES ACT

I might have been about 7 1/2 months pregnant, often tired but so full of sweet life.

We had just repaired our Belizean-built fishing boat we'd sailed home for our Puget Sound fishery. All that was left was to have it admeasured as per the Jones Act requirement: Any foreign built vessel under 5 net tons could legally be used commercially in the United States.

We called the Coast Guard. They sent out a guy.

We lived on a houseboat, anchored out in Eagle Harbor. *Isela* was tied alongside. Paul wanted me to handle this arrangement and I happily took it on. When the guy showed up at the end of Winslow Wharf, I jumped in my 15-foot flat-bottomed "Good Little Skiff" and went to collect him.

Standing there, uniformed and briefcase in hand, he also wore a broad smile. I rowed him out to the boat.

I made tea for him on the wood stove while he did his work. It didn't take long, *Isela* being such a small vessel.

As he left the skiff on his way back to Seattle, he told me it was the best cup of tea he'd ever had. *Isela* measured in at 4.99 tons!

MARCH 9, 1981

We went sailing that gentle Spring Friday, a moment of tranquil privacy, prior to what was to come. I spent Sunday night at University Hospital in early labor. Anxiety surrounding the unknowns of childbirth had brought on a case of herpes and I was advised to get a caesarean for the health of the child. A meeting with the hospital obstetrician and anesthesiologist was a demoralizing and dreadful experience and felt like a kind of baby factory. When I mentioned my hopes for a home delivery, the anesthesiologist moaned, "Oh, you're one of those."

My long-standing experience with herpes told me this outbreak was no longer active, so they gave me drugs to slow down the contractions until test results could confirm. Paul and my midwife stayed with me overnight.

Results took 18 hours and came back "inconclusive." Prudence and the A.M.A. counseled me to proceed with surgery instead of the home-birth I'd hoped for. But the decision was mine and mine alone. Everyone weighed in, pros and cons, but left it up to me.

This was the hardest decision I've ever made. Instinct or faith impelled me to leave the hospital and go home to have the baby. The nurses up to that point had been passive and noncommittal, but raced to unplug me, gushing with enthusiasm and joyous support. Angels. My labor immediately ramped up.

Paul, the midwife and I rushed to the ferry and barely made the 3 o'clock boat. Not having eaten in over 24 hours, I went to the galley and bought a muffin. Cardboard. I threw it away. Navigating through the smoking section on my way to the loo, my contractions only allowed about 15 feet of forward motion until I had to stop and act nonchalant. The ferry matron saw this and followed me into the bathroom. It was clear she knew what labor looked like. All the stalls were full. "Are you o.k.?" "Yes, I'm in labor and trying to get home." Every toilet flushed and women rushed out to surrounded me, curious but supportive. The matron was distressed. She assured me the myth wasn't true, that if you are born on a ferry, you get to ride free for life.

We parked at the top of the hill and slowly made our way on the path through the trees to the beach. Getting from the beach to the houseboat without falling in the water seemed like the hardest part of this labor so far. Our hastily built floating dock was narrow, I was top-heavy and feeling imbalanced, and the dance I was producing was fraught with danger. Needing to pause every 10 feet now, it took some time.

Finally aboard, I tried to get comfy. Unbeknownst to any of us, I was in hard labor. We'd taken the class, but talking about labor and delivery is different than experiencing it. The midwife said she'd be back in a few hours after she went home for a shower and something to eat. Just before she left I managed to stutter, "Ccchhheck me!" Which she did. "Oh dear, you're at 8 cm. I'm not going anywhere."

We had illegally strung a telephone line across the road, through the thick cedars and firs, down and out to the houseboat. She picked up the phone. Only a midwife in training, she needed her teacher and other assistant to attend. The line was busy. I remember thinking she'd get in trouble when she called the operator and said it was an emergency, asking for assistance. It was an emergency!

Somehow, the Seattle team of midwives made the 4:45 ferry and got to the houseboat just in time. My closest friend, Linda, was already there. She was so calm and I was so unsure and nervous. Linda had brought chipped ice for my comfort and was boiling water for the LeBoyer bath, just like in the storybooks. Little Red, our Irish Setter, stood on deck looking in the large windows, worrying.

I started growling, an inhuman, guttural sound, unable to speak. I looked at Paul, unsure what was happening, asking for help with my eyes. A light came on in his eyes, he leaned in close and said, "Is it the urge to push?" YES YES YES, my eyes answered. Now at 10 cm, I left the growling behind and started to push.

They held up a mirror. "Look, you should see this. It's amazing." My water had never broken and the baby was coming out with the caul intact, her long dark hair swimming in amniotic fluid. Miraculously, her perfect body was protected from any thing my body could have possibly infected her with. Concentrating on pushing, I could only barely half shout, "I'm .....bbbbusy."

And just like that, at high tide, she was born at 6:05.

Diana, Kashmira Marina and Paul

The springtime setting sun shone a rich pink glow on that gentle evening. It filled the bay, the sky, the trees; my heart.

LINDA

Linda was also a sailor-girl and had crossed the Pacific Ocean from California to Hawaii with her husband Dick, another deckhand, and four young children. During that crossing their boat was dismasted and the trip turned into an epic adventure. She had immense Momdom experience with keeping young children from falling overboard as well as being a super-cool mom. I was a big fan of her many gifts.

We fell into a deep friendship long before my own Momdom loomed large. Our love of sailing introduced us but we recognized something in each other that fired all our synapses. We would meditate together with a group every week and I learned to chill just a bit being around her. But I'm here to tell you, we could laugh a lot too.

I had asked her to be with me for my home delivery, knowing her serenity would calm my youthful anxiety. Having her there was just the ticket.

Attending a birth is an extraordinary experience, to witness the edge of that precious moment of new life. Gobsmacked by it, afterwards Linda considered becoming a midwife. But she realized that plenty of people would want to experience the moment of a birth.

That same precious moment on the other side of a life, the moment of death, was something few people could or would want to experience. Inspired, she became one of the first Hospice of Kitsap County patient care volunteers. She worked there for 12 years and was a serene presence for the last moment of many people's lives.

Linda Golden

She also took on duties within the organization like community education and fundraising. Linda came up with a unique way to do both in a very special package.

Linda was so supportive of my desire to be a boat builder. She encouraged and helped me to believe in myself. Knowing I needed more experience in the woodshop, she suggested I build a boat that Hospice of Kitsap could sell raffle tickets for to raise money.

Now I was gobsmacked. What a great idea!

And so a new tradition was formed. I would build a 15' 3" Gloucester Gull Dory out of plywood and fir. We would sell raffle tickets until July 4th and then pull the winner out of a big glass bowl at the gigantic celebration the city of Winslow always had.

It boosted my skills and my confidence while raising awareness of the Hospice program and a good amount of money to boot!

Linda's name means beautiful, flexible, soft and mild. Do

parents wish for these qualities, or do children just live up to them? Regardless, she is all of these and more.

MY BOOBS

Anyone who has lived in or near American culture understands the power of a large bosom. Attention-getting and attention-holding, women learn early on what that power can do. On the playground in 4th grade, two boys said to me, "You sure have big tits." And so I asked, "What are tits?" Twas the beginning of the end of my innocence.

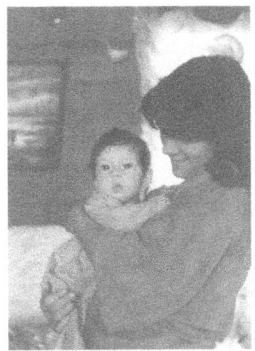

No doubt about it, by my late teens I had learned to optimize my genetic gifts with tight tops and ample décolleté. I used my physicality to get what I thought I wanted – attention from men. It took many years before I realized that wasn't what I wanted at all. But it was motherhood that drove it home.

Holding my nursing newborn, it was undeniable the real reason boobs were invented. Afterwards, I never could think of them any other way.

FISHING WITH *IZZY*

Our business plan was spot on. We followed every rule and did anything required of us, obtained licenses and insurance and developed our own niche markets. Being the only fish-pot fishermen in Puget Sound and delivering lots of fish live, it was a very successful fishery.

Kashmira was 13 days old on her first trip. Twice a week, we'd circumnavigate Bainbridge Island, generally under sail, pick up our string of pots and, one by one, empty the fish into the hold and then reset. Then we'd sail to Washington Street Pier on the Seattle waterfront. This is where we first met Dale Nordland. There was a free tie-up next to the Washington State Ferry pier. He walked over that day to *Izzy* and pronounced, "I see your boat is from British Honduras" (Belize), which impressed the hell outta us. But we found out later, Dale had been just about everywhere.

We would load the catch into 5-gallon buckets and carry them up to Alaskan Way, me with a front pack holding Kashmira, our precious newborn shipmate. Gentlemen of the waterfront always sat on a bench at the head of the dock. They would keep an eye on our business and protect it from loss while we went back and forth to the boat for more buckets of fish. A truly symbiotic relationship. For their consideration, we always shared our bounty.

Once the fish were off the boat, our next step was to hail a cab to take us and our buckets to the International District, where we sold our silver and blue perch, true cod and rock cod to Chinese restaurants there. Several drivers would balk but there was always one who would transport us. The hardest part of the delivery was to get all the fish into the kitchens before the people on the street demanded we sell them the live jumping fish. And in fact, we always did make some cash deals, just to keep the peace.

Once the sale was complete, we'd stack the rinsed buckets and walk back down to the boat with pockets full of cash. Sailing home, it was always just a long, wonderful day.

Someone living on the south shore of Bainbridge Island eventually complained to Fish and Game (FnG), that we were catching their personal fish. So FnG shut us down in inner Puget Sound. "But look," they said, "We're giving you the Strait of Juan de Fuca and Hein Bank instead." And we tried it of course, but finding no fish there, we said, "Screw this. We need to go offshore, where there will be fewer regulations."

Like another light switch, it was the impetus to build our tuna boat, *Ocean*.

〜

CHAPTER 5
ON THE HARD
1984 - 1987

*"Aw, hell. Wooden boatbuilding is nothing more than a million simple
tricks it takes a lifetime to learn. Retaining them is another issue."*
—Ray Speck

RAISING SHEEP

We were beyond blessed with Paul's supportive family who provided a place for us to live as well as to build our boat *Ocean*. Two-plus acres in downtown Winslow, half was a stand of mature cedar trees, the other half a former pasture. A small retired horse barn nestled amongst the trees, wanting us to find a new use for it.

We converted the lower half into a wood shop and turned the upstairs into our new home. 276 sq. ft of living space seemed palatial, compared to our 240 sq. ft. houseboat. Joining the 20th century, we installed a flush toilet!

We turned most of the pasture into a small farmette. Several ancient apple trees still yielded tasty fruit. An annual cider pressing party began, sharing our bounty with friends. The soil had been fertilized by horses for decades, so a large vegetable garden was put in. Everything we grew was stupendous. Kashmira tended her farmstand out by the road, selling fresh seasonal everything. Often selling her paintings too, she was a natural-born charmer. And still there was more acreage to use.

We fenced in the rest and were gifted young ewes, a variety of black sheep who then asked us to acquire a husband for them. We lucked upon a magnificent ram who took charge of the flock, strutting about bleating his signature sound. We named him Foghorn.

Throughout our building of *Ocean*, the farmette required daily attention. This, it turned out, was a happy occurrence. The first year or so was so rigidly "build the boat, build the boat, build the boat every day," our life became very unbalanced. Utilizing this land developed a trifecta as all three of us became a farmer/fisherman/boat builder.

Raising sheep took on a whole new kind of appreciation. We taught ourselves all the maintenance required, including how to call them back from eating the neighbor's rhododendrons with the shake of a can of oats whenever they mysteriously busted out.

Kashmira and Pudgy with a Newborn

Foghorn took his job seriously and we had years of lambing to enjoy. He also protected his flock. This 300-pound god of his species would never hurt or even scare any female human who entered the field. But if Paul ventured in, Foghorn let him know who the alpha male was. Foghorn would wait until Paul turned his back and was next to a fence post. Then he'd butt him in the ribs against it to produce double the pain. The only way to make him back off was to hit his horns with an empty tin can which I can't deny was too much fun. Boinnng! Kashmira would often tie a heavy manila rope around his neck and take him around the block for a walk with other neighborhood children. I should have been thrown in jail, but they always came home unsullied.

Along with our beloved Irish setter, our animal population grew with the addition of a fleet of ducks, a goat and some large, uppity geese.

The geese, named Bruce, Cathy and Pinch-Poke-Goose, were generally self-contained and docile.

But one taught Kashmira a valuable lesson. When Kashmira was a

Cathy, Kashmira and Little Red

little girl, I never saw her afraid of anything. Courage was her middle name until Cathy decided to test her. Whenever they were within 20 feet of each other, Cathy would attack Kashmira, running at her with her wings spread and scaring the bejeesus out of her. Finally Kashmira came crying to me, what could she do? I told her she had to show dominance over Cathy, get bigger, run at her and make scary noises too. The next time out in the yard, she did just that. From then on Cathy was her devoted friend and companion. I've never seen Kashmira afraid of anything since

EGG HUNTS

Taking cues from my Mom, I was always a party girl, though motherhood inspired a different kind of festivity for me. Build it for children. Let them bring their parents and watch us all evolve into the higher consciousness of innocent youth. Easter, with its traditional egg hunt, was one of those holidays my mother had made a big deal of. I continued it, lending my own twist, and the annual event grew huge very quickly.

Paul and I colored hundreds of eggs and hid them all in the open acre meadow that was part of our compound. What a joyous endeavor. Every year I'd wrap one egg with gold foil holding a 5 dollar bill. Mysteriously, it was always the last egg to be found.

Kashmira and Diana with Rhonda the Bunny

Children and their baskets would wait inside the barn and be let out in stages, youngest first. The older ones went wild watching through the windows, testing their patience, while the "babes' '

60

wandered slowly, picking up colorful eggs lying unhid. Parents stood back laughing and enjoyed the potluck brunch that grew larger and more creative every year. We often had an Easter bunny in attendance which brought even more joy.

I have my Mom to thank for these kinds of family traditions that slipped into my bag-o-tricks. I'm sorry I never thanked her.

SPINNING OAKUM

I used to spin oakum for a living, a traditional art. Dave Ullin taught me, along with how to cork* deck and planking seams. Dave was a hero of mine, a mentor and great friend, arguably the best corker in the Northwest and a gifted teacher.

Oakum is a material very much like un-braided manila rope, though softer, like baby hair mixed with long beard whiskers. Made of hemp or jute fibers, it is saturated with pine tar, also known as Stockholm Tar, a distilled thick black goo made from the wood of pine trees. Proven to have immense anti-rot, preservative qualities, it is also used as an antiseptic and in soaps.

Oakum's prime maritime purpose is to be driven into the seams between hull planking and deck seams on large wooden boats, to " harden up" the hull, tightening it and providing a flexible watertight barrier. (It can also be blended with sheep's wool, spun and knitted into a cap for a legendary corker.)

Fresh from the manufacturer, oakum's strands are spindly, clumped, uneven and a proper mess. For an elegant delivery into the seams with a corking mallet, it must first be stretched and spun into a uniform plait. The better the spinner, the faster the corker.

Somewhere along the line, my product excelled even beyond Dave's. At least that's what Dave told me. I still blush just thinking about that.

The surprise of being a female oakum spinner though, was the strong essence of pine tar that embedded in my clothing, my skin, my hair. I became a dude-magnet. While I pumped gas one day, all men within 75 feet were drawn to me and walked over to investigate this delicious scent. I was the best smelling woman in the world, every man's heartthrob just as Dave was mine.

* There are serious disagreements between maritime trades as to which pronunciation is correct (corking or caulking) depending on your coastline. The proper spelling of it is caulking, but this marine tradesperson calls it corking and so chooses to spell it phonetically.

AND WE STIHL LIVED

Almost everything about the building of *Ocean* we chose to do the hard way. Traditional, dontcha know. I later swore an oath that I'd never make my own 1-inch keel bolts ever again. Or drive fasteners with a brace instead of a cordless drill. We did purchase long lengths of Douglas Fir from Jim and Charlie (of the nascent Edensaw Woods) for planking stock, and plenty of dimensional lumber for deck beams and such. It was a rare convenience and saved so much time. But we wanted specialty hardwood, locust for our double-sawn frames. You couldn't source locust other than in a standing tree. We advertised for it.

Locust had been imported, as I was told, to grow for the boat-building industry in Port Blakely. It was perfect for trunnels ("tree-nails") which are clever fasteners that are immensely strong and never corrode as metal does. Locust was a hardwood that tended to rot in the tree but scarcely ever rotted once cut. It is beautiful to look at, honey-colored and figured.

Several farmers replied to our ads. Locust was often planted on a property line as living fence posts. At a certain age (quite large), they became more of a nuisance than a help. We felled 13 of these beasts, cut them into manageable lengths, cleaned up the pastures and brought them home to mill. Along with the locust, we also had miraculously "acquired" two huge, 16-foot iron-bark logs that also needed milling. The largest was 34 inches in diameter.

Stihl makes a quality chain-saw, and we purchased one with a

48-inch bar. Its power and size did the job of milling up all these logs with an Alaska chainsaw mill. We produced piles of sawdust and stickered large amounts of quality lumber to air dry.

Paul's father had a fully timbered undeveloped piece of property. He told us we could mill up anything that was already down. We found a good sized, straight Doug fir, only recently fallen, and we set to it. This log was situated perfectly level but on imperfectly level ground, holes and hillocks with a steep grade under. I operated the dumb end of the mill. Paul managed the motor end as we cut our slab slowly, the bar just at my eye height. When I ran out of ground and had to change position he stopped the cut.

Standing now on an adjacent log, I asked Paul, "What's the chance the chain would ever break?"

"Not a chance in the world," he said.

Fifteen seconds later, after firing up the Stihl, that chain broke and flew off that bar, where moments ago my face had been.

We packed up the equipment, left that fir log laying there with its half cut kerf, to rot in its own time, and never went back to those woods again.

MARIE

Kashmira's paternal Nana, Marie, became my closest friend and deep confidante while I was a young mother. A consummate artist, she was always planning or producing some wonderful piece of joy: calligraphy, graphic arts, baking, sewing and experiential activities. Her seamstress work was superb. Growing up in hard times, she designed and created her own wardrobe. When Marie was a young bride, her strident mother-in-law had complimented her on a suit she was wearing. "Thank you," she said, "I made it myself." Marching across the room, her mother-in-law grabbed the back collar of her suit and wrenched Marie around, looking for the label she expected to find. There was no label of course, as Marie had made it herself.

63

Marie Svornich with Kashmira

A traditional wife and mother, raising four children and keeping the house, Marie never learned how to pump gas into her own car until her 60s and was so proud when she finally did.

Her first grandchild, Kashmira, lived so close by, they saw each other almost every day. They would create some fun together and were best chums. Marie would take an old pair of Matt's work pants and cut them into a new pair of overalls for Kashmira. Or she might create a perfect velvet party dress from a picture she'd seen in a fashion magazine for her granddaughter.

I never fit into this family. I wanted to, but the inflexible gender roles grated on me and everyone knew it. But Marie and I could sit for hours and never lacked important things to talk about. We were best friends.

FRAMING

While we were building *Ocean*, we soon realized that as a couple that wanted to stay together, we should never work on the same project, period. Nothing spoils a romantic relationship like disagreements about how to do something, over and over, every day. So we divvied up the work. Each of us took responsibility for whatever project needed doing. We'd discuss how to pull it off, mull it over, but then whomever took the lead was fully supported and left to make it happen. A very good system.

One of my chosen jobs was framing. We'd cut down 13 locust trees, chainsaw milled them up and after air drying, it was the building stock for our 4 X 4 double-sawn frames. Good, hard, heavy wood.

While Paul was working away from home, I plugged away. Cutting the frames wanted a helper, a "dumb end," though smarts were a necessity. I hired a friend, more than handy, who was seriously interested in boat building as a career. We worked so well together, it was a genuine pleasure.

When the framing was done, she applied for an advertised apprenticeship position at Dunato's Boat Shop in Seattle. I was thrilled and terribly proud of her. But then she came to me as a courtesy, to let me know that she couldn't possibly use my name as a reference. No one would believe a woman could ever be in a position to be building a boat. She'd used Paul's name instead. He'd never worked with her. "You're kidding," I said, heartbroken. Not only was she someone I thought of as a friend but someone who must have understood the work we were doing together. But she showed me she didn't believe it.

She didn't get that job, nor even a call-back. I often wondered if it was because she, herself, didn't believe women belonged in this industry.

PROCUREMENT

There was a small hydraulics shop on a side street in Seattle, close to but not in the fishy part of Ballard. Low-ceilinged, dark and cluttered, smelling of man sweat and oil. Buxom women on the walls wore tool belts and hard hats and not much more. The kind of place I wouldn't want to ask to use the bathroom. But there was the sweetest young counterman who always made the trip worthwhile.

Not living in town, shopping trips for the boat required thoughtful lists of parts needed from several specialty shops for items available in Seattle. It took a lot of time to source and plan a buying trip. I'd take the Chevy 454, baby as my co-pilot, and try to streamline the many stops. I was pretty good at it.

I showed up one day and a different fella was working the counter. I pulled out my order and started to recite it, then stopped and said it would be easier if he just worked off my list himself.

He looked at me with disgust and spit out, "You don't even know what these things are."

Hot and red with anger, I could barely get the next words out. "I don't need to know what they are. I only need to know how to write you a check. But let me show you what it is that I require." Using my body as a teaching tool, I pointed to the appropriate spots. "This is an elbow. This is a knee. And this," I told him as I pulled up my tank top, "is a hex nipple when I'm in the fish hold and it's 35 degrees below zero."

I had given him my anger and now he was red hot. He filled my order and I wrote out a big check. I never went back.

MOVE ALONG

To BUILD a wooden boat is a wondrous thing. A labor of love, regardless of size, shape or pedigree. It requires immense dedication, determination and focus. Many who don't build, still enjoy the feelings such endeavors produce, and want to be a part of it and feel connected in some way. At the very least, they like to watch the process.

While building *Ocean*, our 38-foot traditional wooden fishing sloop, we got a lot of visitors. So many in fact, that I started to keep track. We averaged 7 people per day, 7 days a week for 3 1/2 years. Sorry, that's too much.

This interest and celebration from our community is supportive, but extremely distracting. Several people understood and limited their time with us, but the majority felt no compunction about just staying and staying and staying. Gentle comments from me were ignored. Something had to be done.

I erected a sign on the large cedar tree at the entrance to our site. I dug up a large red beet from our vegetable garden, drove a spike through its heart and attached it to an international sign of no, no, no. Most people didn't understand what the sign represented until I read it for them. "NO DEAD BEETS!" It worked wonders.

NO DEAD BEETS

Many years later, when I ran a shop of my own and felt a strong sense of responsibility to my customers to actually produce, I simply said, "MOVE ALONG!"

THE BATHTUB

Living aboard always felt like home and there were few amenities I missed from living ashore, except one. I decided to design and build into the interior of *Ocean* a proper bathtub.

One of my jobs was to design the interior. This was a working boat and most of the space was taken up with fish hold or engine room. But it was also meant to be lived in and sailed long distances, for weeks at a time. Fishing can be hard on your muscles and hard on your hygiene. There was a perfect space forward of the fo'c'sle bunks and aft of the chain locker. It was just large enough for a deep bathtub. I set out to learn how to build one out of fiberglass.

This was a project uniquely my own. Paul was not as convinced as I that a bathtub was important. I learned about mat, roving, gel coat, colorant, and polyester. I built the mold but realized I'd need a building buddy for the lay-up, what with the time constraints of the accelerant. Dick Golden offered to help, so together, he and I jumped right into the build, neither of us really knowing anything about the process. We pulled it off and were thrilled with the results. The only thing we'd neglected to learn was the importance of wearing a respirator. We both got stupid stoned.

I placed the tub in our un-planked boat, in-frame, with bulkheads fore and aft of it, the first piece of furniture installed. It was clearly visible for all to see. Our many visitors had plenty to say about it too and none of it good. "Girly-girly... stupid waste of space... a boat doesn't want a bathtub... fluff..." Even Paul seemed to bend to the majority opinion and weighed in similarly. But the deed was done, installed, wired and plumbed with a sump pump and varnished rails. I went on to whatever was next on the list.

Our single-cylinder, 21 hp Hundested semi-diesel was cooled with raw (salt) water. Salt water circulated through the engine and discharged through a deck hose – nice warm water to clean up the fish mess and great for cold hands. This is how we filled the tub when underway. Depending on the latitude and temperature of our environs, we could dial up or down the rpms or the load on the refrigeration to increase the temperature of the water in the engine. We had ourselves the perfect bath.

I'd fill a gallon jug of fresh water and float it in the tub with me, letting it warm up for the final rinse of body and full head of hair.

The size and shape of the tub was a product of the hull shape but wouldn't you know, it never spilled a drop of water, even in rough seas. There was room for myself, my little girl and the gallon jug, deep enough to completely immerse up to our necks. A lovely amenity to the end of our long days.

Not long after we launched and began to voyage on the boat, Paul gave me a huge apology for ever doubting my tubby judgment. He spent more time in it than anyone.

DAVE ULLIN

"If I could inspire people to be content... Anything that is purposeful makes me feel content."—Dave Ullin

Dave was the Dalai Lama of watermen and chose an intentional life of simplicity and uncompromising virtues. Living alone he found purpose through learning, teaching, advocacy, volunteering, strength of mind and body, work and play.

He lived on an old wooden tugboat but could not reconcile using fossil fuels for propulsion, so he removed the diesel engine and pretty much stayed put. He commuted by skiff and taught me how to row. And even though I was convinced I already was an expert, I improved a lot.

Not having an engine in his boat made room for his vast collection of tools. Early on he gave away all his electric tools, preferring the intimacy of hand tools and the extra thought and engineering they required. He loved to move huge rocks and stumps. The shovel was his favorite tool.

Story goes that as a young boy his parents gave him a shovel for Christmas which he immediately ran outside with to dig a hole in the backyard. He dug all day until bedtime when his parents insisted he stop. His head was way below ground level.

He tried to teach me proper shovel uses, nuances and techniques. But after his long tutorial I assured him it was one tool I had no interest in learning.

Dave often walked a path that went by a preschool, where 3, 4 and 5 year olds played outside. They would rush to the fence to talk with this gentle giant of a man, recognizing a kindred spirit who felt the same about them. He began his passion for work at the age of four, helping his parents dig up a stump. So he decided to teach these younguns how to put up firewood using traditional hand tools and teamwork.

Neighbors up the street had taken down some trees and did not want the wood. So with a hand cart, Dave and the children loaded the wood and transported it back to the preschool. He brought his bucking horse, crosscut saws, axes, hatchets, mauls and wedges and set up for some serious work with a willing crew.

Working together they bucked up the wood, split and stacked it all, and I'll wager he even taught them how to sharpen, oil, and care for his tools. They sold the firewood to their parents to raise money for the school.

Dave never ate a pizza; preferred apples to apple pie; never drove a car and almost always carried one or two large canvas bags filled with heavy tools. It was a sight to see him walk onto the ferry carrying a cross-cut saw. Almost scary with his serious, purposeful expression, until you would smile at him and he would break out into the most infectious world-class smile.

I am stunned to admit I have no memory of the first time we met as his presence and physicality were remarkable. I only know that he was in my life until he left us.

After knowing him for a few years, he did something that really made me mad. I had taken on the job of building the deck on *Ocean*. He watched my progress silently. Unhappy with how I was springing the planks, (bending them into the shape I desired) he privately went to speak to Paul about it to register his complaint. His concept of chain of command was clearly that Paul was my boss and my better. When Paul told me of it, I blew up like Mount St. Helens.

I walked straight up to Dave and thumped him hard on his chest and stated my position: I was in charge of this particular project and if he had a problem about the way I was doing it, he had better come talk to me. He heard me. He also heard how what he did had hurt so much! He sincerely apologized for his behavior.

Our friendship deepened that day into one where we took much more care with each other to always be respectful. He was my biggest fan.

Dave and Dick Golden planking *Ocean*

ABSENTIA

Unbeknownst to me, I left something behind at a fancy hotel in absentia.

An old girlfriend was having a passionate, extremely private affair with a man. They made plans to rendezvous at a high-class joint, away from the kids and gossiping neighbors. She went out and bought some madly expensive and alluring French underwear. Apparently when she left the hotel, she neglected to retrieve them. I mean this stuff is eye catching, what movies are made of and probably not that practical. But she called the hotel the next day, wanting them back. When asked for her name she panicked and said Diana Talley.

They disappeared of course, but it's nice to know someone somewhere was thinking juicy things about me.

LAUNCH DAY

It should have been a day of celebration. We expected it to be. After 3 1/2 years of dedication, focus and teamwork, we were ready for her splash. Wanting some sense of control over a potentially challenging day, we chose not to plan a party and only told our closest friends. About 50 people showed up.

Several things went wrong from the git-go. The trucking company, that had previously visited the site and assured us they could do the move, found they couldn't make the tight turn out of the driveway. I was ready to cut down the neighbor's tree that was blocking us, but instead they called a tow truck to come and winch the boat trailer into submission.

This worked, and Paul and Kashmira and Dave Ullin scrambled on deck to ride the mile to the water. I drove the safety vehicle bringing up the rear. We made quite a splash just navigating busy Winslow Way.

Mark Julian, the owner of Eagle Harbor Boat Yard, ran the travel lift for us. As he transferred the boat from trailer to slings, ceremony was about to happen. Friends had made a lei, to hang on her stem to bless her, and scored a bottle of Champagne to hang there as well, for tradition, soon to be broken as we launched.

Our extended families were there, close friends and many acquaintances that had watched her development. The local press showed up. They asked for an interview with the builder. Paul went to speak with him.

After the interview, several of us were standing by her bow, including local and regional boat designers, sailors and boat builders. Someone asked if she would float on her waterline, a natural question of a boat built by owners who also designed her and were not professional marine architects. Then someone said, "If Paul Svornich designed her, I'm sure she will."

"Huzzah, huzzah," all around. Paul beamed with pride. He also shot me a look that said "give me this moment." I silently peeled off.

Here we were, more than seven years into our relationship. We'd adventured together, fished together, had a child together, and spent more than 3 1/2 years working together, building this "dream" boat, truly equal partners I thought.

Early on in the build, we'd decided to carve up all jobs, lists and long lists of to-dos. It was a simple fix to the crushing pressure of two partners who enjoyed sleeping together, fighting daily over how something should be done. There were so many mundane as well as glory jobs, we had no trouble carving them up equally.

Essentially, we made a list of jobs needing doing in the near future, and each of us took a lead. Our agreement was, whoever led a project, decided how it would be done. We'd have a staff meeting, discussing pros and cons, lightly arguing about the "If I did it, I'd..." and then whoever had that job, decided how to do it and the other guy stepped back and respected that process. It worked very well and we quit wanting to kill each other. Stuff got done!

Paul chose things like chainsaw milling downed trees, designing and building the horseshoe stern and pilot house, planking, choosing and installing the engine, rigging, spars, metalwork, and so much more. I took on lofting, carving the rabbet, framing, deck beams, house structures, the interior design and build, the deck, electrical, plumbing, and so much more.

One of the jobs I'd taken on was the weight calculation, the purpose of which is to determine the sum and center of all the weights, the center of gravity. It is the counterpart to finding the center of buoyancy of a floating body, the point at which the buoyant force acts. Physics says a floating body reaches equilibrium when weight equals displacement and the center of gravity lines up with the center of buoyancy.

I tackled the time-consuming and particular responsibility of designing a map of the boat, determining every weight of every thing that was a part of it and distributing it on the map in foot pounds. In other words I calculated the weight of the mast and where she sat on the map, the weights of the planking, decking, fasteners, rigging, deck structures, the engine, interior joinery, water and fuel tanks, machinery, sails... the endless list of everything that goes into the construction of a boat. Figuring out where the poundage was and then extrapolating to a place where I could confidently say, "This is how much ballast we need and where it should be placed," was a huge job and responsibility. But if I did it right, the boat would rest on her waterline.

I was wicked proud of that particular job. Just before we were pouring our ballast, I remembered when Paul asked if I was confident with my calculations before we committed to adding or deleting any weight here or there. I thought for about 30 seconds, wanting to give due respect to the decision, and answered, "No, I'm sure."

Paul knew I was responsible for this design application. And yet here he was, taking credit for it. How could this be? Weren't we a team? I was dumbstruck.

Well, wouldn't you know, she did, in fact rest on her waterline.

The rest of the day was a kind of blur. I managed to build a deep wall around myself, pretending I was happy.

The following Wednesday, the Bainbridge Review came out with a photo of our boat *Ocean* above the fold, with a headline that said "Paul Svornich Finally Launches His Boat." The interview didn't mention me at all. That and his accepting credit for my work fostered a conversation. Paul asked me, "What would you have done?"

"I certainly would have given credit where credit was due," said I. And that was the beginning, of course, of our inevitable "divorce."

A KINDNESS

After launching *Ocean*, we immediately wanted to venture out. *Ocean* has an unusual mechanical operating system in that the helmsman is not physically next to the engine controls. The Hundested motor and prop required dial-in directions; forward, reverse, neutral, and power are inside the pilot house. The guy steering the boat is outside. It was perhaps a design flaw.

No doubt about it, I was way behind in experience operating a boat, docking especially, compared to Paul.

After we launched, I can't explain how this happened but it was a huge kindness and gave me the experience and confidence I have used since. Paul suggested I be the Captain of the vessel on paper, but also that I be the guy at the helm and steering wheel, docking or departing. This also meant I would learn what, when and how much power to ask for from the "engineer," or the guy dialing in the prop. We weren't going to fret about a scuff or maybe worse. Here we were, a perfect new boat and I'm the guy possibly taking out a rub rail, sponson or bow pulpit, because of my inexperience.

It was a powerful teaching and learning place to accept my moment. It also showed great self-confidence on Paul's part to share the public perception of who's driving the bus.

I don't remember ever killing a dock. But I do remember my gratitude for his support and encouragement, which led me to becoming proficient at docking.

∾

CHAPTER 6
PELAGIC
1987 - 1989

Photo of *Ocean* by Patrick Roelle

"Every skipper has his own compass."—Irving Johnson

FOG

Fog is an occult thing; there's no science for its fickleness. It can arrive and embrace you quickly, holding so tight that if your luck has run afoul you may never be seen again. Or it can visit with a capricious kiss, leaving you abruptly to notice how precious life truly is.

After rigging the boat, our shakedown cruise was to go fishing off the Washington coast. It was late October and the windless days were warm, with calm oily seas and fog thick as butter. Blue sky was visible directly overhead but in every direction at sea level, 20 feet of visibility was the best you could hope for.

Five days on the fishing grounds and the bite was off. Five days of sweat, thick diesel soot and fish guts. It was a perfect time to clean myself up.

The boat was equipped with a beloved deck hose. Hot raw seawater pumped from the cooling system of the semi-diesel, discharged on deck and made for a perfect outdoor shower. Wrapped in our cocoon of fog, I began a long, languorous break from work to delve into the pleasure of hot water on naked skin.

I was all lathered up when the light abruptly changed almost imperceptibly. Not 50 feet away on our starboard side and clear as a bell, a 58-foot purse seiner sat drifting. The captain was on the flying bridge and his four deckhands lined the port rail gawking at me.

I never caught her name as she motored by at 2 knots, because when she passed, the light changed again and the fog encased her stern, 20 feet away.

LAPUSH

Entering the Quileute River on a good day must be difficult. I'm just guessing, because I've never gone in on a good day.

After several days of fishing off the Washington coast, Kashmira and I still had not gotten over our seasickness. The Quileute Tribe at La Push offered us a momentary respite, so we decided to go in.

Two navigational buoys lay offshore to help guide you to the river's mouth. Depending on the waves and wind and your speed, the course may not be straight; you'll zig and zag. With a heavy following sea, the zag can be extremely wide. As you start to gain James Island the zig will bring you uncomfortably close to wash rocks, rocks, rocks, rocks. The steep sandy beach is dead ahead. Just before the breakwater, a quick jog to the left, then a quick jog to the right

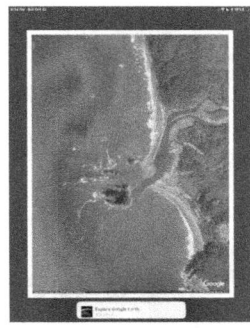

Entrance to the Quileute River by Google Earth

through a tight opening gets you to the mouth of the river. The river is tidal and so may seem wide or very narrow. It silts up regularly and must be dredged often to keep a channel open for deep water boats.

Zig, zag, rocks, rocks, rocks, jog, jog...

Our first approach was in dense fog, no wind or seas of note, and the radar worked fine. Finding the first buoy, we motored ahead for the second. A sailboat appeared, coming close alongside.

They said, "We thought you were the buoy. Your boat has a really strong radar signature," and then they motored off north. This was good to know.

Moving landward and slowly, wash rocks appeared and the surf hitting the beach seemed deafening. Finding the red light at the end of the breakwater, we jogged and jogged and entered the mouth of the Quileute. It was low tide.

Traveling ahead about 100 feet, we went to dead slow. It was salmon fishing season and the river was choked with gill nets. Too narrow to turn around and nowhere to go, we essentially just sat there.

A local man in an outboard skiff, picking fish from his net, saw our dilemma. Immediately he let go of the net and rushed downstream to us. "Follow me. I'll guide you to the marina." Beyond grateful, soon we were tied to the float.

Kashmira

Kashmira, our 6-year-old goodwill ambassador, was on deck and caught the eye of our new friend. He said to us, "Welcome to La Push. We have a new community center where our children are doing arts and crafts right now. Please come and meet them." Because we home-schooled Kashmira on our boat, any opportunities to engage with other children were special. So hand in hand they walked together while I followed behind.

I felt his kindness. I felt as if I were being wrapped in a blanket of openness and friendship by the Quileute community. Because of that, La Push will always be my healing place.

ICEBERG LETTUCE

After our brief stop in La Push we headed out again to find fish. Endless fog, left us feeling alone and invisible. Bottom fishing off the coast for days in these conditions, we were seasick. Kashmira and I never got over our days and days of seasickness on this trip. I wanted to be done with it all.

This was not the outcome I had expected during all the years of building this boat. Our previous sailing adventures, though decidedly dangerous, seemed carefree and joyous in comparison. Now there was a different kind of high pressure guiding me. I was a new mother and had neglected to foresee this possibility.

The first Westport buoy sighted, invited us landward. Crossing the bar in total fog was not the captain's choice. My darling daughter and uncomplaining deckhand stepped to the hatch, leaned over the deck and vomited blood.

"THAT'S IT! We're going in. I don't care what you think," said I.

With radar, luck and stubbornness, we pulled into a slip less than an hour later. Wishkah Valley Doug was there to grab our lines. He had heard our Hundested engine, and knowing there was only one boat on the Washington coast that sounded like that, had rushed to the dock.

Longing to permanently jump ship after our shakedown, I begged Doug to drive Kashmira and me home. He refused. I felt physically beat up and emotionally unsupported. All the decisions regarding when to go, how long to stay out and when to come in, were never mine to make.

On no occasion did Kashmira ever give a hint that whatever we were doing wasn't exactly what she also wanted to do. Her mal-de-mer was just part of fishing with mom and dad. Even this current episode that seemed so dangerous cleared up the moment we both stepped ashore with no signs of continuing problems.

Towards that end, she and I deserted our boat for the local diner. We ordered what seemed like the best meal we'd ever enjoyed: an iceberg lettuce salad.

2,000 MILES

Our family was in crisis. Four years of relentless effort, dedication, and optimistic dreams of our future had only taken us as far as Westport before I was desperate to abandon ship. Mere months from launching, even I could see that I wasn't giving our future a fair chance. But I was tired, beyond tired, and fully aware that I never felt able to take a day off. Wishkah Doug recognized our situation and stepped in to save us.

We both knew Doug from Eagle Harbor where he kept his troller. A second generation commercial fisherman, he'd fished with his dad, then on his own – a valuable addition to any crew. Alaska was his second home. He knew what we were going through.

Both he and Paul counseled me with care, understanding my tender condition. They talked me down off the emotional ledge and made me feel heard. We both accepted Doug's invitation to tour the area the following day, the place where he'd grown up.

It was a shore-side adventure of cranberry bogs, meeting his parents at his family home in the Wishkah Valley and driving on miles of sand beaches. We didn't know you could drive on a beach, and Kashmira and I laughed so much. Almost every place special to Doug, he shared with us for longer than just one day. It felt like a perfect vacation from our daily routines. Doug's intervention worked.

Five days later, we cast off the lines and headed back to Eagle Harbor, done for the winter. But not before Paul and I came to an agreement. Both of us still longed to live our plan of fishing together as a family. We had the boat, the fishery and the family to do it. My fear for the safety of our endeavor with a 6-year-old onboard was all that held us back. I required more say in the where, when and how. He promised to do whatever it took to put my fears at bay. We made a pact. I would commit to 2,000 more miles and reassess then. We spit on it.

LEAVING IN FEBRUARY

A high pressure ridge that settles over the Great Pacific Northwest can often be counted on in February. It brings cold north winds. The west coast albacore fishery generally starts earnestly in July. After our initial shakedown cruise in October, we were faced with the question: do we wait for July, or leave in February and go looking for fish?

Hot to leave, we readied the boat.

Our plan was to sail to Hawaii, shed some clothes, re-provision and investigate the waters west of there. This would be a true test of the new boat and crew and we might even catch some albacore.

Saying goodbye to our family and friends on February 1, it was four years to the day since we had started building *Ocean*. As we watched the weather, it appeared our high pressure hopes would come true. After bucking a strong westerly in the straits, we were glad to pull into Neah Bay where we waited for the norther. Very soon we hauled the anchor and sailed past Tatoosh Island, bound for Hilo, Hawaii.

Kashmira and Paul hanging around on the bowsprit

The ocean was alive and showing us her late winter mood. Large swells and that strong north wind helped us on a broad reach heading southwest. All of our equipment, especially the boat, performed flawlessly. Our standard watches were four hours on, four hours off, which quickly changed as our individual gifts became apparent. Always prone to seasickness for at least the first three days, I preferred being on deck. Any chores down below were extremely difficult. Cooking, especially, exacerbated my mal de mer. Instead, I was a strong, competent helmsman, able to hold a watch for 6 hours before needing relief. This allowed Paul to handle almost everything else needed doing.

My first night watch tested my nerve. The sky was black with heavy overcast. No stars, no moon. The only light to see was the vigilant mast-head light, my only friend awake. It had been awhile, so I needed to re-learn my strengths and weaknesses.

The growing seas rumbled like freight trains bearing down on me and the chorus of the wind and waves were deafening. I'd hear them coming, just off my stern, and every single one rushed to the boat, hit the side and leapt straight up in the air, where they would turn into a creature from a Disneyland ride: bulge-eyed, wide-mouthed, laughing and howling at me, "Hahahahaha. Boogabooga-booga!" Confidentially, I was scared.

And so I returned to that long-running lifelong conversation I had dropped sometime back. "God, it's me again. I need your help. Can I have some guts please? All I need are some guts." I immediately threw up. After a while, I asked the same thing again. Again I threw up. It finally dawned on me that God was giving me exactly what I had asked for. So this time I said, "God, give me courage. All I need is some courage." And that did the trick! The rest of my dark night watches I felt confident and those Disneyland ghouls vanished.

Three days after leaving Cape Flattery, our brand-new autopilot broke. It was like having one less hand to help steer the boat. We had a staff meeting to discuss our options. Turning northeast against these swells and wind to return home for a replacement was out of the question. Service and parts were available in San Francisco or we could continue on towards Hawaii, hand steering every moment. We both agreed, "How hard could it be to hand steer the rest of the way? Let's go for it."

Two days later we both cried Uncle, eased the sheets and roared downwind for The Bay. Quite possibly over-canvassed, we yawed our way south, and was never able to leave the helm. It was one of the most thrilling stretches of ocean we ever saw.

Sailing under the Golden Gate was an emotional homecoming for me. This was where I had first picked up my saltwater path.

We made our way to Napa Street in Sausalito (now called Galilee Harbor) where there remained a remnant of the community I had lived in at Gate 3. True to form, they welcomed us with the generosity and kindness that mariners show each other. Annie, who first introduced me to the waterfront, was there. " Boatswayne" or "Boats," who wore shorty-shorts that are still legendary, lived aboard the 38' *Santa Lucia*. Jeff, Dudley, and Duane, along with other old friends, remembered me and my humble beginnings. All those years ago, Duane had tried in vain to teach me how to sail on his sweet boat *Bertha*. But my sailing synapses weren't firing yet. He had a son now named Simon who was about the same age as Kashmira. They played together while we were in port.

I didn't mind at all returning to this precious place in a vessel everyone admired. We stayed until our repairs were complete.

GALE

Well, of course we left port in a gale. Our time in Sausalito had stretched beyond the simple repairs we came in to make. The old expression, "Men and ships rot in port," was beginning to feel personal. We needed to bust out of our comfort zone and get underway.

I was always easily susceptible to charm and Paul had an uncanny knack for bringing out the youthful beast in me. Heavily laden with too much ego and Yo Ho Ho bravado – and convinced we were invincible – we barely gave pause to the question, "I mean really. How hard could a gale be?" We cast off the lines. Next stop, Hilo!

A friend later told us as he drove across the Golden Gate Bridge that day, he looked down and saw our boat bashing hard into it. All he could think was, "Those poor bastards!"

By then the new autopilot was earning her keep. Down below, legs spread wide to counter the movement, and eyes glued through the pilot house windows, we watched helplessly as everything not welded to the wooden deck flew overboard: flotsam to end up on Baker Beach. To our horror we saw the forestay systematically unwinding itself off the turnbuckle on the stem head with every pounding wave. Without a forestay and in these sea conditions, we would surely lose the rig. We had forgotten to mouse it while doing repairs.

Paul raced to the slide hatch, tools in hand, turned and said, "If I go overboard, be sure and come back and get me."

"No chance in hell." I said. "The best I can do is note the lat/long where I last saw you, to tell your parents."

He made it back safely. Now with the rig intact, I took to my bunk with immense mal de mer. A particularly hard knock down levitated a well secured bottle of sesame oil. It flew across the cabin, hit me in the head and broke when it fell to the floor. It was 25 years before I could stomach that smell again.

WITNESS

I make no apologies. I'm different, exactly like everyone else.

Sailing offshore and taking my watch on deck, I'd often witness that glorious night sky. Sometimes I called the crew to come take a look. They'd bounce to the hatch and squeeze together in it looking up, she and her father. And just as lively, off they'd go to grab the astronomy reference book. Soon they'd be standing together back in the hatch. One by one, each constellation would be identified and its mystical story retold.

Identification never held my interest or curiosity. I merely wanted to gaze upon the billions of stars, be awed by them and enjoy the magnificence. I am a different kind of witness to my world.

OVERBOARD

We were sailing from San Francisco to Hawaii on our newly launched boat, me, my 7- year-old daughter and her father. Four hours on, four hours off. Being more than halfway, we'd picked up the trade winds and were hardly wearing any clothes. Just off watch, I looked around, saw that everything was perfect, and decided to take a mid-day nap.

After sleeping in the pilot house for an hour and a half, I woke to find no one about. This was a small sailboat, 38 feet on deck. There weren't many places anyone could be, but I started looking, because this was unusual. Glancing into the engine room, I could see they weren't there. On deck, I went forward to the fo'c'sle, slid open the hatch and called their names. This was the likeliest place I'd find them, what with having bunks and a bathtub. No reply. I scurried down the ladder. Nope. They weren't there.

The only other place on board was the fish hold. At 35 degrees below zero, there wasn't much chance our 7-year-old would be there. But I looked anyway. I looked and then went down to search every square inch of the tiny frigid hold. Nobody was there.

Back on deck, I was beyond panic. Where could they be? I even looked aloft, because they were both fun-loving and liked to "hang around. "

Kashmira on the bobstay

Of all the times I'd been at sea, the biggest fear I ever had was losing someone overboard. And here we were. I remember standing midships and screaming their names as loud as I could. Nothing.

I was about to run back to the pilot house, disengage the autopilot and turn around to look for them. Look for them? When did they go over? And where? How was I going to look for them?

And then I thought of one more place they could be. I ran up to the bow and looked over the edge of the deck. There they were, sitting on the bobstay chain, laughing in the bow wave. "Hi mommy. Me having fun."

My relief at finding them was immediately replaced with a kind of anger that can only be expressed thusly. The fact that I did not kill him right then and right there, should be noted in my file.

WAY OUT WEST

We found Hilo with our Loran, (an electronic navigational system popular at the time) then sighted the 13,000 foot volcanic mountains lording over mist and clouds so magnificently, it was undeniably land. After several days of eating ice cream and stretching our legs, we bought copious amounts of tropical fruits. Splurging on expense, we took a rental car to Kilauea and Mauna Loa, two of the world's most active volcanoes.

The Hawai'i Volcanoes National Park blew my mind. Driving through tropical rain forests, past steam vents and over black silica lava beds to the Crater Rim, we could feel the presence of Pele, the volcano goddess. It still remains my favorite National Park.

The Hawaiian islands offered remarkable views into a different world than where we were from. Ostensibly heading for Oahu, we wanted to poke in where we could. After leaving the Big Island, we took a magnificent knock-down in the Alenuihaha Channel. Famous for its fierce unforgiving winds, its reputation was not overstated. It woke us right up.

Paul had visited the Island of Lanai several years prior and raved about its loveliness. We dropped our hook there in a small protected anchorage, needing a nap before we went ashore. In less than five minutes, a local in a runabout insisted we must immediately leave. Lanai wasn't open for unexpected visitors. Crying fatigue, we pleaded for a brief respite but the answer was decidedly no. Bruised from this reception, we hauled the anchor and set our course for Oahu, choosing not to visit Maui or Molokai.

Arriving after dark to Honolulu's waterfront, we faced a puzzle in finding the right lights that marked the harbor. Red, green and white blinking lights were side by side the entire south shore. The breaking surf was disorienting as we chose one entrance we hoped would be the Ala Wai yacht harbor, and powered in. Tied up at last, rattled and weary, we were grateful for a place to stop. Immediately, the harbormaster let us know our boat didn't pass muster and we would have to leave. Apparently the commercial basin next door was where we belonged. This time we insisted on an overnight first, before we would leave. She allowed it.

The following morning found us powering into the surf, taking a hard right and a hard right again to enter the boat harbor to the west. This was where the commercial fishing and charter boats moored. It was huge and appeared to have room for us. Secured again, we waited for the harbormaster. It wasn't long before he stepped aboard and claimed our yacht could not stay here either. *Ocean* was brand new, pretty and looked like a yacht, except for the trolling poles and fish hold. She was a commercial boat. Of this, we held firm too. Kewalo basin was where we belonged and we weren't leaving.

The local community wrapped their collective good will around us. A young fishing family made sense to them. By far the smallest boat, we were surrounded by large steel ocean-going fish boats. A Korean boat owner across the dock brought his wife to meet us. She delivered a large jar of homemade kimchi as a welcome gift. A gruff Hawaiian captain who never smiled, always walked past without acknowledgement.

Kashmira was on the stern deck one day in her bathing suit, holding a loaded Super Soaker water gun that another boat captain had gifted her. Noticing the gun in her hands and startled by it, he jumped back quickly until he recognized it as a playful moment. About to get clobbered by a 7-year-old, he went back to his boat, grabbed a bucket, filled it with water and beat her at her own game. They both roared with laughter and he never walked by again without saying hello. Once again, our young goodwill ambassador smoothed our new connections.

Oahu was a treasure of stunning visual feasts. We rented a beater automobile and took in some sights. Snorkeling in Hanauma Bay on the southeast coast of the island, we hand-fed frozen peas to fish. This was wildly exciting for our 7-year-old but its pristine beauty and accessible ease encouraged over-tourism of this small nature preserve. Coconut oil from the densely packed bodies lying chockablock on the beach covered the water with a thick, sweet-smelling sheen. A human oil slick. We didn't stay long.

Several weeks later, re-provisioned and fueled up, we cast off the lines to head west. We were here to find tuna, after all. As we were leaving, a dock-side opinionator yelled out, "You're going to kill a lot of birds with those trolling lines. Better get used to it."

We were horrified at his comment.

Kashmira with a snake mackerel - nothing boring here

This next stretch of ocean proved to be the most captivating water we'd ever seen. I've never understood people who claim to be bored at sea. Every day is different and brings new wonder. We went out there, way out there, towards Midway. Here, at last, before the customary season with its competitiveness, we learned to catch fish in a new fishery, in our new boat, and in a wonderfully tropical environment, on our own terms.

The weather was superb – puffy white clouds and steady trade winds at 8-10 knots. We moved right along, hardly heeling. Clothes were definitely optional, though as I pulled in the very first tuna we ever caught, the barbless hook popped out of its jaw and embedded itself into my calf. Henceforth, I always wore rubber boots and sometimes nothing else. My tan line was curious.

Dolphins were everywhere, hundreds of them per family, playing in our bow wave and as far as the eye could see. We sailed alongside a turtle and lifted it aboard, put it in a large bucket of saltwater and kept it just long enough for Kashmira to name it Shelly. Whales visited us often, swimming so close to our lee side, we could easily have stepped on to their backs. A mother brought twin babies to see us, bragging no doubt. It was stunning the amount of life willing to expose themselves to us.

Later on we would be in a part of the Pacific Ocean that men had likely sullied, for whenever we ran forward to say hello to the visiting dolphins on our bow, they dove and never again came up.

People were there too. Being close to Pearl Harbor, the Navy flew test flights over our area and strafed us for practice. In the middle of the day, we heard a huge explosion of sound, looked up and nothing was there. Wondering what had happened, we continued looking up until they returned. A tiny dot grew to exactly over us in a matter of seconds. There was another huge boom and then they were gone. These fast moving aircraft were deeply sobering.

We came upon two Asian drift nets and their mother ships. Illegal now, it was a hugely impactful fishery at the time. Our first encounter was mid-day. The entire crew stopped work to yell and wave at our 7-year-old deckhand, an anomaly in those parts. These nets stretched for miles. Sailing up to one, luck was needed to determine which way to head to find the nearest end to continue sailing westward. Sailing through them would have fouled our propeller.

Our second encounter was uncanny. Late at night as the autopilot steered, the deep sound of another larger engine woke us both at the same moment. Levitating ourselves to the hatch in concert we watched as we passed by the mother ship, providentially sailing perfectly parallel to the drift nets 100 feet away from us. Grateful for our guardian angel, we stayed awake the rest of the night, until we found the net's end.

There were fish out there too – tuna, our target species.

From the aft deck, I heard Paul scream, "Bird!" Racing to the stern, I saw an albatross being dragged by one of our lines. It was drowning. Faster than fast and two handing it, Paul and I hauled in the longest fishing line, hoping for the best. We swung the bird on deck. It looked drunk. Paul began giving it CPR: tiny chest compressions, squeak, squeak, squeaky noises. The bird finally vomited the Pacific Ocean, regained consciousness and stood alongside us momentarily until it felt present. Just before it took flight, it bit Paul, as a kind of thanks.

We never caught another bird; confirmation that God was watching over us.

CHOOSING HOME

Returning to Oahu, with fish to sell, we came to realize that Hawaiians refused to consider frozen at sea (FAS) fish. They were used to fresh only and it was nearly impossible even to give our catch away, even though we had invested in the highest quality FAS equipment. Hawaiian dogs wouldn't deign to eat our fish. We headed back to the west coast of Washington to engage in our albacore fishery season.

The season was reasonable. We found fish and developed an off-the-boat niche market, turning off the engine at home October 15. We slept for weeks.

Looking forward, I suggested Alaska for our next foray, it being an environment more interesting to me. We rested up, geared and provisioned up and left to go north, again on February 1.

Everything about Alaska was a surprise. Traveling north, at every turn in the channel, the landscape offered me what I was used to seeing: American consumerism. I'd see a Walmart or a condominium adjacent to an airstrip. But it always turned out to be rocks. Just rocks. I came to realize we often only see what our minds know from our learned experience. In 1989, the year of the spill in Prince William Sound, we entered Southeast Alaska, hoping for a chance.

Sitka was a lodestar for me, with its visual beauty and friendly community. I'd never seen so many men wearing front packs carrying babies. I intuitively knew this was where I belonged and imagined I would eventually move there. I am still surprised that never happened. Instead, we bought a license and fished for bottom fish. The summer sun and high latitudes allowed us to wake and work from around 4ish a.m. to 10ish p.m., when the light faded. We were bone weary.

We bought into the derby, the halibut opening where you fished regardless of weather. During the season, almost every boat in the harbor held a permit and went out for it.

Halibut are caught on longlines, not the trolling gear we generally used for tuna. With generous advice from local fishermen, we bought the buoys, anchors, and heavy longline (groundline) that you let out and

Halibut fishing

then hauled back in later after a 6 or so hour soak. Our hydraulic tuna puller worked perfectly for the heavy weight of the haul-in. Short, lighter weight lines, or gangions, were uniformly snapped onto the main longline, connected to a baited circle hook. The whole schmear was neatly coiled into large deep buckets ready to set and returned to the buckets the same way after the fish on the hooks were bonked on the bean (subdued) and put into the fishhold.

I soon learned that a deckhand can still coil down the hauled-in longline into the buckets when they are sound asleep.

A dangerous fishery and exhausting, we had been awake and hard at it more than 36 hours. I was hauling in and something caught. As I held the main line with my left hand, the hook on the gangion uncaught itself and went into my right thumb deeply. We had anticipated this possibility and left a knife handy to cut the line if necessary. But I had to hold the long line solid, so as not to pull me overboard, and the gangion with the hook still required attention.

I yelled for help. I needed three hands. Paul staggered towards me, knife in hand. Drunk with tiredness I imagined he wanted to save the rigging and not my thumb. "Don't cut it off," I screamed. Quietly he advanced and cut only the gangion.

We were spent. All the while, our 8-year-old daughter was down below cooking up breakfast on the diesel stove: pancakes, eggs, and French toast. Never scared and always optimistic, she was a first class deckhand.

We never found our place in Alaska, though we tried. Heading back to the lower 48, we engaged again in the summer albacore fishery.

The king salmon

This season was lean. Including the sparse income from the Alaskan enterprise, our bank account was smaller than before the start of the year. Frantic to dig our way out of debt, we chose to continue fishing late after the equinox, north off of Cape Scott at the tip of Vancouver Island. Sometimes albacore can be found there late in the season.

The weather was rough as one might expect, and carrying reduced sail area, waves crashed over us. It was dangerous on deck and the engine was getting a workout trying to make forward progress. What few fish we caught when we hazarded on deck were limited by the sea conditions. We had to throw out a drogue, or sea anchor, to hold us on the fish every night, yet we continued to drift 20 miles anyway, bashing into the wind and waves.

Standing in the pilothouse all those days, looking out the windows to our watery surrounds, I knew the boat would survive. We weren't going to die. But a sea change was developing in me, every day stronger until I was sure I knew what to do.

Remembering the 2,000 mile pact that Paul and I made in Westport, it could be said I'd fulfilled my promise to Paul fivefold. This life was not for me. "Take me home," I said. He did and that was that. I never fished again.

CHAPTER 7
HELM
1990 – 1994

"I like doing things my own way."
—Kirsten Neuschäfer

BUTTONS

T was beyond fortunate to be asked to move to Port Townsend and join a boat building shop as a shipwright with 3 great men: all gentlemen. The shop owner knew my work and my need to relocate and invited me. I was suddenly exposed to a broader boating industry than where I was from. I sharpened my skills and learned tons, not the least of which was how to get along as part of a team.

Many people know it isn't necessarily the level of skill you may bring to the table, because that can grow along with your rate of pay. More important is how well you can work together and make the workplace somewhere we all want to be. In my three years working there I watched several talented independent woodworkers and shipwrights get hired and then let go because frankly, they were no fun to work with. Somehow, they kept me on.

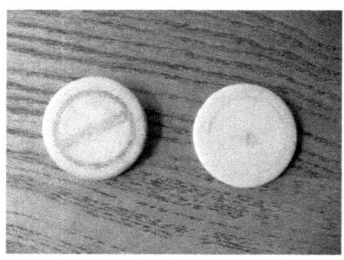

Unbeknownst to me and apparently for some time, the men had learned to walk on tender eggshells around me just about one week out of every month. Finally, one of them made and presented me with this set of buttons. He presented them to me privately, with genuine care and interest in my well-being. The buttons displayed the International Symbols of Period or No Period. I was not happy and fiercely convinced that hormones, my hormones, had no effect on my demeanor or fluctuating sensitivity. But it had been a soft discussion of my moods. I wore these buttons anyway and changed them out appropriately because of the kindness and humor with which they were given.

Things at the shop improved immediately. No more eggshells. I came to understand that if I just tempered my feisty spirit a bit, listened well and opened myself up to constructive criticism, I could learn a lot from these gentle men. (It was entertaining to watch them try to explain to customers what the buttons represented.)

But the men weren't always angels either. There were times when someone would walk through that shop door, and you just knew it was going to be one of those days. I began to understand that on those mornings, most likely he hadn't satisfactorily completed an argument with his wife before he came to work. And through gender extension, I became the brunt of his discontent. Generally I just let it roll off my back, kept myself busy with my work and knew that all that was wrong was that he had not yet fully learned how to speak respectfully to women every single time.

I wanted my work. I needed my work. It was so much bigger than just a paycheck. It was a passion I fell into that drove me. "Last man hired," I knew to take on more than just the hours in the shop at rate per day.

Our shop vac had died. It was a vital tool that everyone used. Early the next day I came in, tore it apart, fixed the problem and completely rebuilt it. When my boss came to work, I was just finishing up. It was clear he was continuing an argument with his wife and I was the recipient of his mood. He approached and said, "Gee Diana, I had no idea you would know how to do something like that and all by yourself." And just like that, I was completely, finally and decisively done with taking condescension from anyone.

Very calmly I looked him straight in the eyes and emphatically said, "I know a lot about Suck and Blow." His eyes went wide; he stood up straight, zipped his lip and went to work. And never, ever again, did I hear one snarky remark from any of my co-workers.

This, it must be said, was the same man who came to me early on and told me, "I can't imagine how hard it must be to be a single working mother. I want you to feel free to come to work every morning after you've got her off to school and to leave early enough to be there when she comes home." Who does that?

I miss that shop. We had great fun producing good work, growing together and laughing a lot. We all learned about men and women, our differences and similarities from each other; Jan Watson, David Vohs and Steve Langhorst, gentlemen all. Buoying each other up, we were a team.

SCANDIA

Something guides me. It's a power I still don't understand, but I never take it for granted. I've walked through doors that never felt like anything I could take credit for, and yet, I decided to walk through them. *Scandia* was one of those decisions.

I had moved to Port Townsend by myself, practically penniless and was kind of couch surfing on generous friends' boats. My free rents allowed me a leg up to save for my own living scene. One particular job netted me a whopping $4,000, so I began to look in earnest.

Of course I wanted to buy a boat to live on, something large enough for Kashmira and me, and it had to be wood. Onshore housing still felt alien to me. I perused boat listings in all the regional nautical magazines and saw there wasn't much available in my price range until a 38-footer stored in Anacortes caught my eye. She was a Kettenburg 38 named *Scandia* with 26' of waterline, 6 feet deep and 8 feet wide, hull number 6 and launched in 1949. Sheesh! So different from the wide, slow boats I was used to. I was completely ignorant of the Kettenburg legacy; it's a renowned boat building shop in San Diego that built hundreds of boats over 40 years of family ownership. I called the broker immediately and went up to see her.

Someone had torn her apart, de-rigged her and barely started to put her back together when they lost their umph. What she had of a hull was half-painted, with long planks on each side hanging half-fastened to her hull, the ends left flapping in the breeze. Her boom and delaminated 47-foot spruce mast sat on horses, and there were multiple boxes of bronze hardware. She had been sitting there, unloved, a very long time. I went aboard and did my own survey.

Surprisingly, not a bit rotten, she boasted nothing but potential. I asked the broker to buy her and he countered that I shouldn't, but we finally agreed to the $4,000 asking price.

Jan Anderson, our local independent boat mover, agreed to collect and bring her home after mighty begging on my part and a kind word from David Langley. Set up in the Boat Haven, I began making her right and livable in my spare time between jobs.

She taught me major lessons in a different kind of traditional boatbuilding than I knew: restoration and repair. Better than boat school! She required a new rudder, floor timbers, bronze drift bolts, and a new engine. A quarter of the hull needed replanking, new butt blocks would need to go in and the whole hull corked. A third of the hull required steam-bent oak sister frames alongside the original broken ones. I needed to rebuild the interior, fashion and install new toe rails, and change out the thru-hulls. She had no water tanks, plumbing or electrical. When all that was done, I could putty, paint and varnish. Her spruce mast needed to be wedged apart and glued back together. The boom, deck and standing rigging looked to be fine.

Still living alone, I kicked butt, knowing as soon as I had a place to live, Kashmira would be able to move up to Port Townsend. The sole reason for choosing to buy this boat was because at 38 feet, she might be large enough to live on and I had just enough money. Very poor reasons at best.

Being new to town and furiously industrious, I was a kind of entertainment for the boatyard looky-loos. People would drive by slowly but seldom stopped to talk.

One local shop owner walked over one day and asked, "I've been watching the progress on your boat. It looks really good. Who's doing the work?"

"You're kidding. I'm here every day, only me. I'm doing the work," I replied.

"No really," he said, "Who's doing it?"

I took a deep breath and finally said, "You're right. My boyfriend comes over after dark and works all night for me." This satisfied his curiosity but all I could think was this guy was probably no fun to have sex with.

A more heartening moment occurred when a young father and his 7ish year old daughter were walking by. I was on the ground, hanging a plank. "Now here's a great project," I heard him say. "Look what he's doing there."

"She!" his daughter said.

"Yes, he's planking now," he offered.

"She!" she said again.

Seven months later I re-launched her. Only then did the fact that she was a racing sloop sink in. I had not much affection for her and saw her only as a stepping stone to something else.

At the rigging stage I reached out to Paul Kettenburg, her designer, with handwritten letters, seeking advice. We became pen pals. I offered him a spot as a foredeck gorilla, muscling around my spinnaker. He, in his 80s, sweetly declined my invitation, but I started to think differently about her. Plus, there was a buzz surrounding her hull shape and pedigree as our town is filled with sailors who love to race. To me, racing was a kind of fluff pastime my serious nature did not appreciate. My mantra was always "Work and Struggle to Survive."

Slowly I entered the fray on the bay, racing with the fleet. As I was totally green, racing rules were learned by the guys yelling at me when I did something wrong. I was a proper mess with all my "dirty air." George Maynard asked me if I knew how to sail. "Well of course I know how to sail!" But in reality, I knew how to steer a course and sail it for 200 to 400 miles, then tack the other way. That was my kind of sailing.

Scandia, with her sleek hull, tall rig and light construction, showed me how to get the most out of the wind and currents. Plus I had yet to install an engine and so sailed in and out of the marina – a neat trick with a 38 footer – which improved my skills. I started to win races, even with my blown out Egyptian cotton jib and sad old mains'l. Winning, or the hope of it, piqued my desire to join every race I could.

This happy ownership was better than going to sailing school and led to a deep love and appreciation of her merits, for she was the true sailor, not I.

Scandia - photo by Linda Dugan

RANDY

My first job at the shop in Port Townsend was laying a new fore-deck on the old wooden tugboat, *Noreen*. A glory job! I was young, not unattractive and had years of boat building experience. But I also brought a heightened awareness and sensitivity to the possibility of my being potentially harassed in my new work environment. It was everyone's topic of concern then. Previously, I'd only worked with friends in a community I knew very well. Port Townsend and the Boat Haven was a different world. I was on my own and confidentially, a bit terrified.

The rest of the crew were all men, big, tough, experienced, and hard to read men. The corker who was brought on for the job was Randy Purdue. He was highly inscrutable, immensely funny and could be quite ribald. He held a twinkle in his eyes.

My very first day, sitting on the midships bulwarks, leaning over and working on the side deck, I was wearing plumber's britches and not presenting my best.

There's a sound in the working boatyard when you know everyone is active in their trade, especially the corkers, who produce a high pitched tonal hammering sound as they drive cotton or oakum into seams. Suddenly I realized that it was dead silent and Randy was sitting right below me.

Jumping up, I turned around and yelled bloody murder, "Are you looking at my butt?" What an introduction! Randy turned 3 shades of red, practically started crying and insisted that he wasn't. He could not have been more mortified. I accepted his apology.

Since I was setting my boundaries rather firmly up front, word got around quickly that it might not be a good idea to "mess with" the new "cupcake" in town.

THE NO WORK CAR

When Kashmira was learning her words I must have said, "my car isn't working" so much that her young brain translated it to the "No Work Car." The moniker fit so flawlessly we incorporated it into our family vernacular.

I stopped at a gas station in Poulsbo to top off the tank in the "No Work Car." Always vigilant on maintaining her performance, I'd popped the hood and adjusted the carburetor feed, just to let her know I had her best interests at heart. A young woman was hitch-hiking and I invited her along.

I re-entered the highway and got about 300 feet before I heard a loud BOOM and saw smoke in my back window. I pulled over. "Get out!" I yelled to my new friend, "The car's on fire!" Rushing to the stern I opened the lid and saw the whole compartment consumed by flames. I quickly closed it, not knowing what to do. A pick-up truck immediately stopped and the driver pulled out a fire extinguisher and doused the fire. And then he was gone. So was the hitchhiker, I noticed.

The only time I ever called a tow truck, I had her delivered to the barn on Bainbridge. Sitting on a milk crate I went about the re-plumb and rewire of the engine. The entire repair took about 37 minutes. The best part was when three female realtors came walking into the driveway. Stilettos in mud. I told them what I was doing and they professed to want to do something like that too. "No you don't," I said. They all giggled.

I worked for an Alaskan halibut fisherman one very cold winter in the Boat Haven. Dave Ullin worked with us. I was planning a drive down to Bainbridge Island. The boat owner was particularly fond of Dave, and he asked me to deliver a whole frozen halibut to him for Christmas. It wouldn't fit in the back so I tied it onto the stern of my VW Bug and wrapped its neck in red ribbon as a kind of seasonal apology for everyone who would be stuck behind me going 45 m.p.h.

Her factory running boards finally rusted away. I decided to replace them with some skookum cha-cha locust hardwood. Handsome, they turned out to be. I had been working on a large project as one of the wood butchers with several other sub-contractors. Brion Toss, our local traditional rigger, was on the project too. When Brion saw my new running boards, he hired me to build some for his classic Jeep. It was the beginning of our many years working together.

VOWELS MATTER

I give people my name when I introduce myself: Diana Talley. That's my name. But many people are lazy with names they think they hear. They'll phonetically drop a vowel; hang onto the consonant living next door. No big deal, right? I strongly disagree, as seeing people paying attention can be a large green flag to building relationships.

Ask anyone with a name like mine. Heck, we could be back-up singers for the group Steam. It's irritating and embarrassing to walk around saying, Na na na na, na na na na, hey hey, goodbye all the time.

The first year I lived here I started to hear whispered rumors about me. Not just in the boatyard, but all over town. Apparently, I was thought to be Nat Natali's ex wife, Diane Natali, not Diana Talley. I am almost no-one's ex wife and surely not Nat's. Poor Nat! Of course I knew him and we were friends and neighbors on the dock. We did lots of fun things together but nothing even remotely romantic.

As a way to mitigate any misunderstandings up front, I started adding the phrase, "like the goddess." Any learned person knows there are no goddesses named Diane. Mirthful in intent, I got serious pushback from several men who could not in any way reconcile the idea of me being anything even close to a goddess. Ok, honestly, this irritated me. But these men were all named things like, Edward, Stephen or Joe; names of saints being honored on the day of their birth. Hence, no doubt, they were just bummed that their parents didn't have the wherewithal to name them Zeus, Apollo or Dionysus.

When someone introduces themselves and gives you their name, they are also giving you a gift of a potential friendship that could possibly change your life in a good way. Listen up and pay attention. You can never have too many friends.

DAVE'S GUURL

"We're given a script by our culture of how to live and all we have to do is change the script."—Dave Ullin

Before they invented buses, I was Dave's occasional driver. Usually it was a trip from Bainbridge Island to Port Townsend, where we would work on large commercial boats together. Traveling with Dave was always a riot.

I'd pick him up in my VW bug at the park in Winslow where he'd rowed ashore from his anchored-out tugboat. He'd stow his kit and every possible tool he thought he would need into the backseat. Then he would fold himself into the passenger seat and off we'd go. These trips were the bonus points of being his friend, deep conversations both ways.

An old Alaskan longliner was getting a major refit and the medicated, hung-over indentured crew only seemed to be shoveling smoke, and poorly. When I would drive up and Dave would get out, instantly, his presence changed everything. Each man on the crew stood up straighter, worked harder, looked and acted smarter. Dave never seemed to notice.

There was a palpable feel of near reverence having Dave onboard, and the work progressed efficiently. This feeling blanketed me as well and I didn't mind a bit. The crew always thought I was "Dave's Guurl," an incorrect but charming assumption, as Dave had never had a guurl. But because of this assumption there were never any misogynistic comments, sexual innuendo or crass vulgarity. They pretty much left me alone.

The captain of this historic fish boat had purchased her for a song, but the song was a lament; she needed a lot of work. Spectacularly thrifty, he cut corners when he could.

Determined to complete the refit in time for the season, he pushed the crew hard. We gave it our all. As thanks one day, he bought an 8-ounce cup of coffee for the 7-man crew to share. The owner was a family man and his wife came to visit one afternoon. Both thrilled to see another woman in the boatyard, she and I walked towards each other to make our acquaintance. But before we were within speaking distance, he yelled out, "I don't want you talking to her. I mean it!" She veered away and we never spoke.

Needing more external ballast, he decided to steal a railroad I beam from the tracks where the Larry Scott Trail is now. Dave carried one whole end by himself while three of the shipwrights struggled with the other end. Dave Ullin was a legend.

When she finally went back in the water, with no spare time to make the season, she was the only boat I ever knew that the travelift crew allowed shipwrights to continue working on as they drove her to the launch slip. Traveling down the road, she swung high in the air as the crew kept pouring hot tallow into the bilge to help keep her from sinking. That rank tallow dripped from her seams while the pack of port dogs licked the street behind the boat.

Once though, as sometimes happens in my industry when the skipper needs to release tension, he blew at me. He decided I was the weakest cog in his machine and likely wouldn't stand up to him. He saw the work I had carefully researched, designed, built and installed: a proper pair of running lights for his worthy vessel. He did not like it. I had lined them off parallel to the waterline and the owner thought they should be parallel to the sheer of the boat. That placement would shine the lights up towards the heavens, not towards any other boat floating on his flat earth. "What are you doing? That's not traditional. I want it traditional," he snarked.

Dave briefly stopped his work and quietly said, "She's right. That's exactly the way it should be done." No muss – no fuss – end of discussion. If everyone had a friend like Dave, the world would be a better place.

THE HEART OF THANKSGIVING

My favorite Thanksgiving was in 1990, my first year in Port Townsend. I was essentially homeless, penniless and friendless, and more than a wee bit depressed.

Brion Toss, who I'd been working with recently, saw me on a street corner in Point Hudson. It was a few days before Thanksgiving and he asked if I had somewhere to go for dinner. I burst into a flood of tears, heaving and sobbing and blurted out "NO!"

Not knowing what to do, he put his arms around me somewhat tentatively and said, "Well, you'll be having dinner with my wife Christian and me then." It was my first indication that this was where I could make a home. I fell in love with him that day and will love him forever.

A CHRISTMAS EVE STORY

When I was a young girl my father always assisted Santa in the most delightful ways. It was one of his special things that I embraced and a tradition I continued when I had my own little girl.

Every year my fiercely determined child stayed awake all night, hoping to catch Santa. It was murder, but it was fun.

When her father and I separated, I moved to Port Townsend. That year at Christmas-time she was to spend the holiday with her Dad and the issue of Christmas stockings came up. He didn't believe in Santa Claus and I wasn't going to be there.

The family home was a small two-story converted horse barn — living space on top, shop below. The stockings were always hung by the window with care. So after dark that Christmas Eve and knowing they would be at Nana's for dinner, I went to the barn and set up a 20-foot extension ladder that just reached the window. Then I tried to sleep on Uncle Bruce's boat and set the alarm for 3 a.m.

When the alarm went off I went back to the barn with my sack of stocking stuffers. This was a really nice neighborhood on Bainbridge Island and as I oh so quietly climbed the ladder, all I could think about was Frank Gunn, the local cop, driving down the street and seeing a second story burglar and me ending up in the hoosegow on Christmas Eve.

I made it to the top, but then I had to open those old wooden windows as quietly as I could not knowing if anyone was awake on the inside. Sqeeeeeeak. It was murder, but it was fun. I heard sleeping sounds coming from the inside and so quickly filled both stockings. But then I had to close those old windows as quietly as I could. Sqeeeeeeak. I got down off that ladder lickety split and drove home to Port Townsend.

Of course the best part – and I heard it from her Dad - was when they woke the next morning and found their stockings to be full. Hers with goodies and treats, but she asked her Dad, "Why is your stocking only filled with coal?" He had a proper belly laugh about it and told her, "I guess I've been a very bad boy this year."

PATTY - A RARE BIRD

Dennis and Pat McGuire - photo by Bob Martinson

I had stopped in Mats Mats to visit with Ray Speck, where I'd heard he was helping a husband/wife team build their new sailboat, *Nellie Juan*, at Dale Nordland's barn. I was miffed that Ray wasn't there, finding only this petite, humble woman, building alone and kicking butt. I even told her I was miffed.

But it was clear when we first met, that Patty and I would under-stand each other in ways few people can. She said, "97 days." I said, "106." It just flowed out of us, the stories of our remarkably similar adventures on much of the same stretch of ocean and at about the same time in 1980. That's how long we had each spent at sea in a small sailboat. We fell into an ease I've rarely felt with a stranger. Competent, accomplished and vastly experienced, she brought no bravado to our conversation. A rare bird.

I claim only one religion: to never interrupt someone's work. I broke my vow of silence willingly that day so I could invest in this new friendship.

BOB

Bob was from Alaska – a big, hand hewn, rough cut commercial fisherman. A staunch bachelor and almost a caricature of the edged autonomy that Alaska sometimes spawns. He never smiled.

He brought his boat to the shop for a major overhaul, to totally gut and rebuild the interior to yacht standards as well as all the other usual stuff. This was a big boat, a big project and with spring and the fishing season looming, extra people were brought on.

We all worked out our own business arrangement with him and mindful of his budget, Bob was also a brutal negotiator.

I told him my rate of pay was $15 per hour. "Puuh!" he coughed. "I'm not going to pay you 15 dollars an hour when I could hire a man to do the same thing for that rate. I'll give you no more than 10."

I'd felt this sting before from men and women but no one had ever said these words to my face. Hot with anger, my temperature rising fast, I up and quit the shop and booked outta there, before I blew.

Sitting in my cockpit on that quiet late winter afternoon, still trying to chill, I looked up and saw Jan standing on the bulkhead. Whether unwilling or unable to walk the extra 100 feet to my boat, our negotiations began from where he stood. This was funny because the entire Boat Haven soon became privy to a conversation that really should have been private as we yelled across that stretch of water to one another.

"Diana, come back!"

"No, I won't!"

"But we need you."

"I won't work for such a horrible person."

"But we can't finish it on time without your help."

"I just can't work for someone like that."

"But you need to know that all of us agreed to a cut in pay."

"I can't do it."

"Please Diana. Come back."

I never really knew if it was my genuine need to make rent or my loyalty and fondness for the shop, but when I showed up for work the next morning, Bob openly smirked. I felt defeated. But then Jan did something really cool.

He did a glue up for the large trim piece on the forward edge of the pilot house. It was huge and nothing about it made sense to my eye except the quality of the joints and how the bottom and forward side fit perfectly to the boat; the parts you'd never see. The rest was a mash up of different sized square blocks of teak, grain going every which way with nothing fair and no hint of how the finished piece should look. I'd never seen anything like it.

When the glue set, it took 4 guys to gingerly remove it, lower it to the ground and set it up on the shop bench.

Jan looked at me and said, "Finish it Diana."

"You're kidding?" said I. I'd never cleaned up someone else's work before. He just smiled and went back to another job.

So I set to. This was all handwork and I carved, whittled and rasped. And just like the monkey with a typewriter, when given enough time, he will eventually type the Encyclopedia, I too finished the sculpture. It looked pretty good, raised back in place to be the forward wrap-around trim of the boat's expansive pilot house.

Bob often held court in the shop, surrounded by his fishing buddies, while we bustled around. During one such time, I needed to give him my first bill. I held out the paper.

He snatched it away, scarcely looked at and threw it on the

bench. In typical Bob-speak, he hissed, "I'm not going to pay you this!"

Dumbstruck, I didn't know what to do. I didn't know what to say. All I could think was that I had done my work, the work was good, and I had never complained nor was ever even sullen.

Then he held me with his eyes and softened his tone and said, "Diana, you're worth so much more than this. I'll not give you less than $20 an hour." My first raise!

I could have done without the histrionics or the twisted rite of passage I managed to get through. But Bob taught me that lesson, to never stop believing in yourself. Someone is bound to come along and believe in you too. From then on he was supportive and kind throughout the whole project and beyond. We became friends and he often smiled.

MATT - THE FISHERMAN

I would always try to be there when my 10-year-old walked home from school each day. One particular afternoon, I waited for her for a long time. "I was worried, you're so late," I said.

"Oh. I met a man," said she.

"Great! Just great! What man and where?" I said, earnestly.

"I was walking by the commercial basin, looked down and saw a tuna troller tied up. The captain was on board, so I went down for a visit." My anxiety dissipated as I too, had noticed the boat and heard of Matt.

He welcomed her onboard; fishermen love to talk story with other fishermen. I can picture her there, feet slightly spread apart for balance, as you would stand on the deck of any boat offshore, hands in her pockets, confident and experienced. They spoke for some time, sharing fish stories, ocean stories, and life stories, this tuna fisherman and ten-year- old girl. Kashmira would sometimes stop to visit Matt on her way home from school and always walked taller, her head held higher, after every visit.

GOING ALOFT

I had talked myself into being terrified of going aloft, even though I'd never even tried it. And here I owned a sailboat with a 47-foot mast that needed maintenance. Asking anyone else to do it for me seemed unacceptable. My pride forced me to compromise.

Jack Finney lived across the dock, my neighbor boy who was also a gifted rigger and boat builder. I broached the subject with him. A natural teacher, he offered to train me how to safely pull myself up, tie myself off and let myself down. He made it sound so doable.

After several attempts at learning "the knot," I finally felt confident. He rigged up my boat with a heavy manila line connected to a bosun's chair and up I went. We worked together, pulling on the single block purchase until I reached the top. He waited until I tied "the knot" proper, felt secure and safe, then off the dock he strode.

I screamed, "Hey! Where are you going? Don't leave me here alone!"

He smiled and said, "You can do it all by yourself."

I was so afraid, I clung to the top of the mast with my eyes closed tight, shaking uncontrollably. For several minutes I was immobilized with fear. Then I opened my eyes and looked around. What a view! Things ceased being scary and became wondrous! I had my own top-down look at boats in the harbor, the Cascade mountain range, our sparkling bay filled with maritime activity and Mount Rainier.

Suddenly I had a new interest and skill to market. I built a top notch bosun's chair and invested in a quality gantl'n (gantline) with a five part purchase (line passing through 5 sheaves or pulleys), which proved effortless to use, even decades later, as I aged.

Well into my 60s, a myth went around at how strong I was, and could pull myself up with such ease. Ha! It's all in the rigging!

SCHOONERMEN

A small fleet of Port Townsend sailboats were heading to Sidney, B.C. for the annual Old Gaffer's Race. Miraculously, I was invited to join the large crew of the scow schooner *Patricia* on its maiden voyage. A kind of sailing crew I had never sailed with before, these were serious drinkers. Not Van or Carol of course, but most everyone else.

Van Hope and Carol Baker sat comfortably in their deck chairs while the young sailing enthusiasts took turns steering and running everything but the navigation. That was left to the ship's resident chickens, Loran and Radar, who were charged to squawk loudly if they intuited rocks or reefs to avoid.

Scow Schooner *Patricia* with Van Hope and Carol Baker

The 43 nautical mile run to Sidney took a good three days, stopping at several anchorages along the way. This was a shakedown cruise after all. Systems had to be tested. We even made time to anchor up in Canoe Cove and have Bill Garden aboard, for he designed *Patricia*.

The Old Gaffer's Race itself was well attended but the winds were lackluster. Halfway through the course, and being dead last (scow schooners are reliably slow), we anchored up, donned our swimming togs and over the side we all went. A perfect kind of sailboat race with Van Hope in charge.

Van was a marvel: gracious, and open hearted. So accomplished and still vigorously curious about everybody and everything. He was an old school gentleman and a pleasure to spend time with. I learned on that trip a way of sailing I'd never been exposed to before. It wasn't the speed, size or pedigree you cared about as much as the pleasure in the doing of the getting there. I was more versed in go, go, go.

After the awards ceremony, how was I to get home? I had a job waiting for me and a need to snub up the travel time. Staying with *Patricia* would take several more days. But there was a faster boat just about to leave that would only take hours.

Rob and Arthur were about to cast off their lines and sail home to Port Townsend. The two had come up on *Belle*, a luscious, everything right about it pinky schooner. It was a bachelor cruise. It never occurred to me I might be intruding, or that I even needed to ask for a ride. I can be such an insensitive lout.

"Hey! Hang on!" They waited but not knowing why. I grabbed my sea bag and ran to *Belle*. Plopping it on deck I said, "I'm having my period. It's a bad one this month. I'm gonna go down below and take a nap. Don't call me on deck except in an emergency." Neither of them knew I wanted a ride let alone that I was jumping onboard. This was my brusque request for passage.

Rob and Arthur did what you'd expect Rob and Arthur to do. They looked down, down at their feet while I stepped aboard and went below. Not a word was spoken between them or to me. Gentlemen both; gracious and open hearted.

Hours later, I emerged to a ravenous Westerly, pushing *Belle* inbound up the Straits. A notably uncommon and glorious sail, it was probably my all-time favorite short downwind scream.

PETER - THE BRAVE

Alan Preston hired many of us to work on his long string of customer-owned Grand Banks classic wooden boats. The shop in the Skookum Building, where several other businesses shared space, was travelift accessible. One of the first big-time professional finishers in town, Alan was known for superb paint and varnish results and was always busy. We learned most of his techniques, but his tutorial on how to clean brushes was life-changing. I have passed along those instructions to dozens of customers and co-workers. The landfill is a happier place. Alan hired me to be his wood-butcher, to do whatever repairs were needed. I liked that.

There were two Grand Banks blocked up side by side; sisters. Early one morning before the building started to buzz, I was on the foredeck of one of them, making a repair. Using my three pound hammer to let the boat know who's boss, I was "WHUMPING it." Quite coincidentally, on the foredeck next to me was a young man making the same repair. He was using a ball-peen hammer and it sounded like "tink, tink, tink." A decidedly lowercase sound.

Someone stepped into the shop from outside and boomed out, "You're hitting it like a ###damned little girl. Just hit it!" This was funny to me so I boomed out, "Come over here and I'll show you how a ###damned little girl can hit!" The shop went deadly silent. The two of us on our respective foredecks were once again, alone.

Weeks later, Peter stopped me on the street. Shaking with nervousness, he leaned in close, his voice cracked and stuttered as he quietly confessed, "Diana, it was me that yelled that stupid remark about hitting like a girl. I am so sorry."

When I let out my signature belly laugh, he knew he was forgiven. I've almost never loved someone more for this show of trust and courage.

BUFF BABE

Eventually, rowing as a pastime became my great love. I had always thought of a skiff as merely a vehicle that got me from here to there. It became, instead, a genuine pleasure.

A good friend and I struck a deal. In exchange for yearly mainte-nance on his stunning 16-foot Whitehall, she was mine for the season. Whitehalls were originally built to ferry goods and people to ships in New York Harbor. Their lapstrake hull, full skeg and wine-glass transom comprise a very sexy design.

I felt grumpy most days. Living on a small sailboat as a single mom, juggling work schedules to please both my co-workers and my daughter. Sometimes it felt like I was neglecting my own needs. I developed a habit of jumping in the skiff after work and going for a row.

I preferred this Whitehall to the sleeker shells. It had heft, but was still very slippery. Using my 9-foot oars to propel us at a very good pace, I'd row the same stretch of marine highway every day. I'd leave Boat Haven, heading eastish. It always took about ¾ of the downtown waterfront before my rhythm caught up with the boat's. Then it became pure magic, as effortless as breathing. I'd row to Point Hudson, pull slowly around the harbor and stop long enough to enjoy a Camel straight. Then I'd off back westish to the Boat Haven, always returning happy, peaceful and rejuvenated. It got me out on the water, privately able to survey my world at my own pace. And without even noticing, my body built muscle and tone. I even slimmed down.

Occasionally Kashmira would go with me, rowing tandem. She too was a strong and accomplished rower. As we came in to the Boat Haven one summer afternoon, a neighbor boy yelled out to me, "Are you what they call a buff babe?"

We both looked at each other and whispered, "What's a buff babe?"

ONE-O-THE BEST DATES EVER

New to town and fresh from an unfortunate "divorce," I was righteously celibate and fiercely opposed to "dating." A single mother, I was also desperately hungry for an adult conversation.

Somehow, a friend of mine, a guy, knew all this and asked me out for dinner.

I said yes! Didn't even think of the "what ifs."

He picked me up after both of our workdays at the top of C dock. I remember wearing a clean pink dress. His vehicle was unknown to me, a black 1950 3/4 ton Chevy pickup truck. Super Sexy!

He drove to the ferry and we went to Whidbey Island. He asked, "Do you know this beach?" I had lived on Whidbey years before, yet never knew the west facing beach at Ebey's Landing. He took us there as the sun was descending. The sky was on fire.

Back in the truck, we drove to La Conner, to a favorite restaurant of his that was expecting us. The owners were his friends from years of patronage and treated us like visiting dignitaries. Five stars! Our conversation was interesting, deep, personal and adult and we languished over it for hours.

After catching the late ferry home, he dropped me at the top of C dock. Not even a hint of a kiss. One-o-the best dates ever!

INGER WITH AN E

She, like me, is an Olsen, Olsen with an e. Our ancestors come from the same part of Norway, though she, herself, came to the U.S. quite recently. We discovered this about ourselves along with other deeper similarities when we both crewed on the maiden voyage of the scow schooner *Patricia*. A 5-knot cruise afforded us lots of time to delve into our new friendship.

Later that same year, the Port Townsend Wooden Boat Festival was promoting a family friendly rowboat race. Kashmira and I felt very confident with our rowing abilities, so she signed up in her age group and I signed up in mine. At 10, she was a kick-butt rower and would eventually clean up the field in her own boat her father had built.

Dick Golden was displaying his two-station, 17-foot Rangeley Boat *Master's Skiff* at the festival and offered it to me to use if I wanted it: a stunning double-ended lapstrake rowboat that stood hands above the rest of the fleet. Want it I did and I decided to ask Inger to row with me.

Inter Rankins, Diana and Kashmira

"Do you know how to row Inger?"

"Do I know how to row?! I was rowing before I could walk." That was good enough for me. We never even practiced, just tallowed the oarlocks to smooth the mechanics and waited for the start.

I'm not even sure we all won, and I don't recall other women or girls rowing that day. But we stood out so much in our respective classes, most of the men racing against us rushed up afterwards to shake our hands and remark on our performances.

Kashmira in her Dad's Skiff

I'll wager five bucks they're still talking about us.

THE SHIPWRIGHT'S REGATTA

When I came to town I could count on one hand the number of shipwrights who did not own a sailboat. The backbone of our fleet, almost all old wooden wonders, were owned, used and loved by our community of shipwrights. Our boats were our teachers, our inspiration and connection to a broader world. They were our family members.

Shipwrights are those who build or repair vessels of all sizes, often working 7 days a week, year round in all weather. There was a kind of brain trust led by Pete Johnson, who noticed our tendency to work first and neglect life. They hatched a plan: the first Shipwright's Regatta. Put down the tools, cast off the lines and remind

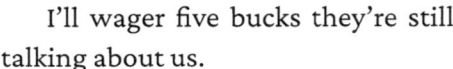

yourself why you love boats, on our bay, mid-winter with almost all of your competitors.

Doug Humes, a shipwright known for his business, "Doug's Shim Shop – We Don't Let Quality Get In The Way Of Progress," was one of my neighbor boys on the dock. Part of the brain trust, he came to see me. "We're all going sailing on Sunday and I want you to come with us."

"I can't go sailing. I have to work on my boat."

"No Diana, you're coming with us! You absolutely have to take this day off for sailing!"

Not happy, never happy, I fought it all the way to jumping on the boat and motoring out the harbor. Of course it proved to be one of my all time favorite days, discovering life beyond work while doing what I loved best – sailing.

Our first awards ceremony was impromptu and proprietary at Rob and Pat's Landfall Restaurant. We huddled around the wood stove and shared a 4 or 5-pack of beer amongst the fleet. Doug cooked up a huge pot of Scow Chow (a tasteless, healthy mix of beans, seeds and cardboard) which we were grateful to inhale. We recognized and celebrated our shipwright community.

Alcyone, Scandia and *Shaman* - photo by Patrick Sullivan

The regatta grew from there. No particular rules of racing, no class starts, horns or flags. A course would be set by a different sailing master each year with changing committee boats and skipper's meeting and awards ceremony venues.

It was a kind of mobile feast. Jim Peacock would sometimes sail out a way, light the fuse, put his fingers in his ears and the cannon mounted on his foredeck would signal the start of the "race." The awards ceremony lasted longer than the race and almost everyone won a prize.

It is arguably the only day of the year that all our local shipwrights can agree on the same thing.

THE FIRST WOMEN'S ROWING CLUB

Port Townsend's waterfront is so inviting, it makes you want to get out on the bay. Inger and I had discovered our mutual love of rowing but neither of us owned proper rowboats so we came up with an idea. The Wooden Boat Foundation was beginning to boast a sizable livery stable of various kinds and sizes of row boats. Surely we could tap into this?

I approached the executive director who loved the idea of getting more people on the water. He couldn't have been more generous and accommodating. The livery was available to us and anyone else who was inspired. I offered that it was likely more women would participate than just the two of us. Still, we both agreed, the following Wednesday at 5pm, we'd all be there.

I have an inordinate natural ability to marshal a throng.

Several phone calls later, our two had grown to every woman we could think of that wanted a go. Wildly excited, the next Wednesday, about 30-plus pumped up women arrived armed with wide smiles. This is when the E.D. made the brave, courageous decision to address our throng, that warm, sunny, perfect-rowing-weather day.

Apparently the board of directors had informed him that the liability issue of allowing anyone to use one of their boats without a licensed captain aboard was impossible. At that time, there was only one licensed captain in the crowd, Ellen Falconer, and she wasn't able to stretch herself amongst all the boats needed. We were beyond disappointed. Such a great idea was thwarted.

Never to miss a surprising opportunity, Inger saved the day. She suggested we all re-convene at the Public House for a beer. Every Wednesday thereafter, for a very long time we all met at 5pm at the Public House. We called ourselves the Women's Rowing Club.

THE FUNKY BOATYARD

Ostensibly, this area in the Boat Haven was set up as an incubator space, to help new entrepreneurs get a start in the marine trades. Prices were reduced for a land footprint and practically anything was allowed. Shops varied in size and scope and trailerable boats could move in alongside. The scow schooner *Patricia* was completed there and schooner *Barlovento* restored.

I was a loyal subcontractor to the shop I worked in, but could see that it was coming to an end. All the boys were about to spread their wings and develop independent careers. I needed to make my own independent plans to move forward.

Systematically I interviewed most of the large shops in town to see if I would be a good fit in any of them. In doing so I understood that my true nature was as a sole proprietor, working for myself. My responsibility and success would depend only on me. No one would tell me how, when, where or what to do. The Funky Boatyard offered that set of wings.

Many original independent Port Townsend trades conducted good business in the Funky Boatyard: David Thompson, Jan Anderson, Bryan Hayes, Barry Stephens, Van Hope, Doug Humes, Roy Wildman, David Langley, Phil Rome, John Huber, Michael Stone Soup, Ray and Roy (the twins) and myself, to name a few.

My cool shop

Randy Purdue and Eric Wilson had built a shop in the compound but had lost interest in it. It was the coolest shop in town by my thinking and I paid top dollar for it, 200 bucks! Located just inside the berm where the railroad tracks were and where the Larry Scott Trail is now. On a high tide, massive southerly storm, the waves would crash over the berm and hit my windows and the whole shop would shake. It was "Whoa, this is livin!"

This shop gave me my start, one of the best decisions I ever made. I had no tools save for several canvas bags of hand, power and mechanical tools. But nothing industrial. I'd always been working out of someone else's big shop, but if I intended to get serious, I needed my own. Jon Gaedke, a commercial fisherman friend from Bainbridge Island, saw my situation and gifted me his original Craftsmen shop tools built in the 40s. It was a set that included a band saw, table saw and joiner. If I needed a thickness planer, Dave Thompson let me use his, which was right down the lane. He only ever asked 5 bucks per use, but whenever I could, I'd sweeten the deal with some cookies. Everyone helped each other and it allowed me to establish myself and build my own business as the incubator was intended to do.

Greed and poor management led to the boatyard's demise several years later. The leaseholder, who negotiated directly with the port and sublet space to all of us, realized he could make a substantial income by renting out more space to more people without shops and businesses. Newcomers were allowed to live in boats and tents and cars. Rats followed, as did less security or feelings of mutual community and so I chose to move to my next shop.

MONEY TALKS

I've been asked how I think cultural changes could come about to promote and support more women in the boat building industry. Money talks, is my answer. Whoever controls it decides the who, what, where, when and how it will be spent.

I've heard it said that generally speaking, more men than women own boats. In my experience and from my perspective as a shop owner (who has hired mostly women) most boats are owned by a husband and wife. If a wife chooses to allow her husband to make all the decisions for maintenance of their boat, that is her choice. But I believe women could do more with the responsibility of ownership.

F/V Duna -photo by Dan Kowalski

Good friends from Alaska owned a stunning, historic and traditional wooden salmon troller. They were in the habit of driving her to Port Townsend at the end of each season to haul and continue their years-long restoration of this very old boat. They were smart about it too, and each year, they only bit off repairs they could afford with the long view in mind. She and he worked side by side in equal measure.

The first year I was in business for myself, they arrived back in town. Taking the initiative, she said to him, "Can we please hire Diana this year? I'm tired of working with male shipwrights. I'd like to work with a woman, someone who will say more to me than just 'I need a cup of coffee.'"

"Of course we can," he agreed.

They hired me that year and every year thereafter I was on the restoration project.

Walt Sonen, Diana, Sachiko Scott and Rick

BOAT MIDWIFERY

Sailors are thought to be superstitious. I prefer to think we are courteous and respectful to unseen powers, cautiously hedging our bets with the unknowable.

Sailing on the ocean, one can easily come to believe there are higher powers, beyond the winds and waves, watching over us, keeping us safe.

Legend has it, whenever a new boat is launched, gifts to these gods must be made. Appropriate alcohol must be delivered to the boat and to the water (champagne for new builds, spirits for restorations) but also a wreath of flowers or greens.

John Huber's Launch of His Swampscott Dory, *Sadie*

Photo by David Jackson

This wreath must stay on the boat (no matter how long), until the vessel leaves the shelter of the harbor. Upon such time, it must be cast into the sea as an offering to the Goddess of Safe Harbors.

Never wanting to test this legend's veracity, I've worked diligently as a boat midwife, building the gifts of wreaths, just in case.

I AM A HOTTIE

My Mom always said that wearing black clothing hides a multitude of sins, and because of that, I almost always wear it. Though confidentially, I fear my sins still show.

Brand new to the boatyard, someone pointed at a boat and said, "Prep that hull for paint." I had brought many skills with me, but paint wasn't one of them. So without direction and armed only with enthusiasm and unearned confidence I happily began my job. No gloves, no mask, no nuthin except a full sheet of 80 grit and a rag drenched with paint thinner. I would merrily sand away and then wipe down the dust. Clever: I kept my rag in my back pocket, always at the ready.

Working up the 30 foot hull, stern to bow, I finished the port side, the shady side, with still a good half-sheet of grit left unsullied. Turning the corner at the stem, immediately, the full force of the sun hit my backside.

Eeeayowza! Essentially and instantly, my pants were on fire. I stripped them down to my knees to find 2nd degree burns outside my little pant's line; extremely painful and beyond unfortunate. Debi Saxton simply said, "You'll only do it once." And she was right.

JESSIE THE DUCK

What do you do when you are living on a 38-footer and your 11-year-old begs for a duck? You "just say yes" (my personal motto since 1982) and drive to Cenex to buy her a duckling. Whereas most people might scoff at a barnyard animal signing ship's articles of agreement, we made it work well for quite a while, her living aboard.

Our first venture beyond the marina, when Jessie was brand new, we cast off the lines and sailed south for a month to visit Kashmira's Nana with our duck as second mate. We tied alongside our old houseboat where Kashmira had been born, anchored in Eagle Harbor.

Sitting on the houseboat deck, a mallard husband and wife drove by. You could see the light bulb flash on in her little baby duck brain. MOM! DAD! Overboard she went, paddling as fast as she could, trying to catch the grownups. As soon as she reached them, they attacked her viciously, almost pecking her to death. I jumped in the skiff and rowed out to save her. This was the watershed moment. From then on, she considered herself just part of our family. Nothing more. Nothing less.

Jessie went everywhere with us: sailing, bicycling, and cruising, as well as long drives, always searching for one more different water experience to enjoy. Sometimes it would be for a row in the skiff, sometimes to eat slugs in a friend's garden.

Kashmira and Jessie

I built a dock box large enough to hold a bale of hay which Kashmira conscientiously used for clean bedding every day. Jessie slept in the hanging locker in a big purple box. The boat smelled of pine tar and the sweet smell of alfalfa.

Jessie would hang out on the dock while we were at school or working, a goodwill ambassador to the tourists, dogs, neighbors and port employees. Amazingly, the port never complained. Because she was flightless, I built a ducky ramp to the water so she could come home whenever she swam in the harbor.

Often, Kashmira would hurry home from school, scoop up the purple box, put Jessie in it and ride downtown on her three-speed bike to Haller Fountain: a tour of Water Street and a freshwater soak for her best friend.

We never imagined we'd want a lesson in duck anatomy, but Jessie gave us one. Jessie was a boy duck. I mean, Jesse was a boy duck! Oh dear. Some visuals just stick but we continued to think of her as a girl.

The day finally came. A neighbor heard the sound of a large splash and Jessie was just gone. The otters took her. Our little boat could not have had a better shipmate, friend, confidante or family member. Quack!

. . .

NATURE AND NUTURE MERGED

Rosetta Olsen and her daughter Frances

Diana and her mother Frances

Diana and her daughter Kashmira

MILTON UTAH

MORMON COUNTRY IS the site of our original homestead and the deep family ties that keep enticing me back. Emigrating from Norway, my great-grandmother Gunda made it just this far and decided to put down roots. Together with Nels Olsen, they raised several daughters and had a good life.

Gifted at cattle ranching, Nels sometimes had to leave the valley and travel to a distant ranch over the mountains to work as a hand for a season. Lines of allegiance were strong and he never shared where his homestead was, nor that they raised sheep. Nels was also a trapper. The term trapper evokes anger and disgust these days, but in the 1800s, trappers were revered in their communities because they protected people and livestock.

Grama Gundy

Grama Gundy held it all together, raising children and tending garden and flocks whenever Nels was gone. This pioneering woman was known for her strength and passed that trait along to her girls, who in turn passed it along to theirs, to theirs, to theirs. Nurture and nature, Olsen women share many undeniable similarities. I now understand and accept that I come from a long line of strong women and no longer feel a need to apologize for my gifts.

My "Uncle" Gale was born, raised and died there. He was an Arabian horse rancher, mink farmer, bishop of the local Mormon church, storyteller, friend to anyone needing one and third generation mountain man and trapper. He had the good sense to marry Nell. Nell had a quiet grace and generous soul, fierce family loyalty and community service dedication. Not born of Olsen stock, she was married to someone who was. She kept it all together and (almost) never complained.

Gale was a talker, told a good tale and often held court by the barn out back. One night, Nell prepared a dinner feast. Her dinners were legendary, often akin to thanksgiving. At the backdoor she yelled, "Dinner's on!" She waited a bit, then yelled again "Dinner's on!" Nothin.

Dinner by then was cold and something snapped. She took the mashed potatoes, gravy and meat and threw it all at the ceiling, then took herself to bed. Gale never missed a dinner call again.

My Mom loved her family connection and wanted to be buried there in the family plot.

THE FAMILY BIBLE

Actually there were two Bibles and both were well-used: Amy Vanderbilt's "The Guide to Gracious Living" and my personal favorite, "Etiquette" by Emily Post. My mother insisted on raising a girl with good manners and it certainly came in handy. I write a very good thank-you note.

When Kashmira was 8, I took her for a long drive to meet our relatives in Idaho and Utah. My favorites were always Nell and Gale Allen in Milton, Utah. Gale was my mom's first cousin, but we always called him Uncle Gale.

Gale was really fun to spend time with. Nell, his bride of almost 50 years, held everything together with her patience and good humor. Straight talking, both of them, you always knew how they felt.

We stayed for several days. Kashmira spent every minute with Gale in the pasture or corral, inhaling his vast natural history and cowboy charm. I spent the better part of our visit sitting on Nell's big bed, looking at family photo albums and hearing her tales.

Every dinner was like Thanksgiving. Nell did it all. After our first dinner together, I rose to start taking dishes to the kitchen. Nell was flabbergasted. "No one has ever lifted a finger to help me in the kitchen."

"What about my Mom? She's who taught me to do this."

"Your Mom! Your Mom was the worst. Whenever she would visit, all she did was sit and expect to be waited on!"

This reinforced what I already knew, that my family had a "Do what I say, not what I do" kind of culture. And yet I appreciated having learned these manners and introduced these bibles into my own child-rearing. Kashmira writes a very good thank-you note too.

Kashmira and Sam

Knowing good etiquette helped me in so many ways. I was faced with a major parenting dilemma several years later. At age 12, Kashmira's best friend was a sweet 13-year-old neighbor boy. They were inseparable and in love, and wanted to get engaged. I knew I had to choose my argument carefully and wondered, WWEPD. (What would Emily Post Do?) Digging deep, I commiserated with my daughter. I told her how happy I was for the two of them but was pretty sure that etiquette doesn't allow engagements to go longer than a year. And at age 12, I was positive she wouldn't be old enough within that timeline to get married.

She was completely down with my explanation and it never came up again.

SHAVINGS IN MY BRASSIERE

This really happens! I've always run hot and usually can only wear tank tops, which is not as much protection for my neckline as OSHA (Occupational Safety and Health Act) standards would want when I'm operating a thickness planer and wood shavings are flying through the air. When it does happen, it's quite a spectacle watching someone like myself prospecting for itchy snippets.

Shavings were deposited in my little pants once and I was none too happy about it. I was holding up a 16 foot, 2x12 Douglas fir board, running it through the large thickness planer. Once the board gets started, you must tend it and cannot let go. A young port employee "travelift cowboy" had been mercilessly trying to get my attention. I simply was not interested. Seeing my situation and knowing I was captive, he rushed over, picked up a handful of planer shavings, pulled the aft waistline of my britches open and dropped them in. Everyone watching roared with laughter. I didn't find it funny.

When the plank was through the machine, I went into the shop, dropped my drawers and tried to clean myself up. Impossible to do and with no privacy, my co-workers witnessed the whole thing. None of them laughed because they knew that when I get offended, I will pointedly state my position.

This "cowboy" almost lost his job over the prank. Speaking on his behalf, I asked the yard boss to just make sure nothing like that ever happened again, for which I did receive a proper apology from the Port.

Very early on in my young 20s, it was clear that my body attracted unwanted attention. Like most young women, I took great care to try and look my best. This attraction never led to furthering my career as a boat builder. I consciously decided to tone it down, leaving behind the extra feminine equipment that objectively attracts attention. Some might say I went too far, but I felt the better for it, even though I was told I was obviously just doing my man thing.

Man thing! What's a man thing? Anyone with an ounce of observational skills will see I'm 100% guurl. I don't want to be a man or especially look like one. I just choose to wear ambidextrous-looking clothes, and have incorporated this "style" into my work-a-day world. People are first judged by their appearance. Associates immediately understand that I am there to work only, not to attract anything more. I mean heck, if I want to slip into something more comfortable, I'll do it at home.

HOWDY

"Here's to it and here's from it, and here's to it again! If you ever get to it, and you don't do it, you may never get to it again."
—Howard Springer

I remember thinking when I met him, what an odd duck he was. I'll wager he felt the same of me. Me, holding a hydraulic post-hole digger, squatting on the edge of the hole I was digging with the pile of loose dirt from it behind me. With the plumber's butt pants I was wearing, I confessed to him that day, "My underwear is filled with dirt."

We got past that and saw each other eye to eye. Mutual friends of equal merit. His knowledge of all things maritime was remarkable, holding degrees as a mechanical engineer, a naval architect and a marine engineer. Howdy had a kind of genius as well, knew what he knew and shared his knowledge generously. Nothing pompous or egotistical about him, a natural born teacher. He and Jeanie moved to Chile with her young children early in their relationship and built the commercial fishing boat building business for Marco in South America. Afterwards they settled in their waterfront Port Madison home. A sailor boy, truly, the waterfront was his element.

We began our friendship working together. He hired me to refurbish his large teak motor-sailer, *Vamos*. I'd sail down on *Scandia* and stay at his dock for a week or two, limit the highway commute time. We'd grill oysters in the shell after work some days, cocktails always at 5. The first bill I submitted to him, penciled on a dirty piece of plywood, he wanted to check my math. A brief overview showed him I'd forgotten to carry the two or some such mistake. He owed me much more money. Another in a series of notifications that we could trust each other completely.

Me n Howdy - Two Peas in a Pod

When he sold that dear old boat of his to its second owner, both he and Jeanie felt the sharp sting of retiring from being able to step aboard. I kept sailing down there and would tie up just for fun after that. Sometimes we'd all go for an evening sail about with Howdy at the helm. It made us happy.

Howard lived a good long life, well past what the doctors imagined. Some kind of medical miracle he was, at the bottom of the Grim Reaper's list. When we finally did gather together to honor this remarkable man, a young relative of his learned how much time we spent together. Incredulously he asked, "You mean you just liked to hang out with him?"

"Howdy was a lot of fun!" was my retort and succinctly worded love report.

THE HANDBOOK OF NAT

There's no handbook given out when your children are born. Even now I remember being a young teenage daughter and tender trouble for my parents, especially my mother.

Karma faced me front and center when my own daughter grew into the same pressures and choices I had tried to navigate.

My first serious romance was with an older boy who clearly did not have my best interests at heart. Clear to everyone but me. My mother, in her zeal, restricted me from seeing him. My mother imported relatives from several states away to talk sense into me. This only served to ramp up my desire. I was undeterred and eventually chose to marry him, if only to prove my point. They were right, of course, I found out soon enough, but there's no sense using reason sometimes.

So here I was 25 years later, facing the same dilemma but the onus was now on me. Like then, I still didn't have a clue but was inspired to seek counsel from someone slightly ahead of my situation. Nat was a friend whose daughter had already graduated high school and seemed a kind of expert. I sought him out.

"What do you do when your girl is dating an older boy who looks to be introducing her to a dangerous path? She won't listen to anything I say."

"You need to go directly to the boy, privately. Appeal to him as a responsible adult and ask for his help to get your daughter successfully through her school years."

So I did. He listened respectfully and understood exactly what I was asking. Very soon after, he just drifted away.

∽

CHAPTER 8

RIGHTING MOMENT
1994 - 2008

"I see the solution for ignorance through example inspired by love."
—Dave Ullin

OLIVE BRINGS HIM 'ROUND

I met Rick through our mutual friend's intervention. I was hard at work on a boat project and she and Rick appeared in the shop. "Diana, come down and meet Rick. He needs your advice for a problem he has with his boat."

"I'm busy! I don't have time! I'm working! Can't you see I'm busy?" A confirmed bachelorette at this point, "I can't give you any time!"

Completely undaunted, she remained steadfast, even more stubborn than myself. After three minutes of her unwavering resolve and repeated dialogue, I finally climbed down to meet this pain in the ass visitor, knowing if I didn't, my workday was done. Rick stood silent, patient and smiling. Not happy and willing to express it, I spluttered, "Ok, show me your boat."

He did need help on his boat. I advised new structural knees in his cockpit. But while walking to A dock, those 200 feet, we just started to talk. It took all of two minutes, even walking slowly, for me to transform from a hard-edged, pissed off, independent woman, burdened with responsibility and feeling no room for joy, to a gushing, soft, mesmerized, young, alive, pile of warm electric feelings inside and out down to my toes. It was beyond sickening, but I happily went for it and never looked back.

And so it began. Is this what you call love at first sight?

The righting moment on a boat is the force that tends to restore a ship to upright equilibrium once a heel has altered the relationship between the vessel's center of buoyancy and center of gravity.

This was a righting moment for me, when I first felt supported to live life well and balanced.

CATCHING THE BOUQUET

That tradition of catching the bride's bouquet has something so right and so not-right about it. Yet almost every bride participates, along with all her spinster girlfriends.

Early on, as a lark, I took to bringing a catcher's mitt, decorated with ribbons and flowers, to every white wedding I attended. All gussied up and holding that mitt, I immediately began to catch each one, possessing an inner confidence that understandably intimidated the field of competitors. A mother of the bride once told me, "It was a supreme waste of time since you have no interest in ever getting married." Mothers of the bride did not think this was funny.

At Auman's wedding, my belt already full of bouquet notches, I decided to sit this one out. Having seen me look longingly at Rick who was also in attendance, Auman had other plans for me. She insisted I join the large group of women vying for her bouquet. I stood in the back, determined not to make a scene.

She began calling my name, waving the flowers and calling my name. "Come and get it Diana." This went on for so long, it was clear she wasn't going to throw it. Not really knowing what to do and wanting to get on with it, apparently I ran a pattern, weaving quickly in and around the group of women until I made it to the front and grabbed the bouquet. Huzzah! Another notch.

Taking my cue, I walked straight up to Rick and held the bouquet to his nose. "Want to smell my flowers?" Smiling, he took a step back and said, "No." Undeterred, I decided to set the hook and hit him with the very best pick up line I could muster. "Hey, you're a man. There's a dance class I want to take. Would you like to take it with me?"

He stepped forward and said "Yes."

THE COOKIE JAR

Invited into Rick's house for the first time, my perfunctory observation was that his was a well loved home. Many details caught my eye, but one thing in particular was the cookie jar.

As the jar already possessed a sense of proprietary standing, I walked over to it, cracked the lid and looked inside. It was full of cookies. "Huh," I thought. This was a huge green flag and enticement to really get to know this man.

OUR FIRST DATE

"Put together whatever you'll need for an overnighter and I'll pick you up at 9 a.m. tomorrow."

Uncharacteristically, he showed up right on time. We drove to our local airport where a chartered four-seater sat waiting. That alone was shocking to me. Rick's thoughtful mode of evacuating Jefferson County was so out of the box. In no particular hurry, the pilot let us choose our path on the way to SeaTac. A blue bird day, we followed the shoreline towards Point No Point, over Port Madison and Blake Island. Once in the big airport, we were shuttled to the car rental stall where a shiny, black Lexus was reserved. Snazzy.

We drove south to the Olympia Brewery in Tumwater, a place I'd seen for 40 years, every time I drove past on I-5. I always wondered about what went on there and so did Rick. It felt almost reverential for this Seattle guurl entering such an iconic Northwest business. The full tour included an Oly tasting. **"It's the water."**

Afterwards, lunching at the historic Falls Terrace restaurant, we both ordered fish & chips. Overlooking the brewery and the upper Deschutes falls, the scene was pretty romantic. Midway through the meal, Rick suggested I take a moment to look at the view. Turning back, most of my food was now on his plate. He just smiled, so I let him keep it. He was playfully pulling my leg and this character virtue was a new look for him. He could hide the deep humor I later learned to expect from him beneath his stoic Yankee demeanor. All it seemed to take to bring it out was my signature kind of can-opener personality. I loved to mine deep for what lay below his reticence and he was thrilled to find a fascinated me to open up to.

After lunch we walked the charming Olympia waterfront where

boats, music and artists shone in a fading autumn sunlight. Things just seemed to get better and better. It was all pretty dreamy.

That evening found us at the Tacoma Dome for an NBA game between the Seattle Supersonics and the Phoenix Suns. Fans were screaming and laughing and jostling each other whenever a basket was made. Three pointers, half the crowd went wild. I'd never experienced professional sports like this and don't even remember who won. I was mostly wild about this charming man who was sitting next to me.

After the game it was back to SeaTac, turned in the car and checked into a very nice hotel. After coffee and our continental breakfast the following morning, we hopped on a bus for downtown Seattle. Every mode of transportation so far had boasted differing views. This bus was slower and required no attention save to each other which we spent lavishly.

Treating the day like we'd never seen the city, we visited the Pike Place Market and the Seattle Art Museum, deciding to save the Space Needle for another time.

Walking to Lake Union we were early for a check in at Lake Union Air, planning to saunter over to the Center for Wooden Boats to kick around the livery and suss it out.

Seems we weren't booked at Lake Union Air but Kenmore Air instead. A simple mistake perhaps but Kenmore is 13 miles north, a long way to walk with less than 2 hours until our reservation goes "Poof" like Cinderella's pumpkin coach at the stroke of midnight.

Teaching ourselves to navigate the bus system, it was a scramble and a full-out run, but we arrived at the head of Lake Washington just in the nick of time. We boarded our seaplane which loudly deposited us on the pizza beach in downtown Port Townsend, apprising all of downtown that we were back. Stepping off the pontoons onto our home-turf pebble beach in my fancy city shoes, I felt completely transformed. I had left town with a handsome stranger and returned with a man I was aching to learn more about.

GINGERBREAD SHIPWRIGHTING

In 1994, Rick was living in Jim Blaiklock's 15 x 15 three-story phone booth. At least that's what his house felt like, angular and compact.

Jim had bought this place several years before but had yet to extricate himself from California. He and Rick were friends, so Jim often made the trip up. He came that year to spend Christmas in Port Townsend.

Jim's Phone Booth

Kashmira and I decided to pay them an early Christmas visit. In a pit of fashion, I bought one o' them do-it-yourself gingerbread house kits to take along. I imagined she and I would make some holiday fun while the boys watched us. It didn't quite turn out that way. When the package hit the table Jim grabbed it and said, "Well lookey here. This isn't right – let's fix it."

The default gingerbread design was a simple single-story Craftsman style house of low-pitched gabled roofs with overhanging eaves, patterned window panes and a covered porch. Jim's house was contemporary with unadorned lines and windows, lacking ornamentation of any kind or even a covered porch.

In no short order, these grownup professional shipwrights filled the table with measuring implements, tri-squares, Japanese and Gent's saws, bevel gauges, chisels, bonkers, straight edges, pencils, paper and a plan. Starting on their first building project together, they cut, fit and fastened the gingerbread into a scale model of the 15x15 three-story phone booth home with windows, a door and sugary snowdrifts, all traditionally fastened with icing and crafts-manship.

Kashmira and I just stood there grinning and watching because, there really wasn't anywhere extra to sit in a phone booth.

YIN AND YANG

In the scheme of things and barely knowing each other, we moved in together fairly quickly. At our advanced age (he was 39 and I was 42) we decided to not waste precious time. When we married our fortunes together, it was clear we had several major differences. He was the yang to my yin.

Always wanting to live simply, my entire trousseau consisted of a few cardboard boxes of family treasures, two canvas bags of tools, a dozen or so articles of clothing and a handful of books. Rick's house was filled to the gills with art, music, furniture, a closet filled with clothes for all occasions, a fully equipped kitchen and an extensive library. It was surprising how much stuff could fit into this "phone booth."

Being a minimalist, I was in the habit of passing along books I'd read, keeping only the few I could never part with. I had kept resource materials, boat building manuals, a dictionary and thesaurus, photo albums, magnificent sailing yarns and "Siddhartha." Taking stock of my tiny library, I'm certain he came to think of me as his lovable illiterati.

He came to me one day, this voracious reader, to share his joy in discovering what he called the best seafaring yarn he'd ever read – an obscure, hard to find novel. Like a child on Christmas morning, he laid out the gist of the story, wide-eyed and enthusiastic, voice inflected with delight.

The protagonist was a young sailor man who is cursed, after a spectacular act of cowardice, to wander "the wild waters till all the seas run dry." He sails through time with many famous captains: Sir Francis Drake, Henry Hudson, Henry Morgan, James Cook, William Bligh and Horatio Nelson. Serving aboard a Grand Banks codfish schooner or fighting as flag-lieutenant aboard the *HMS Victory* during the Battle of Trafalgar, this sailor inhabits every imaginable kind of vessel on every ocean for over 200 significant years.

After Rick's complete synopsis, I said, "Oh, you're talking about the story of Mathew Lawe!" "You've read it?" he asked. "Of course," said I.

It was a turning point for us that day. He thought of me differently from then on. I was now lovable and literate. (The book is "The Master Mariner" by Nicholas Monsarrat.)

UNCONDITIONAL LOVE

After Paul and I separated, his mom Marie made it clear that she would never choose sides between us. She loved us both. We remained deep confidantes as she helped me to be a better family member.

Her first and lasting advice was to never speak poorly of Paul in front of our daughter. Kashmira knew she was half his and half mine, any criticism would tear away at her self-confidence and confuse her understanding of family love. I broke that vow only once over a small indiscretion he had made and the blow-back from Kashmira was immediate and fierce.

Marie's health was failing, her heart was weak. I visited often, collected her and took her out, but living hours away, our time together wasn't the same. I got the phone call late one night from Kashmira, that Marie was in Bremerton in the ICU. It didn't look good.

I practically flew, in my old car, early the next morning to be with her. We had some hours alone before the rest of the family got there. Until then I spoke long and softly to my dear friend, reminding her of the love she had gifted me for so many years. She lay unconscious and hot in her bed, brain dead, the doctors told me. Constant seizures racked her body as I changed out cold compresses, pressing them to her forehead, her temples and neck, tenderly caring for my Marie.

When her family arrived, we sat together awkwardly, not knowing what to do. A young doctor told us too matter-of-factly that if her seizures were distressing to us, they'd be happy to break Marie's neck, which would calm her body for our comfort. I lost it! Crying uncontrollably, I begged them not to do that.

Marie's husband and some of her children and Kashmira were there now, so I chose to leave before her next heart attack would take her. We were told to expect it soon. Her family spoke to me privately in the hallway just before I left. "What did she want done with her remains after she died, Diana?" No one had bothered to ask her. Foolishly thinking it would keep death away, I hadn't either.

She is the only person I have ever known who lived and breathed unconditional love; a majestic inspiration but something I have never been able to live up to.

JIM BLAIKLOCK

I made a T-shirt for him once as a prize for the Shipwright's Regatta. A huge NO emblazoned on its chest. Jim was so generous with his time, he never said no to anyone for anything. I understand he hung the shirt on the wall at home.

An OG shipwright, Jim was superb at all aspects of traditional boatbuilding. The Wooden Boat Festival had enticed him to move from northern California, and once he got here, he embraced life in P.T. It took him a while to move. Jim had a large fleet of boats and American made trucks that had to move with him. All the while,

Rick and I lived in his three-story phone booth, becoming some of his first friends here. We were family.

Sweet on women, he was a prolific chick magnet. Women were drawn to him by his respectful nature and stayed for his deep heart. He began bringing me tulips every year on my birthday. I called them Jim's Two Lips and there are hundreds of them planted around my yard now.

Jim and a friend were having lunch at the Blue Moose Cafe. I came in, saw them, stopped to say hi and leaned down to give Jim a kiss. I always greeted him this way. Surprising us both, this particular kiss was so much more than a friendly peck; electricity shot down to our toes and back up to our hearts where it stayed as we struggled to say, "OH!" The earth shifted momentarily and everyone in the room noticed.

Kind and gentle, we worked and played together for 25 years. In all that time, only once did we ever have a disagreement. It was a doozy, though.

He being a devoted sailor boy and brand new to town and our friendship, I invited him along as a "decorette" aboard my K38 on the Shipwright's Regatta. Before we even left the dock that cold wintry day, we fell into an argument about local politics. Motoring out, it escalated as we set the sails and entered the race. All the while, our voices got louder and shriller, and we were heard by the entire fleet. Sound carries over water. Rick sat between us in silence, trying not to look at either, embarrassed for us both.

"You're wrong!"

"No, you're wrong!"

"How dare you even..."

"Oh yeah!"

"Yeah!"

"Why I oughta!"

"No I oughta!"

Jim Blaiklock - photo by Robin Dudley

We continued to yell at each other the entire racecourse.

Emerging from that temporary blip apparently unscathed, we never shared harsh words again. I can speak of it now that Jim has died and is no longer with us. Because it is very likely that Jim was right!

MONEY WELL SPENT

Marrying our fortunes together included several boats. Rick and I owned three rowboats between us. I had *Scandia*, a Kettenburg 38 racing sloop, and Rick owned *Kah Tai*, a 26-foot pocket cruiser built by Sam Connors. Our "fleet" was in tip-top shape, because we both shared "the sickness."

That first year together, I offered to help Rick with *Kah Tai*'s spring haulout. We immediately fell into the argument about what products were superior. Both of us were "supreme know-it-alls" and neither would yield. I was a fierce proponent of traditional varnish; he boasted his use of Log Oil.

After four days out of the water and on the hard, his boat was perfectly refinished with fresh paint all around. It was then that I thought, someone should make a law forbidding any boats to be built larger than 26 feet because boats that size were so fast to maintain. And, confidentially, his spars and brightwork looked stunning. Log Oil may be superior to varnish, but you never heard that from me.

By now, we were working together as wood butchers on a long term project in the boat yard. Adjacent to our day to day was an abandoned boat inside a well-built temporary building. Without a door, it begged for visitors. I would often step in there and look long and hard at this sad old wooden boat. What I saw was nothing but potential. There were definite signs of love and legacy emanating from her, but her deck was rotten and the house was all wrong. A brand new, 47-foot spruce mast built by Ernie Baird sat on saw horses, hoping for a go. I spent way too much time crawling through her, surveying her, wondering about her. "Someone should save her," became my mantra. Every day, a meditation, "Someone should save her."

We asked around and learned her story. *Taku* did indeed have a legacy. Built in 1947 and designed by Bill Garden, she had raced in the Swiftsure in 1948, raced again in San Francisco Bay, and been re-rigged to a yawl from a cutter to aid her racing handicap. For her time, she was competitive. Sometime in the '60s, she came to Port Townsend, purchased by Glenn and Margie Abraham. Together with the Daubenbergers, they helped build the nascent Port Townsend sailing and racing culture with one of the first sailing yachts in town. Racing her locally, they also ventured north, family and crab pots onboard, cruising the American and Canadian San Juans and beyond. They perfected the complete family boating experience.

We found her present owner, who had bought her from the Abrahams when Glenn's illness required downsizing. He had been a boat school graduate and bought *Taku* with the hope of restoring her. It was a noble first project. Somehow he lost his umph and moved back to his native country, Oh Canadah, and instead bought a 44-foot Hans Christian with a full on down below interior: staterooms, a shower and commodious galley. It would be a wise alternative purchase for his new fiancée. And yet, he was still paying dollars and cents every month to house *Taku* on port property.

Rick and I talked about acquiring the boat, the responsibility and dedication it would take to "do her right." ("Someone should save her.") So we contacted the owner and asked to buy her. This, and it must be said, was within the first six months of us even knowing each other. Dumb, dumb, dumb. Talk about a commitment! Purchasing a wooden boat fixer-upper is akin to adopting a child.

Taku's owner immediately drove down to Port Townsend to seal the deal. Sitting in the cockpit of my K38, we finalized it and handed him a Canadian one dollar bill in payment. We found out later it was way too much to pay. It turned into many thousands of dollars and seven years of saying, "Thanks for your kind invitation, but we will be unable to attend," our new mantra, now that we were restoring an old wooden boat. And yet it also brought us closer together, because we teamed up as "parents" for our "adopted orphan."

As inspiration in the rebuilding, we traveled to Friday Harbor to catch a look at *Rain Bird*, another Bill Garden design that we highly admired. Stuck in Anacortes waiting for a ferry, we remembered that *Taku* had been built there. Knowing the builder's name, we decided to look him up in the phone book. And there he was, almost 50 years later. I called him.

"Hello. We are looking for the builder of the sailboat *Taku*. We own her now. Is that you?"

S/V Taku - photo by Nick Reid

"Why? What's wrong with her?" he brusquely said.

He thought we were looking for warranty work, 50 years after she had launched.

We managed to navigate past that moment and he invited us to come to his home, where he shared his story.

A pilot during the Second World War, his route had been from Seattle to Alaska delivering goods. Every return flight had taken him over the spectacular Taku Glacier where he'd look down upon it and swear, "If I live through this war, I'm going to build a sailboat and call it *Taku*." And he did and we now owned it.

Margie Abraham learned of our purchase. There's a familial relationship to the boats we own, especially the ones we own for decades. Margie, an OG boat babe in Port Townsend, still held *Taku* dear. She invited us into her sailing tribe. Her gracious support held us sway while the boat taught us so many lessons, especially that no dollar bill was ever better spent.

TAKU MARINE

When we bought our sailboat *Taku* for a buck, a large, sturdy building came with it that we turned into a serviceable shop. Having chosen to leave the funky boatyard, I needed another commercial space to work out of and together, Rick and I made it our own.

Shop rules and boundaries were established. It would be kept organized, tools could be shared, and we would be equally responsible for tool maintenance and replacement. We never worked on the same job together. He had his customers and I had mine, with separate businesses and bank accounts. Of these non-negotiables, shop tidiness was a hard learn for me. No doubt about it, I liked things neat but there was a severity about his rule that daunted.

Our local marine hardware store was named Admiral Ship Supply. The Taku Marine shop wall of fasteners contained in oyster jars was so vast, well-designed and maintained, it became locally known as Captain's Ship Supply. Several Sundays when Admiral was closed would see neighbors stopping in to "borrow" needed hardware. In short order, I came to understand that if everything was put away after each use, less time and swear words would be spent finding things later. Saving time saved money and I became a believer; this was one of many apologies I gave over the course of our friendship.

We worked in that location until the Port had to re-ballast and resurface the whole boatyard. The shop and our boat inside had to move. Doug Lockhart, our wise yard boss, engineered a way to move the shop first with one travelift and then move the boat next.

We were relegated to the extreme northwest corner of the heavy haulout yard which was still underutilized. It was as far away from the eyes of the world as it could be. Several other long-term boat projects and their buildings were also sent out back. A blessing, as it turned out to be a quiet, friendly niche location. Old and new customers still seemed to find us, but there was one decidedly distracting environmental flaw: Jake's Restaurant, on the hill above us. The smell of their sumptuous steaks grilling would waft down and encourage us to bushwhack up to savor them. The smell could shorten our workdays as we wore a social path into that hill.

All too soon, the port administration decided to evict all temporary buildings. They didn't like the unprofessional look and were rigid in their decision. Given very little notice, we scrambled for a new home. David Langley had, at that same moment, decided to move out of the 800 sq. foot shop he'd been occupying for years. Shop space was difficult to come by. He offered it to us, said we could just take over his monthly rent. It seemed so easy, we jumped at it. We gave away our building to someone who tore it down for the lumber, then gladly moved into our new space.

All the small blue sheet-metal buildings in the Port were owned by someone named Bill Sperry. The rent was less than what we'd paid to the Port before, and the footprint out back where we parked our boat was part of the deal. It came with liability insurance, cooperative use of a forklift and an outdoor hose. And, it had a flush toilet! This alone elevated us into the ranks of becoming the smallest "big time operator" in town.

Things were looking up. The building was prominently located close to the Boat Haven entrance from Sims Way, and suddenly our customer base began to grow. We needed a proper shop name, a dilemma since two people naming one thing could be contentious. We mulled it over for weeks and finally agreed to name us after our boat *Taku*, discovering later that the Tlingit word for Taku meant "fierce winter winds." Powerful.

Several months later a man stopped in who didn't seem like a boat owner. Barely giving him the time of day, I asked him if he needed something. He smiled and softly declared, "I'm Bill Sperry. How is it you are in this space now?" 'Twas the beginning of the finest relationship with a landlord in my lifetime and stayed that way until Bill decided to sell out to the Port.

When that happened, everything changed. The Port immediately raised the rent and removed the space out back as part of our lease. We were required to hold our own insurance and the forklift went away. Every year, our rent was raised.

When Bill left town to relocate to Forks with his wife, Kitty, he stopped by to say goodbye. He confessed that in all these years, he had forgotten to raise our rent.

BEST HIKE EVER

Rick and I were new and in love, but fairly sick of each other. You know how it is. It was early March after a tough winter spending too much time indoors. Something had to change.

He suggested I hike the coast trail from Lake Ozette to Rialto Beach, by myself, alone, without him. He knew that the Washington coast was a kind of heavenly place for me here on earth, somewhere I had wanted to hike, but this really pissed me off. Everything out there in that wild lonely environment – wind, waves, trees and rain – is extra-large and holds your attention. Why wouldn't he want to come along? I stewed a few days until I realized this was the shake up we/I needed.

This trail is listed as difficult in the hikers guide. Twenty miles of mainly beach walking can be hard on joints, but it is the headlands you must cross that keep it interesting and can be dangerous. Some of the larger capes on this route are never navigable at water-level. The trails over these headlands are steep, primitive and often muddy. It can be a scramble. Fixed ropes are in place and maintained for the most precipitous routes. Even during the summer months, few people will interrupt your solitude. The month of March would prove to be almost completely empty of humans.

Stopping at Brown's Outdoor in Port Angeles, Rick preceded me into the store. Proud as all get out, he announced to anyone listening, "My girlfriend is going to hike the coast trail." All I heard from the salesman was, "Wow, she must be in really good shape."

This really concerned me. I've never thought of myself as being in really good shape.

Dancing on the Coast

After the three-hour drive from home, we hiked the three miles of slippery cedar-planked boardwalk to the beach through the winter-wet maritime forest. Once there, we set up camp and enjoyed unusually fine weather. The sun set golden after a strong showing of late winter warmth and we danced together, as if no one was watching. The next morning we woke to a cold drizzly downpour. It was time to set off alone, by myself without him.

Twice in my life I've worn a watch: when I was breastfeeding and needed to keep track of the time, and now. I carried a tide chart because people die out there trying to hike around headlands with a roaring incoming tide. When the shoreline is flat, the water can very quickly flood the beach. I respected the tides.

After an hour of walking in the rain, I decided to try climbing the steep bluffs, wanting assurance that I would not drown in case I got stuck on an incoming tide. Clay, it was. One step up, slide down, step up again. Repeat.

I gained the top and it felt like a win. Then a terror hit me. A bear poked me on the shoulder! I turned quickly, he poked me again! Turning frantically, I couldn't see him; the bear. My loose head gear had poked me, and I realized I was afraid. Afraid of nothing. So I chose to never be afraid again, such an easy thing to do and so beneficial.

Sliding back down to the beach, I continued south, rain-soaked and euphoric. Passing the Three Fingers of Death, whose names I didn't know the meaning of, I only knew that I was too inexperienced to understand the extent of my poor decisions. Bunches of brightly colored fishing floats were hung in the trees here and there on the beach above high tideline. It was several miles before I discovered they marked places to access fresh water.

Unable to walk around a small headland and impatient for the tide, I climbed up to its top. No ropes or trail was offered. Walking on the steep, slippery route that showed no trace of human feet before me, one false step would have delivered me the 60 feet below, to a dangerous mess of rocks piled together from years of wind and waves.

Only one other person braved the entire stretch of beach that cold, wet March day. As I headed south, he was heading north. It was pissing rain. We shared one minute of "Hi, how are you? " Then the coast was empty again. It was heaven.

As I passed the Norwegian Memorial and the Chilean Memorial, I stopped at each to read the markers placed by their countrymen, to honor the lost crewmen who died so long ago in shipwrecks. This area is part of the Graveyard of the Pacific, a treacherous coastline that has claimed more than 2,000 ships. Its wild inaccessibility is what drew me.

Farther south, there is a shake-roofed three sided wooden shelter, still holding tough in this fierce environment and large enough for several campers. I got to share it with the resident raccoons for two nights, wanting to stay on the coast  an extra day. I take out my secret stash fire starter: bone-dry cedar shavings from the shop, tinder for the fire I'll build to keep the wet cold at bay. I investigated inland a bit the next morning. Built next to a small stream, a small industry of some kind used to be located here; metal and wood are scattered about. Three days later, Rick was very glad to see me at Rialto Beach.

Alone with tides, wind, sun and moon, and the crashing surf booming its hello. Hands down, it was the best hike I ever took.

RITA - THE SMART IRISH LASS

As Rick and I planned our first St. Patrick's dinner together, he called his Irish mother and asked for her soda bread recipe. I'd never heard of soda bread, having descended from a different ethnic background. Apparently I was a Square-Head, from proud Norwegian ancestors, unknown to me in my youth. Mom identified as 100% American, which to her meant we bore neither allegiance nor nod of awareness to any other country.

Rick and Rita

Wanting to please Rick, I followed the recipe exactly, baking several loaves for him and our guests. When he tasted it, he summoned a smile, saying, "It's good, just doesn't taste like my Ma's." I continued to bake it and every year twas the same. "Not gravelly enough, not like my Ma's."

After his parents both died twenty years later, Rick and I were cleaning out the family home and I found Rita's recipe book. I read every page and felt her love in each word. But wouldn't you know, she had a personal recipe for soda bread and it was completely different from the one I'd gotten all those years before. Smart Irish lass!

This is her recipe and how she wrote it.

Irish Bread
3 tea Baking Powder.
3 Cups of Flour.
¾ cups sugar.
1 ½ tea salt.
1 egg
½ box of Raisins
Handful of Caraway Seeds
1 ¼ cup of Milk with 1 tablespoon oil
350 degrees for 1 hour

Now when I bake it, Rick takes a big bite, smiles broadly and says, "Not bad for a Norwegian."

DIANA GONE

Even living with a fun cop (Rick's job was to enforce fun) who consistently coaxed me away from gainful employment, I struggled with my original work ethic to never take time for myself. Habits are hard to break.

Looking around my 'hood, few other marine trades were noticeably good to themselves either. "Work, work, work," their mantra. But there was one individual who noticeably stuck out.

I went to see him and asked, "I've noticed you reliably take time off, go on vacations. How do you manage to get away?" Laughing, he simply explained, "I go to the calendar and write **Bene Gone**. And then I go. It's as simple as that."

Life-changing! Now my calendar reads – **Diana Gone** all over it.

ADROIT

In our very beginning, Rick and I spent the first of many visits with my longest time friend and her new sweetheart, in Oh Canadah. Lynn and I grew up in West Vancouver, B.C., were neighbors as babies, and still stayed in touch.

Rick and Leo had never met and fell right into a mannish conversation, taking the measure of each other.

Quite abruptly, Leo turned to Lynn and said, "WELL! He certainly is adroit!"

Without skipping a beat, Rick turned to me and said, "DIANA! He just called me a droit!"

NEW ENGLAND

Family was important to Rick and he showed me how to honor it. Every summer solstice on his Ma's birthday, he would visit Massachusetts. I was the only guurl he ever brought home and for over 20 years, we traveled there together.

His parents were very welcoming to me. Both were first generation Americans; his Dad was 100% Polish and his Ma was 100% Irish. Cultural cuisine and holidays of both heritages were celebrated equally in that home. But in truth, Rick seemed 50% Polish but 100% Irish. Jumping into foreign customs was wicked fun for me.

New England had never drawn me to her, nor had I ever known a "Yankee." My attitude about everything east coast was tentative and learned through meritless sources. It is very different from my west coast home, but equally attractive and exotically charming. So many of my assumptions were shattered, as one by one we methodically explored every state on two-lane roads and lanes.

Every trip "home," we hatched an expeditionary plan. Our first year we drove through Maine, stopping in every historic waterfront town that grabbed us, up the rugged coast to Acadia National Park.

Acadia National Park, Maine

Subsequent visits spawned new explorations: the "Boat Shops of New England Tour" (where not surprisingly, whenever we introduced ourselves as boat builders from Port Townsend, doors closed to most tourists were magically opened to us.) We were thrilled to search out the legendary shops we'd read about for years. The "Hairs-Off" museum -- the docent corrected us -- in Rhode Island, that generously displays the Herreshoff boatbuilding legacy. Lowell's Boat Shop in Amesbury, Massachusetts, built in 1793 by Mr. Lowell himself. The birthplace of the dory and the oldest boat manufacturer in the U.S., Salem's Maritime Museum built a 171-foot replica of the East Indiaman *Friendship*. We were specifically invited aboard by the park ranger who had heard of Port Townsend's maritime trades and had several questions about problems they had with *Friendship*. But my favorite shop of them all was Harold Burnham's yard in tiny Essex, Massachusetts. Everything about the Essex boat shop and Harold Burnham was right.

We looked long and hard for another Port Townsend every time we traveled east. And what we found was that although the region is filled with remarkable boat building shops, they are spread out with miles between them. Unlike Port Townsend, where everything maritime is within walking distance, each return home reinforced to us the magic that our small town holds.

The "Geography and History of the American Revolutionary War Tour" was staggeringly vast. We started in Concord, Mass., where the "Shot Heard Round the World" was from; then back to Boston, Bunker Hill and the *U.S.S. Constitution*. I climbed the 294 steps up the Bunker Hill Monument because I was there. Rick declined to join me and sat on the park bench beside the monument. He'd been there before.

Visiting New York City, where my two brothers lived, opened my eyes to its wonder. Both Rick and I were gobsmacked by the style and beauty of the women on the streets.

Every "Tour" and every topic we dug into with zeal and were paid back tenfold with a deeper education unobtainable through the books I'd read in school. There is nothing like a proper field trip or "surfin safari." And all these gifts were made available to me, merely in exchange for my acceptance of New England's seasonal humidity.

THE MIRACLE MILE

Of Rick's many gifts and interests, perhaps his most defining desire was to be in the high country. There, he found what he needed and felt at home. We had many favorite hikes but early on we discovered the Sol Duc/High divide, perhaps our favorite-favorite place in the Olympic National Park.

Always on his birthday, the second week of July, we'd be going up and usually there. We would pack and go, no reservations were required and no other people sullied our alone experience. The mountain was our own. So fortunate a time to be alive.

We'd read of the "Miracle Mile," a south-facing scree slope, cut through with a narrow path, over-looking the Hoh River Valley thou-sands of feet below. Too far down for us to hear the restless river. At just the right time it would be covered in wildflowers, with mighty Mount Olympus in full view to the south. We had to go.

The High Divide

That first time, the winter had been bountiful. Even well into July, the trail was covered with snow. Sunny and warm we had to post-hole; every step we'd sink into the old crusty snow up to our knees. Rock cairns showed the way.

Just as we reached the decision place, whether to go left or right, a park ranger emerged heading down the trail. "Don't go right," he said, "it's too dangerous. The switchbacks leading up to Mount Bogachiel are solid ice. One false step, you'll fall thousands of feet to the river valley." We hesitated, thanked him and stood still, while watching him leave. Good counsel perhaps, but disappointing.

As we considered our next move, three young European back-packers appeared from the right, our desired destination. "We were told it was too dangerous. What do you think?

"It's something no one should miss," they all chimed.

Turning right, we found the Miracle Mile, hot in the sun and free from snow, burgeoned with millions of mountain wildflowers. It was a miracle to behold.

UNFATHOMABLE

Long before the depth sounder was invented, seamen needed a fast and efficient way to gauge the depth of water as their ships entered shoal territory. This was best served by using a lead line, measured and called out in fathoms. A guy on deck would throw out the weighted line, feel for its hitting the bottom and then pull up fast, counting the length in six foot increments. Some guy originally realized that by stretching wide a piece of line between his outstretched arms, the measurement was always about 6 feet, or a fathom. This guy, no doubt, was 6 feet tall because generally, this widespread arm measurement equates to a person's height. Most mariners know this.

I needed a short length of wire for a project at the shop. At my local chandlery, the owner watched me stretch and cut my piece. "Whatcha got there, Diana?" "Six feet." "That's not the way we do it here." "Ok, ok, it's not 6 feet. It's 5 feet, 4 inches." Beyond dubious, he grabbed his countertop tape rule to measure it proper.

He was not a mariner.

Moments later and feeling chagrined, he said, "You're the kind of woman men love to hate." And though it was said with a wink and a smile, there was much more than just a smattering of truth in his remark.

ED CLARK MEMORIAL RACE

I won a trophy once. Didn't get to take it home, put it on the mantel. But my name was engraved and added to a long list of prior winners and hangs at the Center for Wooden Boats now. It was a big dang deal for me and the Seattle boats I beat. My Kettenburg 38 can take the major credit for our performance. She was a slippery beast and truly taught me how to sail.

The race was at the 1996 Wooden Boat Festival, July 4th on Lake Union. Celebrating our country's birthday, every manner of boat filled with humanity was enjoying this fresh-water destination. It was an overwhelmingly crowded stretch of racecourse. When told the sailing directions at the skipper's meeting, their design was new to me. It was a kind of scavenger hunt, not really A to B to C to Finish. More like search for hidden marks in an exact order. An exact order that confused me mid-race, so I followed the *S/V Carlyn* just long enough to reset my directional synapses. She seemed to know the way and looked to be in the lead.

Sailing on a port tack, we were approaching the upwind mark. The hull was well heeled and the 20-knot breeze was driving her hard. Smoking the fleet, we were screaming out in front. My fiercest regional competitor, a man used to winning in a very fine boat, was coming up on the same mark on a starboard tack. He had the right of way. But as I looked to my windward side, another fast moving sailboat was so close, there was no room to safely tack. He called out "Starboard!" I called out "No Room!" He held his course anyway so I was forced to jibe to avoid a horrible collision. This put tremendous strain on the mast and rigging as we let out the boom as fast as we could. Our boats were so close; we could have shared a jar of Poupon. Jibing to avoid collision we immediately tacked back, made the mark and chased this fella who just took the lead.

Now we were sailing downwind, neck and neck towards the finish line, our mutual destination. The speed changed along with the tilt of the boat and things got very quiet as I edged ahead. No more angry water shooting past us, we silently wished her forward. My competitor was screaming at his crack crew to

Ed Clark's Daughter and I

(fill in the blank). I was nervous and dry mouthed. My ancient, blown-out Egyptian cotton jib was underperforming to the eyes of my deckhands. "Diana, your jib is luffing." "Thank you," I whispered back. The jib was luffing but the boat was performing perfectly so I held my course, inching further ahead.

We crossed the finish line, way ahead of the screamer. I admit, it felt good. After tying up, the other captain came running over to *Scandia*, right arm outstretched to shake my hand. "I am so sorry I made you jibe. It was very dangerous. I couldn't see the other boat next to you." This apology fostered my forgiveness.

At the awards ceremony, Ed Clark's daughter handed me the trophy and silently started to cry. "I've never awarded it to a woman before. I'm so happy." I cried also.

I never raced again, never wanting to become a screamer. Whispers are so much better on deck.

JOHNNY ADAMS - THE COMMODORE OF COOL

After World War II, several sailor-boys created the "Cruising Boozers," a casual club of serious intent. The founding fathers had schooners or similarly beautiful wooden sailboats and their girlfriends lived on houseboats in Lake Union; a handy, mutually beneficial arrangement. Several of them went to Gompers, the original boatbuilding school in Seattle. Johnny Adams, Ed Kennel, Bill Garden and Jack Kutz were deeply connected through their passion for sailing; Port Madison on Bainbridge Island was their "home port."

All had distinguished careers, married their girlfriends and raised families. Ed had a large photographic studio (Kennel-Ellis) which, coincidentally, was where I landed my first job in high school. I remember interviewing with him; I was wearing a school uniform, knee socks and saddle shoes. Bill became a prolific, well-known designer of boats of every type and size. His catalog of designs is housed at Mystic Seaport in Connecticut. Jack started out as a boat builder but was known as a marine designer/engineer and historic-vessel expert. His last long-term sailboat was named *Ocean*. Johnny was an architect, had his office in the Smith Tower and was a lifelong friend of Ivar, the Seattle restaurateur who knew how to "Keep Clam." Johnny would race with the Port Madison Yacht Club. He always brought up the rear, while the fleet enjoyed the guitar playing, singing and laughter from his cockpit.

But Johnny Adams also saved our "marriage."

On the rebuild of our sailboat *Taku*, we decided to design and build a doghouse for comfort in our PNW climate. A doghouse on a boat is essentially a small pilot house: more structural than a canvas dodger and just large enough to get in out of the rain. We also wanted it to be attractive.

Here's where partnerships may struggle. If you're sleeping together and want to continue sleeping together, differences in how to do things can become dicey. We disagreed very strongly as to what the design should be. It was bad at home!

At loggerheads, we called our friend Howdy Springer from Port Madison, figuring he'd lend a designing hand. "Call Johnny Adams. He'll know just what to do," was his advice. So we did. And Johnny drove to P.T. the next day. Up front, Rick and I both decided to defer to his suggestions and that would be that. No more arguments.

He sussed out our situation and immediately knew what to suggest. Coincidentally, *Taku* had been designed by his close friend Bill Garden, so he was intuitively able to draw something that would make Bill happy and the boat as well. It took almost no time. He lent a certain familial bridge from yesterday's world to today's. We couldn't have been happier with the entire process and were able to stay "married" after all.

MR. JOCHEMS

I was late to the game of business acumen. I paid my taxes, though, and even kept a separate savings account to collect them throughout the year, a hard-learned lesson. But realistically, my business plan was to have faith and hope for the best.

My projects overlapped with almost every specialty shop in town. More and more I was sharing jobs with the engine sales and service guy, Mark. It's quite possible we may have started off on shaky ground as my demeanor was very different from his. He was quite direct to his problematic customers while I was still a recovering "Just Be Nice Girl" to mine. I yelled at him once over it. But from then on, we were always on the same page, mutually respectful.

I took great pride in always paying cash for everything I needed, didn't need much and had a non-credit history because of it. When we decided to buy a new diesel engine for our sailboat, I was way short of funds.

Of course Mark wanted to sell me an engine. But he went the extra mile to make it happen. He counseled me until I truly understood about credit and the pros it could produce. Then he spoke with his personal banker on my behalf, convincing him to bend all the rules and take a chance on me, to give me a loan simply on good faith. At almost 50 years of age, I got my first credit card.

Mark was also an executive officer of the active Economic Development Council, deeply engaged in boosting local business. An EDC business development class was being offered and he insisted I enroll in it, even acquired a scholarship for me. Not needin no stinkin class on such stuff, I attended begrudgingly but I found it to be so powerful and rewarding, I humbly apologized to him for my stinkin attitude. I paid off the bank loan in half the time and now have a not-bad credit rating.

SEXRETARY

I was asked to join a kind of community think tank because of my status as a stakeholder and resume as an activist.

Walking in for the first meeting, one of the men smiled broadly and said, "Oh good, we have a Sexretary."

Very much past showing my boredom at these kinds of inane comments as well as raising my voice to grab their attention, I tried something different.

I looked him in the eyes, also smiled and quietly said, "Be careful. You don't know me."

Instantly, my simple declaration completely disarmed him and we developed into a good team.

MR. PRATT - MY GO-TO GUY

David has always been my go-to guy, anything boats. He still is, whether it's contemporary or traditional; he knows more about boats than God. And God will agree.

I first met him on Bainbridge Island after he completed a stunning build of a one-off Scott Sprague sailboat; *Annie* was her name. He and his wife Amy took off cruising and we met up again in Port Townsend years later, a place many of us immigrated to.

We were both summoned here to pursue our respective careers in boatbuilding, me as a sole proprietor and David working in the big, big, big shops, building the big, big boats. He became a partner of my favorite boat building shop, Townsend Bay Marine, with Paul Zeutsche, David King and Bill Nance. They were affectionately known as "the Evil Empire."

TBM earned my admiration. They followed the triple bottom line framework, operating equally with respect to social, environmental and economic concerns. The owners were all gentlemen and the neighborhood knew it too. No drama. They were my next-door neighbor boys for years.

I worked for them on various projects as a subcontractor, which literally sharpened my pencil. David taught me that. I also learned about environmental stewardship in a terribly toxic industry and how to mitigate its dangers. Safety on the job site — protecting employees — was displayed in ways a sole proprietor might never consider. The other David, David King, was the safety officer and actually got up from his desk regularly, walked through all the shops and made sure protocols were in place. In all those years I can't remember any accidents.

Because they were the largest employer at the time, often the jobs they took on required outside help. David Pratt championed the wood end of the business and occasionally hired me to do pitsy, intricate high end joinery. This was an ultimate gift to my education and eventually my self confidence. David demanded excellence. I heard that loud and clear and my joinery expertise vastly improved.

MY A.C.L.S

The Anterior Cruciate Ligament is a vital component of the working knee assembly. Every body has two. I've blown out three of them.

The second time was on an 18-mile loop hike in the Eagle Cap Wilderness of northeastern Oregon. Perhaps the most spectacular of all the trails we've ever hiked, it was almost worth the pain. When it happened we were still five miles from the truck. Rick looked at me and pleaded, "Please don't make me carry you out."

The third time was in our own fair Olympic National Park on the Moose Lake Trail from Obstruction Point next to Hurricane Ridge. Descending a steep hill was always my knee's Kryptonite. Moose Lake is only four miles from the trailhead, but the path down to it is so arduous and vertical, I re-injured an earlier A.C.L. blow-out. We rested by the cold alpine lake while I soaked my knee until it was numb. Then we evacuated to the truck. It took a really long time. The only way out was with me walking backwards up the steep slope. Rick didn't carry me that time either.

I always pack a knee brace and an ace bandage now, just in case.

My first blow-out was self-inflicted because I chose to blissfully ignore my body. Killing ourselves during a particularly intense pre-Wooden Boat festival season, Rick and I was undone with fatigue. We chose to ditch sea level and everything boats. Our first crossover in the Olympics, we exchanged car keys with another willing couple who went the opposite way. They drove our car and we drove theirs to trailheads on opposite ends of our crossover hike.

Our route led us in from the north shore Quinault trailhead, over the Skyline Trail and out the Elwha River drainage; 6 days, 60 pounds, 60 miles. Being Labor Day weekend, it was hot and high-country blueberry season. The air was thick with the intoxicating scent.

We passed 34 black bears that were oblivious to our presence while they gorged themselves on fruit, systematically stripping it from the bushes. We stripped handfuls of berries too, to put in our instant oatmeal. Fresh water was nowhere to be found so we rationed ours until we made it to Lake Beauty. She lived up to her name.

My knee bothered me going in. I'd sat funny too long in the bilge of a boat. "It'll be fine," I said, convincing myself regardless of the pain.

Imagining the Skyline Trail to be a kind of ridge-top path, I pictured it steep going up, but once there, only vistas. It was nothing like that. It was very strenuous, steep up and down the whole way until we hit the Elwha River trail. The Elwha and that one lone alarming black bear. He appeared to be wearing a toilet seat around his thick neck, but it turned out to be a radio collar. He wore a collar because of his known troublesome behavior. Passing him at the developed campground where he was digging through human stuff, his demeanor was very aggressive to us. We walked past him backwards so we'd know if or when he was going to charge us and commit armed robbery.

As we re-entered humanity in the darkening evening driving through Sequim, the lights of the cars and the businesses seemed foreign. Our perspective had been seriously altered, and we liked each other a whole lot more than before our mountain sashay.

There was a swing dance class being offered with several weeks of instruction. Early on in our romance, we'd spoken of trying it and now seemed the time. We signed up, spruced up and showed up.

Our first lesson, he's twirling me, I'm smiling. He's twirling me, I'm beatific.

There's a sound your Anterior Cruciate Ligament makes when it blows, just before your knee fails you and it hurts bloody hell. Still smiling, we both heard this loud THWAP, just like a wide rubber band and I start to go down.

He literally sweeps me up in his arms and rushes me out the door, drives me home and puts a bag of frozen peas on my knee. How romantic is that?

MR. WINKLER

Head down and sitting at my desk in the shop doing paperwork, I sensed a presence behind me in the large open door. When I turned, there were three presences, two men and a four-legged mammal of some kind. It turned out to be a Leonburger, the largest dog I ever met. A cross between a Newfoundland and St. Bernard, she had a distinctive kind of bad-hair day.

All three looked like they just walked over from Kah Tai Lagoon, a park across from the boatyard that was full of native history, controversy, migrating birds, and more recently known for homeless encampments. The soft-spoken, polite ringleader of this trio said, "Hello there. I'm looking to buy a boat." Dizzy with work distraction and up to here with dreamers who would stop by and treat our shop like a kind of interpretive center for wooden boat enthusiasts, I didn't want to engage. Assuming they meant a kind of liveaboard so they could move out of the park, I spit out "Yeah, I'll bet you do. Can't help you. Buh, bye."

A few days later, the ringleader showed up again. This time he was alone. "I bought a boat," he said patiently. He seemed determined not to leave.

"Didja now? What did you buy?"

The name *Terrier* slipped out of his mouth like a broad smile.

That stopped me cold. *Terrier*?

"Yup," he almost beamed.

"Damn," I said.

Terrier had been built here in P.T. by Mike Logg and was well known. A looker of our fleet, she was as traditional as you could get for a fiberglass boat. Everything about her was top notch.

One of the first designs I'd fallen in love with had been a plumb bowed Bristol Channel Cutter designed by Lyle Hess. There's just something about a plumb bow for me. Plus, her design had been so right, more than 200 of them had been built and were known as Lyle's masterpiece. *Terrier* was a Hess design, but Mike Logg had added features that set her above all the rest. I think I loved her.

I found myself speaking to this person differently, with newfound respect and I was mortified by my former behavior. "How can I help?"

That was the beginning of the best owner/client relationship I ever had in this industry. I did 15 years of annual work on this wonderful boat for this wonderful man, Tom Winkler. Over time, he had me do everything that needed doing. The painting and varnishing, where the design details were so elegant, added time to a yearly reset but was worth the effort for the ooh-ahhs it produced. He had me build a nesting dinghy, install his auto-helm system, new thru-hulls, and strange weird stuff.

Once, he wanted his "engine room" fully insulated to cut down noise and temperature variables. This wasn't exactly an engine room but more of a basic-training obstacle course I needed to negotiate to complete the project. When he saw my work he asked me, "How did you do that?" To which I had no explanation.

I installed a proper icebox for the galley too. I built the wooden mold and Cape George Marine helped with the fiberglass lay-up. The fit was so "perfect" when I installed it; I had to get inside to push it down into place. I told Tom, it wasn't an icebox, it was a bathtub. Everything he ever asked me to do for the boat I "just said yes."

Except for the otter shit clean-up. Words can't express the horrors of otter shit. Tom and the otters had a weighted war for a very long time. Since he lived in Oregon, I kept an eye on the boat while he was gone. Finding healthy personal boundaries within myself, I cleaned it up once after the otters visited, and then let him know I would never do it again. It's a topic we still don't like to think about.

About three years of haulouts into getting to know him, I finally asked what he did for employment. Living out of state, we only saw each other annually when he hauled *Terrier* in preparation of sailing her

S/V *Terrier* in Trumbull Cove - the Broughtons - photo by Tom Winkler

to exotic places such as Juneau. We concentrated on technical sailor-boy and sailor-guurl stuff, never delving into the personal. But since it seemed we had a stable working relationship by now, I decided to go a bit deeper. He wouldn't tell me, and I could tell it was a tender subject for him. So I dropped it though it didn't seem right since he knew what I did. Years passed and someone local told me he was a doctor. For the life of me I couldn't figure out why he seemed embarrassed to admit it to me.

The next time Tom and I walked down the dock together, we bumped into a friend I wanted to introduce him to. "This is Mr. Winkler. He's a podiatrist," I shared. Indignant, Tom exclaimed, "I'm not a podiatrist! I'm a heart surgeon." Well, now I knew, but can still only call him Mr. Winkler, and may be the only person in the world who does.

MARGIE

"We're going to go visit a new friend of mine today. She and her husband owned *Taku* for 25 years and traveled extensively on it with their children. I know you'll like her," I told Kashmira.

"Great. Just great. Like I want to spend my day visiting with some old woman," said my 14-year-old daughter.

Shortly after we acquired *Taku*, Margie heard of our plans to rebuild her. Deeply attached to her old boat – it having been an important family member -- she decided to bring Rick and I into the fold. We met Margie at a party she held in our honor, where her family members and close sailing fellowship welcomed us with warmth and a familiarity like we were long lost loved ones. Photos and ship's logs came out; stories, history and immense laughs were shared. This was a tight-knit Port Townsend sailing community, happy to embrace us as two of their own. Through it all, Margie held us all in the palm of her hand, warmly, graciously, inclusively and with such genuine care.

Years later, it came time to re-launch our boat after finishing her rebuild. Feeling unusually shy, we chose to do it silently and privately. No big whoop-te-doo port party. But we knew Margie had to be there. We needed her blessing.

There are traditions in the sailing culture. These traditions are important to honor.

Margie Abraham blessing *Taku*

As the travel lift held *Taku* suspended for a moment over her new saltwater home, I handed a bottle of Jack Daniels to Margie. "I was hoping you'd take a swig and splash some on her stern and in the water." Not knowing her that well, I queried, "Do you drink?" "DO I DRINK?" As always, Margie knew just what to do.

All these years later and two hours into our visit with me sitting mostly on the sidelines, I made a suggestion that maybe it was time for Kashmira and I to leave. "Mom! I don't want to leave."

Margie was holding Kashmira so wondrously, in the palm of her soft, warm hand. A hand you are lucky to be touched by.

SAG HARBOR

Unable to find our size and styles of brassieres in Port Townsend, Kashmira and I started a yearly tradition. We'd meet in downtown Seattle, hit all the good stores until we found exactly what we wanted, then choose a great restaurant for lunch. It was always a happy mother/daughter outing.

Wearing the same size, I'd cruise the aisles picking leopard, zebra, red, black, purple. Handing them in to her for her consideration, I was always met with, "MOM! Those aren't my style!"

In truth, most of my choices really looked like a very bad upholstered couch, but they gave me a giggle so I always bought them.

My Girl and I

One year we had just finished our purchases. Walking towards the exit I ran straight into a clothing display for Sag Harbor. "Kashmira! Can you believe this? Who would name a line of women's clothing Sag Harbor? Hahahahahahaha!!!"

She perceptibly tensed, being kinder than I. A saleswoman appeared and explained how respected the line of clothing was.

"Hahahahahahaha!!! I've just spent the better part of an hour standing in front of a full length mirror, naked from the waist up. Hahahahahaha!!! What an unfortunate brand name choice for a woman's line of clothing."

We've continued shopping together since, but I've promised to be more restrained.

A GOOD TRADE

Whenever I made time to take stock of my partnership, I could see the gifts Rick gave me were enormous. He is the only man to ever give me flowers just because and not for some special occasion. The only man who silently and strongly stood behind me. Always observant, he had my back, while never insinuating himself into trying to protect me or fix things. He gave me a deeper appreciation of the importance of family and showed me it is more than ok to take time to witness my world. Living a full, rich life and not just working makes life worthwhile.

Through his friendship and abundant curiosity, I learned so much! It never felt like part of a bucket list but more of a daily meditation. We would take regular "surfin safaris" of exploration (going anywhere farther than Chimacum,) to investigate more about geology or marine biology, or art and poetry and how world history has been affected by it. Our thoughtful, open, and conscious political dialogue helped me to see our world more compassionately, through a positive lens. Sharing a love of cuisine, we worked together in our vibrant kitchen as we researched and built new culinary experiences. His love of the high-country took us hiking and backpacking where we found solitude and communion with the natural world. We learned to care for each other with equity, celebrating each other's gifts and enjoying life by simply opening our eyes and taking it all in.

And for all of this, I have given him the gift of laughter. A very good trade!

PAYBACK

It was time to teach Kashmira how to drive and was to be the "No

Work Car's" destiny. My Dad had taught me in his VW square-back, so now was my comeuppance. Teaching a stick-shift and the pedals for a manual transmission is when a parent takes in a deep breath and may or may not ever exhale again.

With me riding shotgun, we started in the usual places – school parking lots and such on the weekends, eventually ramping up to the highway. Driving up the Elwha River Road, I let her practice backing up and turning around but lost my nerve quite abruptly when the river itself got way too close. All in all, she did very well and only took out one mailbox during her training.

Rick and I were late for a boat launching. He was driving fast down the hill at Arcadia Road which was littered with deep potholes. Suddenly his seat fell through the 34-year-old rusted out floor. Fred Flintstone, Yabba Dabba Doo. The brake line was severed and we couldn't stop. He had to navigate a sharp right turn at the bottom which led to Discovery Road. We could only pray that there'd be no traffic. He cruised it to Second Street, where it finally came to a stop. We hitchhiked to town and after the launch I drove her back up the hill and rebuilt her insides. She was on the road again in no time.

I saved her for when Kashmira was 16 and needed a car. "Mom! It's the only car I've ever known. I want my own car." So I sold her for $375 and miss her to this day.

PORT POLITICS

I've been labeled a rabble-rouser but I think community-builder is more apt. Almost from day one working here in the Boat Haven, port politics were important to me.

Coming to town in an election year, I fell in with a group of concerned port patrons who wanted more say. Helping to champion the candidate who was running for commissioner, I read pie charts and budgets and walked around fostering discussions. I always felt comfortable engaging in local politics.

Money was never my god. Happy enough to have a footprint once I secured a proper shop, I called myself the smallest big time operator in town, a "full service shop." With boat haulout facilities next to my location, I could attract any sized job because if I couldn't do part of it myself, the guy across the street or a tail-gater could. Big businesses boasted being "full service shops," but from my perspective, no single business at that time honestly had it all.

The independent contractors or "tail-gaters" were the unsung heroes of our industry. Coming in all kinds of flavors, they might be surveyors, finishers, riggers, shipwrights, designers, electricians, plumbers, systems, corkers, consultants, project management or anything – the full gamut. Named tail-gaters because they generally worked out of a pickup truck, they were unable or unwilling to secure a port lease. In truth when I started I was a "running boarder" working out of my Volkswagen Bug, a perfectly good substitute for a truck.

Tail-gaters benefit from reduced infrastructure costs and so generally charged less than the big boys who gave customers of different depths of pockets, more choices. Regular folk and not just millionaires could secure quality work for their boats.

The big boys who hired these independent contractors to fill in for their lack of services could make an extra few pennies paying less for labor, but charging shop rate. There were no health care or retirement benefits to pay into. Every single independent elevated what Port Townsend's maritime industry had to offer. Tail-gaters helped put P.T. on the world map.

Adam Henley was then the manager of West Marine. He and I would carpool to port commission meetings, listen and weigh in when moved to. Both of us were dedicated to helping promote and build the wooden boat repair and restoration market. The current commissioners openly dissed wooden boats, said it was a "dying industry," and said "Bayliners are the wave of the future." They summarily voted to remove all boathouses and openly laughed at the argument that historic, classic wooden boats were better served in covered moorage. "I don't get what's so special about an old wooden boat," one said. We both felt kicked in the gut with their lack of interest, curiosity or imagination, so we set about to educate them.

Adam and his wife, Diana, took it upon themselves to conduct the first of several boat surveys in 1999, and the results were heartening. Counting every boat, regardless of material, in the water and on the hard, including Fleet Marine, the Boat Haven, East View Storage and Cecil Lange, 274 were wood or 42.75% of the 641 boats found. Seven were Bayliners, or 1%.

We continued to attend port meetings. Despite these statistics and clear anecdotal evidence such as the powerful county-wide financial boon of the Wooden Boat Festival, our presentations fell on deaf ears. We spoke with anyone in the community who had a foot in the game but few others attended the meetings. We were a pebble in their shoes.

The commissioners then decided to legislate against anyone working who didn't have a lease with the port: tail-gaters. Unaware of their worth to the business plans of lease-holders, the commissioners demanded liability insurance of them all. Without a footprint, insurance is much more expensive, and they posited that this rule would clean up the boatyard of riff-raff. I don't remember any large companies coming to the defense of independents, but I did. Having started as one and grateful for that first step, now as a "full service shop" owner, I depended on them for my success. Hell hath no fury like a woman scorned.

My community-building began in earnest. Being the smallest big time operator, I realized no one in business, large or small, was intimidated by me or saw me as a competitive threat. This became a kind of superpower as I felt completely at ease and welcome to enter any other business in the port to talk about current affairs. Everyone was nice to me.

I organized a well-attended port meeting of almost every sole proprietor and tail-gater. The regular commission meeting was moved to a larger room to accommodate the packed crowd. I was the current ringleader, so I began the public testimony on behalf of all small businesses. After that, several people felt legitimized and spoke passionately about their significance in the port's economic development scheme. Economic development is the primary port mandate.

The large shops still wouldn't commit to any public display of support, but the commissioners were suddenly faced with a loud, invested, and vocal constituency. They eventually backed down from their insurance rule and only required a hold-harmless agreement be signed in order to work onsite in the port. After this large win, participants felt deeper connections and more secure in this community. But the Port administration's design for an "even more perfect" working waterfront required relentless observation and participation.

HER VOICE

From the moment my daughter was able to speak, she used her voice with strength and resolve. One of the first sentences uttered out of that tiny mouth was, "Stop it!" I had been leaning over her crib and tickling her nose with my braid. Not prone to understanding subtle messaging, I sure understood that one.

Around age five she let it be known to her father and me that she was running away from home. Not knowing what triggered this desire, instinctively I knew we had to let her go.

It was dark outside and past her bedtime. She grabbed her favorite teddy bear and quilted blankey and said good-bye as she closed the door. Keeping her in view, I followed silently down the outside stairs and around the building, watched as she opened the barn door, closed it behind her and made a nest in the pile of fresh hay we kept for the sheep.

I peeked in the window to see her beloved Irish setter, Little Red, cuddled up alongside. When I knew she was asleep, I covered her with a proper blanket.

Kashmira and Little Red

Living on the boat, we had homeschooled her, but in third grade, when she started to attend public school, she discovered her name wasn't Marina. We had chosen Kashmira as her first and Marina for her middle name. I, and everyone else up to this point, had called her Marina. My father had never in my life called me by my first name, always by my second, a private love connection between us. Being enormously sentimental, I was continuing that tradition.

But it was a tradition my daughter didn't understand or didn't want to repeat. She came home from school that first day and laid down the law; I was never, ever to call her Marina again! And I haven't! At age eight, she scared the crap out of me.

This child of mine, through nurture or nature, has found her own voice. While I often feel a kind of bruising when she uses it, I am deeply proud of her for being able to state her own opinion, as I was well into my 40s before I could.

She is also a competent, take-charge kind of leader. At age 14, she decided to move away from home again. This time, she pitched a plan to live with her dear Aunt Brenda. Brenda had a fine home and family and emulated many things Kashmira said she wanted now. After her father and I separated, her sense of family was crushed. Struggling as her single mother, I was unable to provide her with what it was she wanted, which she claimed was a more conventional home life. But I knew that my partnering up with Rick only exacerbated her deep unhappiness. This new love we were building had dramatically changed our family dynamics.

All of us – Paul, his sister Brenda, Kashmira and myself, went to a family counselor together. We sat nervous on the wide, faux-leather couches. Our body language said it all as Paul and I leaned closer and closer to each other with every pro and con discussed. Like a cohesive team again, we were resigned now to letting her take charge of this decision. Having discussed it privately, we knew the power of our daughter's convictions and never blamed each other. She made a strong argument and presented it respectfully.

I honestly felt beaten down. I was horribly conflicted but could no longer try to disagree. Neither could Paul.

It was the second hardest decision I've ever made and to this day, my biggest mistake in life, to let her go. She will always think I didn't want her and there could be nothing further from the truth.

LYNN - A TENDER ADVENTURER

She wasn't always confined to a wheelchair, a paraplegic drinking gin with a straw. As children, we ran the roads of our hood chased by the boys, climbing trees and foraging for fish in the crick out back. We had a clubhouse where we wrote, "boys not aloud!"

Born mere days apart, Lynn and I were best friends from age three and inseparable. We always shared big neighborhood birthday parties. Our mothers were fiercely competitive, always trying to outdo each other, so the parties became ridiculously epic.

At 21 Lynn was diagnosed with MS (multiple sclerosis) and began to walk with a cane. But never wavered in her ambition to travel the world. Her greatest gift, aside from her indomitable nature, was her writing.

As the years and her illness progressed, Lynn was always single, as one by one her arms and legs ceased to function. Her writing gave her meaning, purpose and adventure. Along with MS, she also suffered from FMS (Fear of Missing Something) and so became a travel writer for people with disabilities.

Well into her mobility constraints, she met Leo online. "It was her voice that aroused my curiosity," he would say later. Knowing she was dependent on a wheelchair, they decided to meet for coffee. He was drawn in by her eyes, charmed by her wit and that was that. At age 55 they married at her parents' home. It was a lovely ceremony and Rick and I were fortunate to attend. I walked the old neighborhood while I was there, even making it down to the crick in my high heels while Lynn was left in the house in her wheelchair.

She had come to visit me years before she married. There was a private moment we shared when Lynn offered how difficult her life is just getting up each day, dressing, eating, and bathing. I felt so sad for my friend, I sat quietly for some time to honor her struggles. But then I said, "Wait a minute. You've been to the Caribbean, Tahiti and Spain this year, and I've only been as far as Poulsbo!" She just beamed for it was true.

Leo and Lynn - Their Wedding Day

BETWEEN WIND AND WATER

Seven years of dedication and drive to finish our restoration of *Taku* also gave us seven years of dreaming of how we'd use the boat when launched. Once we refreshed our memories of how to dock a boat, anchor, set and tend the sails, we felt confident to go anywhere inshore and used her extensively.

She was always provisioned, with water and fuel topped off, just in case a crazy destination offered itself. We liked being spontaneous. The mooring buoys at Fort Flagler or the peaceful anchorage of Mystery Bay on Marrowstone Island were regular haunts. We could work most of a Friday, then let go the lines and be ready for cocktails with the engine turned off, in about an hour. So close to home, it always felt like we were hundreds of miles from it. We'd pull a skiff behind us and row in for long walks along the shoreline or into the woods, privacy and affection our sidekicks.

Mystery Bay was the first anchorage we shared together that Christmas Eve on Rick's sailboat, *Kah Tai*. Anchored that night, the stars were brilliant in the frigid air. We'd had the bay all to ourselves, sitting in the cockpit singing carols, wrapped in wool blankets and sipping hot buttered rums. I'd surprised Rick with a string of battery-operated multi-colored lights that I hung on the boom. We learned that night, that both of us loved the Christmas traditions we were sharing.

Heading to the San Juans took a larger time commitment, but we managed it on our calendar. Watmough Bight on Lopez Island was our favorite anchorage. We'd row ashore and walk the miles to the store mid-island, always waving at the cars that passed by, the mark of a local. There we'd buy some ice cream, sit in the shade and enjoy it before our hike back. In season, we'd pick wild blackberries along the side of the road, make a cobbler in the diesel stove, cocktails in the cockpit. You could climb to the top of the hill there and watch to see if the fog had lifted in the straits before committing to pulling the anchor. Or we might anchor in Fisherman Bay on the other side of Lopez Island, rent bicycles and tour every hidden gem.

My birthday was approaching and he asked where I wanted to go. Calendar days were generally short that time of year. Spring haul-out jobs hoped for a snubbed-up timeline. Tentative in his query and expecting me to want to head north, he asked nevertheless. I was hit by a pit of fashion and suggested Poulsbo, a place we'd never tied up. Little Norway sounded exotic to me. We could visit the bakery and see Howdy and Jeanie Springer. A few long hours of perfect southerly sailing, and we were at the marina, sitting on a park bench, feeling hundreds of miles from home. Suddenly Dan Kulin, a rigger from Port Townsend, appeared out of nowhere and gave me a big smooch on my cheek. He must have been visiting the bakery as well. Rick was not happy! Not jealous, but not happy. I was thrilled!

PAINT AND VARNISH

Eventually I learned the art and skill of finish work, attaining at the very least some level of marketability. Avoiding it for years, I thought that if I became proficient, I might be pigeonholed professionally. Then like a character actor in a bad series of bad movies, I'd never be able to cut, fit and fasten again. But I came to understand how finishers take the work of a shipwright to the next level, the level that grabs your eye. Often under-appreciated, they are the unsung heroes of the boat building industry. I'm proud to have worked with them all.

I chose to only do finish work if the boat and the owner asked me nicely. There was a particular boat, a real beauty. I had done some minor repairs and systems work that segued into paint and varnish. It all felt right.

Two years later the owner decided to sell. "Diana, you're the best. I want you to do your magic and get her ready for the market. Oh, and I plan to aggressively advertise her with a website, so I want the premium Port Townsend Marine Trades names who worked on her listed. You aren't well known enough so I'm just going to list '(large established well advertised boat shop)' as who did the finish work. You understand, right?"

Beyond offended by such an insulting comment, I let him off easier than I probably should have. I simply laughed out loud and walked away.

PUMPKIN LOVE

I love a good party and enjoy sharing one with my friends but when motherhood hit, parties took on a different significance. Children: the blessing that allows you to relive a childhood.

For Halloween, I spent years building costumes: fairies, witches, geoducks, ghosts, Dalmatians, butterflies, Nefertiti ... I was the type of mom who gave out boxes of raisins to the marauding kids in the neighborhood. Such an embarrassment to my girl.

New to Port Townsend and with childhood enthusiasm, I started throwing an annual pumpkin carving contest party. Everyone I knew was invited and generally everyone came. B.Y.O. pumpkin and carving implements. Everyone wins a fabulous prize.

For weeks prior, Kashmira and I hit the Goodwill regularly, amassing enough goofy prize stock for everyone and generally individually chosen for each attendee. We handmade and hand-delivered every invitation. Adults and children with adults were invited but we all acted like children. Serving only hot apple cider, it was entirely a childlike celebration.

At the first party, Steve Chapin brought a pumpkin pie as his entry. Wildly popular, the next year and from then on, it became a pumpkin carving/pie contest party. Never held in the same place, the event grew larger and larger. I had to rent a venue. The competition was fierce, not just for the artistry of the carvings, which were stunning, nor the

Olive, Elvis (Julian), Nancy and Diana

quality of each pie, which was sublime. The greatest competition was for who would get to be the pie judge. It was ruthless. People tried to bribe me! But I never saw so many adults in one room become so lovable. Often heard, "I haven't carved a pumpkin in 30 years, Diana."

At just two years old, Rangi Ferris wielded a large kitchen knife upon a small decorative pumpkin. I watched in semi-terror as he made a near perfect jack-o-lantern. Pete Langley won first prize one year with a wickedly innovative design. He lit a flare in his pumpkin and won a multicolored tutu (one size fits all). Julian Arthur showed up one year dressed as Elvis. The women went wild. I mean they went wild! Brion Toss became a human jack-o-lantern. He lit a match and held it in his closed mouth and his whole face and room lit up. Bill Curtsinger brought a perfectly decorated, hot, 4-pound deep-dish chicken pot pie. Jim Blaiklock brought a pie one year no one would even try. He was glad to take it home and swore it was delicious.

Young Reed Sigmond was helped by Rick to use an electric drill motor with some Forstner bits (razor sharp). As Reed's grip slipped, I heard Rick say, "I'm bleeding." But the blood just added to the Halloween theme. They lit it up with a bicycle strobe light and Reed won first place that year to enthusiastic applause.

The year Kashmira was at Seattle Pacific University, she rowed on the university's crew team. She approached her coach and said, "You know how most people will want to go home for Thanksgiving? Well with my family, I want to go home for Halloween."

Tristan in the Dark

The very best part of every party was at the end when we lined up all the pumpkins. With the lights turned off and quiet as the dead, candles were lit and the warm soft glow of dozens of carved faces stared back at us. There would be a deep collective Ooh.

I don't do these parties anymore unless Kashmira comes home with her children specifically for carving pumpkins and eating pies. But next time I do, I'll consider anyone who bribes me with a five dollar bill to be a pie judge.

FOUR WINDS * WESTWARD HO

Four Winds * Westward Ho is an historic summer camp on Orcas Island for boys and girls ages 7 to 18. Established in 1927, thousands of children have enjoyed their outdoor adventure programs. Carlyn Stark had been one of them. A camper in her youth, she returned for years as a passionate Camp Director. When we met Carlyn, she still held sway there and visited often. She and her partner Dale Nordland, who was a retired boatbuilder, were our close friends.

Carlyn was a riot. Wildly gifted and enterprising, she always had something to champion or lead. One of the many aspects of camp activities was on-the-water training: swimming, sailing and rowing. Camp housed a large livery of 14-foot cedar rowboats. Over time, their maintenance had fallen flat and many were in disrepair and unsafe to use. Carlyn hatched a plan.

Dale would design a flat-bottomed skiff, similar to the traditional camp boats and construct a jig to build them with. Carlyn would purchase the red cedar, fasteners and what-not needed for the build. All of it would be loaded onto her sailboat and north it would go.

Rick and I were wrapped into the deal as volunteer teachers/boat builders. We loaded our tools onboard our own sailboat and headed north in tandem. Once there, we would teach the eighth-graders how to build a boat. In exchange, we got food and moorage for the week it took, and several camp perks to enjoy in our spare time. Rick was gifted a ride on one of their horses for his birthday, a delightful present that made him laugh. Especially when he hefted his 190 pounds onto the saddle and his mount let out a stiff exhale. The horses were used to carrying small children.

Fixing the Red Skiffs

A natural teacher, Rick taught the first-year class. I took on a restoration project of an unhappy skiff, teaching that class to different eighth-graders. Boys and girls came in with pencil skills and finished the week having used drill motors, a band saw and chisels. Only once did my 1" chisel get dropped onto the cement shop floor – T-boned! Then they all learned how to sharpen tools. Next year we traded jobs. It got so our sailboat could almost steer herself to camp.

NANCY

As Nancy is a kind of Renaissance woman, I've never seen her attempt anything without producing the highest level of excellence: canvas work, cooking, portrait painting, hard cider or fun.

The first time we ate at her home, dinner was fantastic but the dessert was over the top. "Where did you buy this?"

"I made it."

"NO!" Incredulous, I forgot my manners long enough to insist she show me the dirty pans.

Nancy Bishop, Cathy Langley and Diana at Storm King

Right away we discovered we shared a love of backpacking into the high country. In conversation we also realized how hiking with our spouses, while adventurous and fun, wasn't exactly the kind of fun we both looked for on our hikes. With them it was always go, go, go and we could never stop at a stream to sit and soak in the beauty or soak our sore feet. A plan between us emerged.

We started hiking and backpacking, *sans* our men, to high-up places. The destination generally was an icy lake, river or tarn where we could swim naturally, in nature. Lotsa trails and lotsa miles. And then the plan grew. Seems many other women wanted to hike their own pace too, so a kind of group formed with Nancy at the helm.

Nancy was blessed with a beautiful face of eternal youth which belied an innocence she outgrew decades ago. Her deep humor was served by it. Walking together on C dock one day, an older friend rushed up to ask if this was my daughter. "My daughter? I'm only three years older than she is!" Nancy liked that.

I was to build a coffee table for her mother-in-law. Together, we went to Edensaw, our favorite local wood supplier. At the sales counter, she announced, straight faced and all innocent-like and with just the right tone, "We're here to pick up a piece of ash." They all politely stifled a laugh and almost swallowed their tongues, thinking she was such a nice woman who no doubt didn't know what she had said. Nancy smiled demurely. I could never say something like that without being called out.

Twenty some years ago, I snapped a picture as we stopped for lunch on our way to Silver Lake. We both hated it and I was about to delete it when she said, "Wait! In twenty years we'll want this. We're bound to look worse." Maybe for the first time, I think she was wrong. Twenty years later we look better than that photo. I should have deleted it.

Me n Nancy

HIGH HEELS IN THE HANGING LOCKER

Rick's nephew was getting married in Kirkland at the Woodmark Hotel, which had a yacht harbor named Carillon Point. The carillons there rang often. Family from New England was traveling out to attend so we made plans as well. Rooms at the resort were upwards of over $250/night. Moorage in the marina was $1/ft/night, or $36 for our *S/V Taku* which made a charming transport vessel.

We loaded up the hanging locker with Rick's suit, dress shirts and wingtips, my gowns, wraps and high heels. We headed south in our foul weather gear and Xtratufs rubber boots. We had a week cleared off our calendar.

Navigating the Hiram Chittenden locks and Seattle's bridges, Lake Union, the canal and Lake Washington, we entered Carillon on a calm, warm early evening. There was only one other wooden boat, a mascot of sorts for the hotel. All other boats were various sizes of go-fast fiberglass and all carried black canvas covers. It must have been a thing that year. With me at the helm, Rick whispered quietly, "Be careful Diana, no one here is our friend."

Later, sitting in our cockpit, potential friends did walk by. Couples would head our way, the wife was always in front. As she passed she looked away from us and quickened her pace. Her nose looked disjointed, so high it was held. Five paces behind, her husband smiled widely at us, eyes bright with wonder, and waved like we

Sailor Guurl

were sitting on the deck of the Queen Mary. But never a word was spoken. Come to think of it, with the exception of our family, none of the guests in the wedding party spoke to us either.

CONCEPTION

My personal relationships with each of the Port commissioners and the Port's executive director had always been unfriendly at best. I was very rarely treated as such a powerless, inconsequential person. Considering the rest of my life, that spoke volumes. Open disrespect and condescension were the norm and they lorded over me the stark differences in who was in control of my ability to work here.

Over time, I began to get worn down. The port administration had made me jump through hoops continuously as an independent and even now as a lease holder. Fighting just to be able to go to work was burdensome. It was clear that only big business and big money received their respect in this environment. My lifelong insecurities started to buy into the belief that small businesses couldn't count on support of any kind from this administration and that I should just keep my mouth shut. And then they pushed back against the wrong businesses.

The two largest shops in town, Townsend Bay Marine (TBM) and the Shipwright's Co-op, both tried to negotiate different footprints to their leases. Business was booming and more space was needed to accommodate it. Additional employees could be hired with larger shops. This is textbook economic development, one of the most important mandates of the port authority. The commissioners said no to all avenues of discussion. Huh! What's wrong with this picture, I puzzled.

I had talked myself into accepting that small businesses didn't deserve regard, but why not the big businesses? My head exploded, so I sought out my two best advisors regarding all things heart and business: Tim Lee and David King. Each brought a different perspective and I trusted their judgment. Tim was the lead instructor at the boat school, which benefited from our robust working waterfront. We had served together on the board of the Wooden Boat Foundation. David King was the CFO of TBM, served on the board of the Maritime Center and was an elected City Council member.

Tim Lee and Diana - photo by
Elizabeth Thomson Becker

Meeting with both of them separately, I pitched my concerns and they heard me. I intuitively knew it was time for a radical change in the constituency dynamic with the port, but didn't know how to proceed. All businesses, regardless of size, needed to be represented and heard. In conversation, they both offered that what I wanted to do was form a kind of trade union or business association. Understanding this through their counsel, the next step was clear. Tim, David and I were figuratively in the same room at the moment of conception of the PTMTA: the Port Townsend Marine Trades Association.

Seeing a path, I spoke with every marine trade or supportive business known to me, organizing the first of many large gatherings which quickly led to members of the community stepping up to write a mission statement, articles of incorporation and bylaws, and developing leadership. People were ready for this collaboration and goodwill.

When the association was up and running, many of us attended another commission meeting to inform them how this unified voice would be used to promote economic stability and resolve issues that threaten the livelihood of the marine trades in Jefferson County. A commissioner offered, "There can't be that many members. It'll have no power." But immediately, everything changed. The commissioners were finally held accountable by their own large constituency.

TIM, LINDA AND TAZ

Taz and Tim - photo by Tim Nolan

I met Tim in the early 1980s when my boat *Isela* was at the Wooden Boat Festival. Kiwi, my only friend in town then, suggested I join him and his friends for dinner. "We'll motor by and you can just jump aboard. We're going to the Ajax Cafe." Standing on the deck of my boat and seeing *Heather* putt-putting by, all six people onboard yelled "JUMP!" Where, I thought? This is crazy. It was only 16 feet long and every spot on deck seemed taken. So I jumped.

This was my introduction intensive to a part of the local sailing community few know: a deck-load of delightful ne'er-do-wells, in no particular hurry to go nowhere in particular.

The Ajax Café was our destination and only eight miles south. *Heather* is rated to go 4.5 knots top speed but it was slow as she goes that day. And with nary a pee bucket in sight, it was "A three hour tour. A three hour tour."

Fifteen years later, Tim would walk Taz every morning past Rick's and my house. Taz, the Pomeranian, really was a sweet little dog. Few people ever knew that. Though unsure how he got his name, he certainly could be a little devil. He didn't like people.

Tim, Rick and I would fall into the best conversations to start a day many mornings. I would make an extra cup of coffee each day to refill Tim's cup in case he stopped by. That's when I wormed a way into Taz's heart with cheddar cheese. I was his only human friend outside his family.

Whenever he could break out, he'd hot-foot it to our house. If I left the front door open I could be sure of his smiling, pint-sized presence in

S/V *Heather* - Photo by Clinton Cleveland

my kitchen, always scaring the crap out of me. This is how Linda and I became friends. She'd come to collect him and we'd fall into wonderful conversations that were funny, deep and real. She was the only friend who thought to bring me flowers when my mother died.

Tim and Rick had both served in the Peace Corps, Tim in Ecuador and Rick in the Congo. Both of these remarkable men shared an understated decency that informed their notable lives. Neither of them swaggered but their fine moral values were plain to see.

This is why Tim is one of my "girlfriends," a title relegated to precious few men. There is never an ounce of tension that is some-times found in the boy-guurl way. He has more than a full tank of humor and is always present and deep. Being around him helps me want to be a better person.

JENNIFER

I met her when she came to the shop, looking for employment. "I have no experience but I'm good with my hands." I liked this. This was exactly how I secured my first woodworking job. I looked at her hands and into her eyes. The entire package was beyond lovely but I could also tell she was equipped with a fine mind. I hired her on the spot and immediately the conversation at the shop got smarter.

I began teaching her the business of varnish and eventually, along with my old chum Rita (who had taught me how to roll and tip when painting), Jennifer and I started in on a small gold-plater, a boat that demanded excellence. Combined with a strong work ethic, attention to detail and being a very fast learner, she proved indispensable.

Rick walked out of the shop one day and called me down off the scaffolding. "Don't you see what's happening?" Stupid with concentration, I didn't have a clue but took a moment to survey my 180-degree view behind our shop. Every single stopped car, sidewalk bench, shop

Jennifer Boutilier Driscoll

door or shop window was filled to capacity with men, stationary and staring at my crew. This felt just wrong. In retrospect, I should have walked around the neighborhood, engaged each man and explained how uncomfortable they made us feel. But I chose a different path.

I sent a hand-written letter to the CEO and CFO of our next-door neighbor, the largest boat-building business in town, which also owned the greatest number of employees and windows. I thought of these business owners as personal friends, gentlemen and the very best neighbors anyone could hope for. Directly and succinctly, I explained our discomfort and pointed out how much I cared for their business, understanding full well that distractions like these seriously impacted their efficiency and ultimately their bottom line. If this behavior persisted, I was willing, for the payment of a bottle of Jack Daniels, to ask my crew to wear more clothes. (It must be said that our work attire was always professional.)

A few short days later, the CFO was semi-running towards us across the back lot, letter in hand. All work stopped. "Diana, we got your letter. Are you serious?" The three of us burst into infectious laughter, the poor guy. He never really got my sense of humor. After we all calmed down I convinced him that no, I didn't require a bottle but yes, I required him to speak to his crew. Thence forward, the windows remained empty.

Months later, Jennifer proved herself so competent, I passed a job on to her, *sans* my involvement, figuring in no short time she'd decide if this was a career she wanted to pursue. "I bought all the tools I need to start my own business, which probably means I won't do that," she told me. Which is exactly what happened. She soon moved along towards a more intellectual and altruistic path, went to graduate school and earned her PhD. I am so proud of her!

She left a mighty big hole and conversations in our shop aren't nearly so smart.

KURT

He entered our shop with his signature limp, shrapnel from the war still embedded in his leg. Holding a bouquet of flowers and smiling, he was hoping for a welcoming reception. Returned now from years away, he was looking up old friends one by one. The flowers were for me but he found only Rick's curious reaction.

Hair askew and dressed like the gentleman of the coast that he was, Kurt's appearance wasn't commanding. Feeling like a man reduced in time's assessment of a long life lived hard, he decided to leave.

My back was to him but I had heard his entry. I spun around and saw my old friend leaving. "Hey! Where the hell do you think you're going?" I said.

Kurt stopped and offered me his flowers. I gave him a big smooch. Rick was befuddled. I had spoken of Kurt to Rick in terms that set Kurt above all others. A world class sailor and top notch boat builder, he had been the first instructor at the boat school. I semi-worshiped the guy and here he was, an old man diminished with age. Rick thought of Kurt as a kind of god the way I spoke of him. This human person did not equate.

Kurt had been an early guide, mentor and supportive friend when I was a developing boatbuilder. He'd advised me, watched me, cared for my progress and certainly celebrated my accomplishments. I was proud to call him a friend.

Back in Port Townsend, again close to his chosen family, he had sold his last schooner *Ratbag*, which he'd built in Dale Nordland's barn in Mats Mats Bay many years ago. Since Kurt was now physically limited, it was the right decision.

Kurt Ashford - photo by Janet Millar

The next years he rowed as much as he could, the elemental way to get out on the water. When his body wouldn't let him do even that, he learned he had brain cancer. Mad as hell about it, he decided not to die.

At first, his friends went to his downtown apartment to help take care of him. When that became untenable, he moved to Kah Tai, the nursing home by the lagoon. Kiwi and Auman took care of all the details, good and loyal friends. Kurt had a penchant for rum. Routinely, it was smuggled in. The nursing staff was kind about it.

I had always had a fear of nursing homes. Silly really, since I'd never been in one. Like my fear of going aloft, once I did it and looked around, it wasn't bad at all. My love for Kurt helped me bridge that fear.

Our house was mere blocks up the hill from the nursing home. I drove by it twice a day, minimum, to and from work. My first tentative visit was more guilt than desire, but his trademark charm roped me back.

Still building cool things in my shop, I took to visiting Kurt often, asking advice and for tricks of the trade. His aphasia made communication challenging but he always got the design or scantling out in a way I could understand. Full circle, it was, to sit by his bedside and still learn from the master. What a guy!

ABC - ALWAYS BE CAREFUL

"It is better to be careful a hundred times than to get killed once."
- Mark Twain

There's a particular sound a high-powered industrial tool makes when the material being cut changes from wood to human flesh. I know that sound. Three times I've been present when a major shop accident occurred: two different table saws and one half-inch router. It was always the left hand.

Initially it was my own foolish accident. The last cut of my first boat when I was excited and in a hurry. When it happened to me I heard that sound, felt the pain, turned off the machine and yelled, "It's a bad one!" My partner upstairs knew exactly what had happened. He grabbed the baby and drove me to the local medical center. Only given Tylenol, the next drive and ferry ride to the hand clinic in Seattle was long.

I came to understand that push sticks were a vital part of proper table-saw protocol and that industrial machines had more brains than I did.

The second accident was worse. My shop partner took a half-inch cove bite out of his left thumb with a router. All of us in the shop that day watched him lying on the floor and yelling/moaning in a voice that was part deer, rabbit and coyote being murdered; in-human sounds. One of the men kept screaming, "I don't know what to do. I don't know what to do." He got an ambulance ride to Harborview in Seattle and later admitted that when he picked up the tool, he knew something wasn't right but planned on fixing it after this one cut. We threw that router away, smashed in the garbage can so no one else would ever use it.

My Finger-Finger - photo by Bruce MacLay

The third time was very trauma-tizing to me, because it happened to Rick. I heard that sound, deeper than the others and immediately knew. The table saw kept running and sud-denly Rick came down the stairs, hand wrapped in his handkerchief. He looked at me and simply said, "I gotta go." Rushing him to Jefferson Hospital, driving through the red light and speeding up the hill, I was in my own state of shock; this was a very bad injury. No insurance or money for a helicopter, I ended up driving him to Harborview, a really long trip to Seattle. Prescription in hand from the ER doctors for "aid in transport," I requested preferential boarding at the Winslow ferry. The ticket taker refused my request and told me to get in lane 12. So I drove to the front of the line and demanded of them what I needed. One look at Rick, and we were the first to board.

I've since made peace with the table saw and it is in fact my favorite power tool now, though I've never been able to get past my fear of big routers. When someone turns one on I literally have to leave the room. I should probably get counseling for that.

ANOTHER USE FOR IT

I worked for a fella many years ago who had a small sailboat with a smaller budget. It needed a lot of work including new cockpit coamings. He chose Honduras mahogany, beautiful but not my first choice of wood for the exterior.

Being clever, I built a jig to bend the coamings around with a little extra umph for spring back. I carefully fashioned the shape and curve, the angles fore n aft, and the bottom, to the camber of the deck. I even cut the limber holes, then slathered them up with linseed oil and threw them in the steam box. It was a Sunday. The yard was empty of distractions and the steam-up went well.

Walking home through Kai Tai Lagoon Park, an epiphany struck me. I had neglected to notice which piece was port and which piece was starboard when I fastened them to the jig. It was such a beautiful day, the sun was out and warm, I decided there was a 50% chance I'd done it right. I wasn't going to worry about it. If I'd done it wrong, both pieces would be bent opposite to the curve of the boat and would be unusable.

Monday morning I was up at Edensaw, our premium lumbermongers. I bought all new Hondo (Honduras mahogany) at no extra charge to the customer. I stashed the unfortunate coamings in the shop's mezzanine, hidden from the world for another use some day.

Months later, Tana, who owned the Blue Moose Café, asked me to build an outdoor waiting bench. Not wanting fine furniture, but folksy funk, I had the free wood to do the job. A coupla hours and fasteners later, I produced a proper bench that many a butt has sat on, waiting for a Tomba or Veggie Hash.

Years after that, I worked on a large gold-plater with an excellent crew of first class craftsmen. Teak was the flavor of choice for this budget. One of the finest shipwrights Port Townsend ever spawned, made an intricate cut and went to fasten it. "Oh well," I heard him say. "Maybe I'll find another use for it, like in my wood stove tonight."

SNOW SPORTS

Round about early December each year, a large group of friends who all work in the Boat Haven meet up at the Quilcene ranger station to buy their permits to go in search of the perfect five dollar Christmas tree. We then caravan up Penny Creek, an access road to the Olympic National Forest. Everyone hopes the appointed day occurs after a heavy snowfall in the mountains. When this happens, those with two-wheel drive park as high up as possible with safe turnaround space and the four-wheel drive vehicles stop and carry the rest of us to "the staging ground." This tradition has evolved and grown since Rick and I started doing this.

The first year, only two of us brought food, me and Kelley Watson. Everyone else operated solely on hydraulics and came home cold, wet and hungry. Groups that went the following years boasted mounds of firewood with a raging burn pile, chairs, blankets, pots of bubbling chili, as well as the ubiquitous thermos of hot buttered rum. Children started to outnumber the adults, but this was a day for all to be young.

After the ideal trees were found, the light faded and the embers died down, we would mass evacuate and meet up again at the Whistling Oyster in Quilcene. Fortifying ourselves for the long drive home, we drank bad beer, ate horribly unhealthy food and played shuffleboard. Breaking into teams, my "boyfriend" Pete Rust and I always partnered up. Suhweet!

The first year Kashmira joined us, she brought along her new husband, Iven. She always deeply enjoyed the Christmas traditions I introduced to her. This was a new one. Driving to Quilcene that day, the radio was tuned to NPR's "The Vinyl Cafe." Stuart McLean was reading his celebrated story, "Dave Cooks the Turkey." The four of us became so engrossed it was a kind of bonding experience. Rick slowed his driving to be sure and finish the tale before we would have to go tree hunting. It was the birth of another new tradition.

Kashmira and Iven

ONE YEAR the snow was exceptionally thick on a calm, crisp, clear day. Every imaginable snow toy made it up that hill. Gus hooked up a gargantuan inner tube (from the travel lift machine) to his truck and towed loads of humans up the road, over and over. There was a short, steep hill where anyone with a sit-upon was sliding down, then trudging up. Repeat, repeat. With nothing to slide on, I decided to improvise my fun.

Never having gone to war, even I knew the military advantage of standing on the crest of a hill and looking down on the sea of faces below me. Inextricably, I began an epic snowball engagement with the closest adult, a person unknown to me. Though I was never very good at baseball, quite improbably, every one of my snowballs hit their mark! The head and shoulders of one man. Giddy with snow-madness, I just rat-a-tat kept obliterating him. I could not miss.

Me, laughing! Him? Not so much. Fighting deep snow gravity, he yelled, "I don't know who you are, but you're going down!" I continued the onslaught. Eventually, he made the crest of the hill and running the short distance, the sport changed to football when he tackled me. We both went down. When the snow dust settled and Peter Sigmond opened his eyes, they were two inches from mine. He was horrified to realize he had just tackled a woman older than his mother. Still laughing and lying on my back in a thick bed of powdery snow, with a handsome man less than half my age lying on top of me, I could not have been more charmed.

TYLER'S LATHE

Christmas was coming on quick and I had not yet decided on the perfect presents for Rick and Kashmira. Many years prior, Len Zeoli, a gifted woodworker and bowl turner, had given me two unfinished bowls: a huge maple and very large yew. They were just waiting for the final step.

In my youth I'd turned chisel handles, bonker heads and whatnots but currently had no lathe. Tyler Thompson had one, so I asked if I could come to his shop to make my presents. He was generous to a fault but a highly principled fella. He said, "Absolutely not, because my shop is for men only and no women were allowed." He would, however, discombobulate his lathe and re-constitute it in my shop. It was a lotta work, but very kind, so I let him.

I chucked up the bowls individually and brought them to completion. They were stunning! Feeling rather accomplished and invincible, it occurred to me that I was looking at a rare opportunity to turn a bowl for myself. I mean how hard could it be?

There was a beautiful piece of wood I roughed out and chucked up in the lathe. Just as I started my first cut, the wood left the machine with such force and kinetic energy, it proceeded to hit almost every surface the length and breadth of the shop – except me. I mean, it continued bouncing back and forth for what seemed like 5 minutes and twas the luck of the draw where it would hit, so I just stood there dumbfounded.

I hid that piece of wood under my bench for years. I never told Tyler and only recently told Rick, now when we could laugh about it. Once again, the lathe, like the table saw, both insentient industrial machines, taught me: that they have way more brains than I do, that it is OK to not excel at everything, and to be happy with what you are good at. Kashmira told me the yew bowl was by far the best Christmas present I ever gave her.

∾

CHAPTER 9

MAYDAY-MAYDAY-MAYDAY

1967 - 1969

My Dad and Me - 1967

"Our lives begin to end the day we become silent about things that matter."–Martin Luther King, Jr.

MOM

Frances Talley

I was once a young Republican. I went to meetings. I even wore the red, white and blue faux straw hat and helped line 4th Avenue in Seattle when Nixon came to town during his election campaign in 1968. I shook his and Pat's hands. At the time it was a thrill. But I soon got over it.

My political leanings were not by choice. My mother made a bargain with me: if I had any hope to ever "date" or attend proms or see my friends on a Saturday night, I would follow her dictum to do meaningful work for the Republican Party. And, along with attending church on Sunday, I also had to go to a church-led youth program every Friday night. There was no discussion or recourse. This was just the way it was going to be.

I like to think that my mother was different from other moms, but I can only imagine. An imperialist, she ruled our home with authoritative inflexibility that lacked any imagination or concept of compromise. It was her iron grip on my tender spirituality that finally broke her spell over me.

During one of those Friday night gatherings in the basement of our Ballard church, something big snapped. I couldn't breathe and bolted for the door. Several miles later I stepped into a restaurant, bummed a dime and called my Dad who never attended Friday services. He came and hugged me with his compassionate understanding and brought me home.

I never knew what magic he performed on my behalf. Our family members weren't communicators, but I never had to attend those meetings anymore. Shortly after, my politics took on a distinctly different personal perspective.

This was the beginning of decades of struggles between my mother and me. Wanting to find a balance between familial loyalty and keeping myself independent was extremely difficult.

People say I'm strong and few could disagree. But I earned my strength through nurture and by nature. No doubt I inherited genetic material from a long line of strong Olsen women, which in turn gave me the power to bust out of this stranglehold we called family.

MY ABORTION

Of course I got pregnant the first time I did it. So young, I knew nothing about sex nor what it might bring to my life. Once my mother found out, I was completely left out of any discussion. Never was I asked what I wanted to do or told what my options were.

She was strong and decisive – a hard right, evangelical Christian — and righteously anti-abortion. But she made a call to someone out of state, who knew someone. I was then told to start telling my school chums I'd be vacationing in Mexico for spring break, for that was where she and I were headed.

And then, just like that, I had a miscarriage.

A watershed moment, I fully learned about hypocrisy as my

mother returned to her righteous, vocal anti-abortion stance. But I also began to embrace a different kind of faith, something private and completely my own.

OH! HE'S NEVER COMING BACK

I wouldn't be lying to say our home life in my later teens was sad. There were serious money issues which had led to a loss of face between my parents and the public persona that had been so important to them both. Our conventional new routine was to share a dinner, make light conversation and then retreat to our own bedrooms privately.

Late one night when I was 17, my father knocked on my bedroom door, popped in, smiled and sweetly said, "I love you and just wanted you to know that." This was an unusual occurrence. He never visited me after I'd gone to bed and the words "I love you" were never heard in our home.

Dad and I had an unspoken understanding that we deeply loved each other. We thought words weren't necessary.

I smiled back at him and replied, "I love you too."

Two hours later he was dead from suicide.

They wouldn't let me see him. My family decided I was too young to look at my dead father's body, as they all had been able to do. No matter how loud and forcefully I had pleaded my case to see Dad, they could not square with the idea that I could be able to choose to see death. I was doubly bereft.

Born a girl in the early 50s, I grew up without a sense of agency, nor hope I'd ever have any. My mother and two brothers had always treated me as meritless and unworthy of regard. I longed to take control of my life and to make my own decisions. This family dynamic damaged me so deeply it would be another two decades before I was strong enough to put myself in a place where I could.

A different time then, families didn't speak of hurts or trauma. We were pressured to put on our best public face and hold it all silently inside. This and the fact that we felt duty-bound to live within our cultural expectations, is why I can forgive them all. It was just our time. Now we speak of closure, coming to our understanding, the finality of death. But for me then, without that visual experience, I went somewhere else. This deeply troubling recurring dream explained his absence and haunted me for too many years.

Dad had disappeared mysteriously. It wasn't like him. He was a creature of habit and always reliable. I could count on Dad. There was only one reasonable explanation. He'd fallen and hit his head, had amnesia, couldn't remember his name or where he belonged. A beautiful woman from Brazil had found him, nursed him back to health and together, they were living happily in South America. Then one day, he woke to remember who he was and how much he missed me. I was standing at my kitchen sink, looking out the window in my busy city neighborhood. A car drove up and parked across the street. I watched as the door opened and my Dad stepped out. He saw me standing in my window. His smile was joyous and his eyes held mine. I watched in awe as he stepped into the road. Distracted, he didn't see the car coming, the car that hit and killed him. My Dad died right in front of my eyes and is never coming back.

It still troubles me.

∾

CHAPTER 10
SQUARED AWAY
2008 - 2018

Photo by Jan Halliday

"God made the old world lovely...and we must keep it so."
—Jae Proctor

A FINAL BLESSING

Mom and I had a complicated relationship; there was nothing easy about any of it. Fiercely independent and competitive, it was difficult for her to openly show warmth and affection. Criticism and a deep unhappiness permeated her being; a thick wall protected her from intimacy. No doubt she had reasons for her great sadness, but it kept everyone on pins and needles.

Bit by bit, her life began to unravel in her early 90s and it became clear she could no longer remain independent. Neighbors called to complain of her driving antics. She refused to give up the car so I disconnected the battery. Neglecting to update her senior status with the state, her property taxes soared. When she read the new amount, she couldn't square it with her reason, so she threw away the tax bill, almost losing her house because of it.

I was fortunate to find an in-house caregiver who managed everything until her health took a dive. It was time to move her to a group home where she had real 24-hour care. I had spent decades promising myself that when and if this time came, I was not going to step up and care for her. So damaged from our relationship, I felt no ounce of familial loyalty.

Rick simply said to me, "She's your mother, Diana." Always reticent, I'd learned that when he offered an opinion it was something I needed to hear. I re-thought my whole outlook and chose compassion and grace, instead of hatred. The outcome was surprising.

We moved her to Port Townsend; she lived in a group home with a population of one. Without the hours of roundtrip traveling to Seattle, I was able to give her time and attention. I'd load her in the convertible, tuck her in with blankets and drive around town, top down. This, I came to realize, was the real reason I had bought that car. Driving down Water Street, she'd wave Rhody Queen style. I'd never seen her so happy, nor so fun to spend time with.

Our final year together, almost to the day, swept away every unkindness from the previous 56 years. A bit of a wait, but worth it.

Days before she died, she handed me her prized diamond ring and left me with this blessing, "Your Daddy would be so proud of you!"

MOM'S FUNERAL

My funeral for her was unstructured, unplanned and shoot from the hip. More like me than her, but I think she would have approved. She was firm about wanting to be buried in Milton, Utah, near her family's original homestead. I wanted to honor her wishes.

Gale Allen, Me and Kenny Nelson

I had pored through endless granite gravestone markers and tombstones in the local Salt Lake City website. Nothing seemed right; I just couldn't buy one online but I could build a humble wooden carved cross instead. This gave me a greater sense of participation in the process. There were thirteen carved letters in her name!

Mom and I took our last trip together. Her ashes in the plastic urn sat on the passenger seat of the Miata all the way to the historic cemetery in Milton. Getting out of the car, I cradled Mom in my arms and addressed the few attendees.

"I've never buried a Mom before. I don't know what to do."

"Uncle" Gale, his wife and the two cemetery officials, knew exactly what to do. They were there to witness a momentous passing of my loved one. "We'll do whatever you want."

I suddenly realized this was a 100% Mormon cemetery. No non-

Mormons before had been buried there. "Oh my gosh." They all smiled and said not to worry about it.

I took the time to witness the mountains around us, the cattle nearby and the soft autumn afternoon warmth, then chose the perfect spot. The young 70-something-year-old gravedigger handed me the shovel to dig the first bite then finished digging the rest of the hole. It was then I learned no one had been cremated and buried here; it definitely went against church customs. Again I was aghast and again they just smiled and said it was OK. "We want to do whatever you want."

Unsure what to do when the hole was ready, I knelt down, looked up at my companions and declared, "I don't want no stinkin plastic between my Mom's ashes and this sacred ground." They smiled and agreed. I poured her ashes through my hands; my last caress. Then again, completely taken aback, "Oh gosh, I should have contacted a minister to be here to say something for my mom!"

My 90-something-year-old favorite "Uncle" said, "I'm a bishop in the Mormon Church. Will that do?"

"YES PLEASE AND THANK YOU."

I'm sure Mom would have approved.

COMMUNITY SERVICE.

Rick and I used to lend our time and talents (muscle) to the Olympic National Park for various projects needed doing. Our park was so giving to us, we wanted to give back to it. We spent several days at the Quinault ranger station working in their large, well-equipped shop to build dozens of picnic tables - I worked on the table saw; he worked on the router.

One particular day we were developing a new ADA accessible path along the shore of Lake Crescent. Working alongside the park's volunteer coordinator, Ray Lovely (who deserved that name), we were armed with a wheelbarrow, picks, shovels, rakes, a peavey and everyone's friend, the scotch broom-eradicator. It was a wonderful project and fun day.

A group of six hikers came wandering down the path and seeing me, exclaimed, "Diana, what are you doing?" They were old-old friends from Seattle I hadn't seen in decades. "We're building a new path," said I. "Why?" they queried. "Community service," I replied. Collectively, their expressions turned aghast, they huddled closer together and scurried past. HUH, I thought? Until I remembered that the term community service is often used with the adjudication of an unfortunate criminal conviction.

It did make me smile, knowing that even though we weren't wearing orange jumpsuits, this story would be bandied throughout my old-old Seattle friends. At least they're still talkin about me!

GET OUT

Standing at the bathroom sink, mouth agape and looking into the mirror, I'm squeezing the eyelash curler. Rick accidentally opens the door and sees this. "What in the world are you doing?" he wondered aloud. I let out a girlish scream and say, "Men are never supposed to see this. GET OUT!"

I'm really laughing but he backed out so fast and apologized so profusely, because he was always such a gentleman. He never did get to see how that contraption worked.

E. L.

We were about to cross the Canadian border and were asked, "Who are you traveling with?" I replied, "Try and follow along; my partner, my daughter, her husband, her father and his wife. It is an unusual modern-day nuclear family reunion."

"OK," said the border agent, "You and your partner go sit on that bench." I start tittering internally and thinking - Oh Rick - you bad boy. Look what you've got us into. Once again, I proved the nickname Rick had given to me to be true: "Our Lady of the Assumption."

A while later, a young man comes out, points his finger at me and says, "YOU! Come with me."

"ME?" says I. "I was sure it would be HIM."

"No, it's you we need to talk to."

He takes me into the interrogation room where he and another fella say, "It seems you were arrested once and we can't figure out what it was for. All it says about the arrest are the initials E.L. Can you tell us what E.L. stands for?"

"E. L? I'll tell you what E.L. stands for. IT STANDS FOR EXTREMELY LUDICROUS! When I was 20 years old I was arrested for trespassing and stealing garbage. I was fingerprinted, mug shotted and STRIP SEARCHED! When it came to trial, the prosecutor — and I'm not making this up – introduced aerial footage. It was one of the "biggest busts" the Whidbey Island Sheriff's Department had ever experienced.

The judge reasoned this was the stupidest waste of time and county money he had ever seen. He apologized to me and my attorney, threw it outta court, chastised the sheriff's department and prosecuting attorney. He made me pay the one witness to the crime the eight dollars for his time and told me he would erase my record. That I should consider myself unsullied heretofore and forthwith a person who had never been arrested. Well, you know that never really happens, does it? You end up with a record that says E.L."

By now, these interrogators were busting a gut and all they could say was "Welcome to Canada!"

NANA BANANA

Rick and I got the call after hours on pins and needles. Izayla had been born, Kashmira and Iven's first child. I had become a Nana. To say we were all relieved that everyone was well is a supreme under-statement. Being 8,000 miles away, it's hard to touch the moment.

Kashmira and Iven had asked for privacy, so that none of the grandparents would disturb their moment of specialness. I wanted to see them so bad it was almost funny, but I knew my job was to hang tuff, put their needs first! Them, them, them, Diana. Not you!

I asked counsel from Inger, "What should I do?"

She firmly explained, "You book a flight and then call them and tell them when you are coming!" What a miracle Inger is! I'd have never thought of that.

Rearranging the order in some faux-pseudo kind of caring motive, I called Kashmira first to tell her I was booking a flight in a few weeks to come see the baby. I was scared as all get-out as to how she'd react.

This is what she said in an unexpectedly animated way, "You must come a week sooner so you can experience Songkran – the Buddhist New Year Water Splashing Festival."

I felt welcome and so booked my flight.

I had visited Bangkok once before. Being in my adult child's home then, as her guest in a foreign country for the first time, my eyes had been opened. Watching the two of them navigate their life, it was clear I never needed to worry about them again. They were good people, living conscious lives.

The flights always seemed to arrive at midnight, and April was at the beginning of the hot season, so it was 105 degrees when I landed. The Suvarnabhumi International Airport is surprisingly quiet. I found them standing at the top of a ramped walkway, with a tiny baby girl that smelled so sweet and perfect, the world turned pink as she was handed to me. Nuzzling her ample head of angelic baby hair with my new Nana nose, I was euphoric.

My hotel was across the street from their conventional 250-square foot Thai apartment. I had splurged on wanting air condi-tioning but being a PNW guurl, I had zero experience with the remote that controlled air temperature. Turning it to its highest setting, I was stifling hot. Trying to sleep naked and splayed out was impossible. The next morning, Kashmira explained physics to me and we turned down the heat together by remote to its lowest setting.

It had been close to 30 years since I'd held or cared for a baby. I felt all fumbly-like. Since this was her first child, Kashmira may have felt similar. When she visited my palatial hotel room with her, we decided to give Izayla her first bath. I've yet to see a bathtub in Thailand.

In that special moment when the two of us were both hoping for guidance and leadership, we felt more comfortable washing the new baby as a team. Curiously unskilled, we stripped down to our underwear and stepped into the shower stream together, one of us held the sweet babe while the other gently washed the important parts. It felt like the real reason I had made this intercontinental flight.

And yet Songkran was upon us, the Water Splashing Festival. Kashmira insisted on taking me to Khaosan Road, a two-mile walk from their quiet neighborhood. There, she knew we would be immersed full throttle in the New Year celebration. We left the baby home with Iven.

Picture a national celebration where everyone who deigned to step outdoors, including the King, would be hit with water from numerous delivery apparatuses. The splashing of water is a New Year blessing, symbolizing cleansing, reverence and good fortune. Kashmira armed us both with 12-ounce water bottles, their plastic caps punctured with several small holes, to be used to return any blessings given us.

Khaosan was crowded and raucous. Thailand never looked so untamed. We entered this special neighborhood together, walking slowly and taking it all in. Famous for partying, it is a haven for world travelers on a budget and known for the epic water fights of Songkran.

I noticed Kashmira's face was slathered with a white paste. Called Din Sor Pong, Songkran revelers wear it as a symbol of protection. "What's with the white stuff all over you Kashmira?" "It's all over you too Mom." I had never felt a thing.

We made the loop, getting hit from time to time with buckets of water. Everything seemed happy and mutual. A young Thai girl was armed with a garden hose. She hit me full frontal/full blast. It grabbed my attention. Her Khun Yaai (Grandma on her mother's side) sitting next to her, roared with laughter. I collected myself, straightened my full-length dress and walked up to her slowly. Her eyes were wide, full of apprehension wondering what this farang (foreigner) Khun Yaai would do to her? She waited with typical respectful Buddhist silence.

I nodded to her grandma and quietly said "Kor Tot Kah" (excuse me) to the girl. Picking up the garden hose, I aimed it on this wonderfully joyous young person full frontal and turned on the valve full blast. This time, she and her Khun Yaai both bellowed long and loud.

A funneled roadblock met us as we left Khaosan road. An older, stately couple stood waiting by the narrow passage for us. There was no going around. Walking up we paused as the woman emptied around eight ounces of water over our heads. When I raised my apparatus of water delivery over hers, she flinched, her face skewed and stiff, waiting for my returned blessing. Just three or four drops of water sprinkled over her head! She relaxed as I whispered to her, "Happy New Year."

"Happy New Year to you too," she replied in English.

A very Happy New Year, indeed.

"RICK! RICK! RICK!"

Sitting in the backseat of his brother-in-law's Cadillac, Rick and I were double dating to a hip-hop techno club in Salem, Massachusetts. Historic and captivating, Salem also has some pretty rough neighborhoods. We were stuck motionless in traffic in one of the roughest.

Looking out my window, not 10 feet away, someone was beating the crap out of a guy, pummeling him, because he'd taken his parking spot.

I reacted as I usually did in circumstances like these (though this was an unusual circumstance.) "RICK! RICK! RICK!"

Following my gaze and train of thought, he jumped out of the car and ran to the scene. And just his presence scared the pummeler enough that he ran away.

Nonplussed and in unison, the front seat occupants both chimed, "Ricky, are you crazy? Get back in the cah."

And he did, for his work was done. No fisticuffs for Rick, just a strong, silent, present backbone, for whoever needed one.

MOOSE
"There's your way, there's my way and there's Norway." – Eric Wilson

Eric "Moose" Wilson - photo by Joni Blanchard

Moose was one of my rare "girlfriends" in the boatyard. He

enjoyed that label. Like many of us in the trades, he presented as uneducated, unkempt and rough cut. But he was so many things, he was unlabel-able.

Don't know how we came to such a deep friendship, but I know this. Men had a completely different opinion and appreciation of Moose. He was seen amongst his male peers as an OG: tough, manly, vastly experienced in shipwrightness, corking and a leader of the traditional trades, a teacher and mentor, someone to be carefully respectful of. We women who were fortunate to know him well, found a sensitive ear, a deep heart, and a kind friend who honored women and appreciated our differences. He treated us with dignity and respect.

One of my favorite moments with him was a February 14 get-down in my shop. He sought my counsel. "My girlfriend and I had an argument today. I don't understand why. I thought that as we got older you wouldn't have to work so hard on relationships."

I laughed full-throated, "Do you know what day this is? Valentine's Day? Could this have anything to do with it? No matter how old you are, relationships require work!"

He left my shop a better boyfriend and I may have become a better girlfriend too because of this deep conversation with him.

I noticed that he was ill. We were working a job together so of course I noticed. I didn't go to his house, insist he go to the hospital or get help. He didn't have health insurance and was concerned about the costs. One of my lifetime major regrets was I didn't throw him in my truck, take him to the hospital and insist on paying.

GIFTS FOR THE TAKING

We studied up about the Broughton Archipelago in British Columbia, bought all the books. In his youth, this is where Dale Nordland had built one of his Aegeans, his ocean-ready sailboats. Tucked in a hidey-hole, next to his gyppo (independent) logging enterprise, he and his wife Betty and two small children carved a life while building the boat together. When it was finished, they set off sailing. This seemed as good an excuse as any to go north, looking for Dale's roots. In tandem with another cruising couple, we headed that way.

It didn't take long to discover our pace was unique and not partner-friendly. They left us in their wake while we moseyed through the San Juans, Desolation Sound and Johnstone Strait, learning of the associated multiple tidal rapids and their many charms. These rapids could be transited, but only when it was slack water. Boats would anchor on either side of the rapids and then there was a kind of rush hour.

On the eastern side of Johnstone we met up with our chums and had picked up another Canadian boat to travel with. As we passed by Alert Bay, a favorite native village we had visited the year before, a large and powerful inflatable left the shoreline and headed straight for us. I held my course and watched them approach with two big, grumpy-looking guys onboard. Rushing right up with their strength and proprietary nature, they scared me. But claiming *Taku* was the most beautiful boat they had seen, they welcomed us to their home and asked us to visit the village. Our two sailing companion partnerships kept us from saying yes, which I regret.

We found Dale's hidey-hole and met local legends, Alexandra Morton and Billy Proctor. Alexandra is an activist and field biologist in British Columbia fighting against fish farms for the sanctity of wild salmon. She is also soft-spoken, gracious, and terribly dear. Billy is also a passionate defender of BC's wild salmon stock and their habitat. A lifelong "upcoast man" of the Broughton Archipelago, he has been a fisherman, trapper and hand logger. A natural born beachcomber of "junk," we spent the day in his fascinating "junk" museum and learned his story. He and Alexandra were very close friends.

We learned never to pay much heed to the cruising books that might suggest not to mosey up an inlet because it would be so overcrowded. More often than not, it was empty.

The *S/V Taku* took us places where only she knew we needed to go.

HONORING VETERANS DAY

For too many years, I was stuck in my generational mindset to shun all Vietnam veterans. Self-righteous and ignorant, I felt better than all of them, without ever acknowledging how as an American woman, I had never had to make those same kinds of decisions.

Inadvertently, I invited a veteran to a dinner party in 1982. Over the course of the evening, he talked about the pain and trauma he had experienced, not only as a soldier but especially about how his countrymen/and/women treated him upon his return. It was clear he felt that every Veteran's Day he should be able to walk into any restaurant in the United States of America and be offered a free lunch.

My eyes and heart were opened that evening and humbled by a debt of forgiveness I'll never be able to fully pay. I've been buying a veteran lunch every Veteran's Day since.

'TIS THE SPIRIT

My daughter and her family live 8,000 miles away in a tropical, Asian country, a long way from The Great Pacific Northwest. Though she loves her foreign home, in her heart, she remains a Northwest Girl.

I quit buying Christmas presents for anyone a long time ago. Seems counter-intuitive since I now have enough grandchildren for a robust volleyball team, but it seems we all have plenty of stuff. I send them a taste of our home instead, a festive Christmas swag.

The first year I posted one to Kashmira, a group of her ex-pat friends gathered around, excited and curious to see what her mother had put in the Christmas box. As she tore it open, the rich evergreen scent of cedar and fir floated out and filled the hot room with everyone's childhood memories. They were delighted.

Kashmira looks forward to these packages every year.

Last year when she received the box, her children gathered round this time. What had Nana mailed? The same scents filled the room but the children asked why there were no presents? Their mom simply said that Nana had sent something even better than presents. Nana had sent them all Christmas.

ANTIQUE BUTTONS

My mom gave me the button box 50 years ago after owning them herself for 30 years, after my Nana gave them to her after who knows how long. Everyone I know with a grandmother from the depression era has a similar box. I've used some occasionally but mainly just made sure they always moved wherever I moved. I'm very sentimental.

On a trip to La Push, Rick and I were invited to join the Quileute community for their Wednesday evening drumming, dancing and singing gathering. It's a rare look into the culture of the Quileute Sovereign Nation we were guests of.

Today the Quileute people live on the Pacific beaches alongside the thick majestic rainforest of the Olympic Peninsula that gets around 115 inches of rainfall annually. Traditionally they fished and hunted sea mammals and were known as the best sealers on the coast. They hunted for whales out of masterfully engineered ocean-going red cedar canoes, traveling as far north as Southeast Alaska and south to California. They are also known to have bred special woolly-haired dogs and spun their hair into yarn for their highly prized blankets.

Many families of all generations participate in these Wednesday evening tribal gatherings and all visitors are welcome. I was particularly drawn to the beautiful women dancing in their red and black button blankets.

These striking button blankets are created by the First Peoples of the Northwest Coast. They serve as statements of identity of the wearer's clan, status and hereditary rights and privileges. They are worn during celebrations and ceremonies.

Sitting there watching the women dance, I remembered that button box. It contained hundreds of abalone shell buttons sewn onto paper cards just sitting in my sewing room.

I met an elder that evening and asked if she and the Quileute tribe would like to have them. They would, she allowed, and also told me that many people scatter antique buttons on their children's graves.

La Push is our healing place and the Quileute have been welcoming to me for over 30 years. We go there when we are really sick or when we are really well. I moved the box to the coast, a better home for the buttons.

RED LIGHT DISTRICT

Kashmira and Iven have lived in Bangkok for 15 years, raising a wonderful family, and they're happy there. Many spectacular Buddhist temples are scattered around the area where Kashmira and Iven live. The people and culture are foreign to me. Almost no one speaks English. I like that a lot.

Bangkok is historic, crowded and hot. Traffic is fast-paced and it can feel like you're challenging the Angel of Death when crossing a wide road. The first time I did Kashmira she said to me, "hold my hand." My immediate thought had been how sweet it was that as grown-ups now, she still needed to hold my hand to cross. I quickly realized the tables had been turned and it was me who needed a grown-up hand to hold.

Early in my visits there, Kashmira helped educate me on Thai culture and how to be a respectful guest in their country. Wearing long garments to cover my décolleté and knees, people seemed more interested, friendlier, and kind to me.

Each visit I tried to learn more conversational Thai. Even though I would make mistakes, everyone seemed to appreciate my efforts and patiently helped me find the words. Searching for dinner on the street one night, I was shopping for Kashmira and Iven, who were too sick to go out. She had directed me to a particular food stand two streets away. I loved this. Lost, I needed to ask directions. "Ba may? Bah meh? Baaah Maeee? Baaa Maaa?" The recipient of my query was dumbfounded and couldn't understand me. Thai is tone specific and obviously I was tone deaf. Finally I said, "Soup?" "Oh, soup!" and he pointed me the right way.

Thailand has many draws. Ohmygosh, the food! Also the traditional art and dance, the silks, midnight flower markets, beaches, the carved royal barges – the royal fleet spoke deeply to this boat builder. And then there is the sex trade. Thailand is known internationally for sex tourism, a big draw and economic driver. In Bangkok there are so many districts, all distinctly different. I understand you can get whatever you could possibly want there.

Kashmira and Iven chose to live in a colorful, bustling, historic neighborhood, very close to the Grand Palace, the Thai, heterosexual red light district. It was made clear to me up front, this neighborhood was distinct.

I've always thought of myself as being terribly sophisticated, educated and worldly. Yet the first five years I visited them, I never once noticed a working girl on the street. Finally I asked her about it. "Look Mom, look at the side of the road." And there they were. About every 8 or 10 feet, a woman sitting in a chair, quietly waiting. Any transactions that may have occurred were always invisible to either of us.

These women looked nothing like the American sex workers I'd seen in Seattle or San Francisco who were flamboyantly dressed and showing lots of skin. They were all dressed conservatively and it stretched my perceived mundane sophistication.

Kashmira introduced me to her favorite working girl. This woman had made a life working within her industry maintaining very long term relationships with "returning customers." Her outward calm and dignity and the graciousness she showed to me helped dissuade any personal judgements I might have had. Scant years younger than I, she reminded me of Kashmira's paternal Nana, a woman of great wisdom. I liked her very much.

PRECIOUS

"I call every wild thing I encounter 'Beloved,' and think how interwoven, and delicate and how holy this all is." —Jan Halliday

I decided to follow through with my annual birthday ritual hike at the Dungeness Spit.

The spit juts into the Strait of Juan de Fuca and is 11 miles roundtrip out and back. Sailors had nicknamed it Shipwreck Spit until the historic Dungeness Lighthouse was installed in 1857. The lighthouse used to be at the end of the spit but the sand spit continues to grow about 15 feet per year and is the longest sand spit in the United States.

It is part of the Dungeness National Wildlife Refuge that was established in 1915 by President Woodrow Wilson, and has been managed by the U.S. Fish and Wildlife service off and on since then. Its primary management purpose has been to be a sanctuary for migratory birds and marine mammals. The public demand for access led to a shared use of the spit in 1956. Local ranchers from Sequim used to take an annual ride out the spit to the lighthouse on their horses every year before it was a state park. It was called Voice of America back then. Long before all of this, native peoples of the North coast used the spit extensively with villages nearby. The Jamestown S'Klallam tribe native treaty rights afford them fishing in

Dungeness Bay and shellfish harvesting adjacent to the spit. Perhaps they will be able to manage the sand spit someday.

Navigating the beach at a high tide is impossible jumping from log to log. I tried that once, having forgotten that tides wait for no birthday guurl. Its stunning solitude and unblemished natural state keeps calling me back. Walking it as a birthday ritual reminds me regularly how the world we live in and the life we make is precious.

Several years ago, Sue Nelson and I walked the spit and it poured, and I mean buckets, all the way out and back. We laughed the whole way, drenched to the bone. Many other women have made this hike on my birthday, good sports all. This year even though there was a 92% chance of rain, there were also super low tides. My friends Beth and Pam joined me.

Well, it rained 100% of the way out. Your elevated right hip can burn heading north to the lighthouse, but after turning south and home again, your elevated left hip can burn just as much and so equalizes the pain.

You keep asking yourself, does getting to the lighthouse really matter?

Today, even though the hike hurt more than I remember it used to, the afternoon was spectacular. Nesting birds strafed at our heads to warn us away, sea lions barked to brag of their prowess and the soft springtime rain was more comforting than abrasive. I felt alive and refreshed on the trek back. The sun came out, the water turned blue again and twas a perfect day.

It does matter.

RICKY AND JULY

His mother Rita hated July and wanted to rip the page off the calendar and lock her son Ricky in the linen closet every year. He had an uncanny ability to end up in the E.R. every July. All the doctors and nurses knew him on a first name basis, his entire youth.

Early in our relationship, I meticulously toured his body (as new loves often do) and found through exploration, his sizable amount of scars. "Tell me about this one," and each told a story about a long ago accident in July. This was my favorite tale.

Young Ricky had received a bow and arrow set for his birthday and was target practicing in the backyard. His father Dick was on a massively tall extension ladder, cleaning the gutters, three stories up.

Ricky had been aiming at his basketball and one of the arrows hit, but instead of impaling the ball, it hit the round surface and bounced back towards him. Miraculously, when it struck his face, the point entered his eye socket, just missing his eye.

"DAD!"

I can imagine Dick's horror to see an arrow sticking out of Rick's eye and how he surprisingly didn't kill himself getting down that ladder lickety split, to take him to the E.R.

Now where is that key to the linen closet?

CLAM DIGGING

When your child leaves your home and starts their own, you wonder if anything you taught or presented to them made an impression. You watch for shadows of your influence and delight in any you may see.

Kashmira claimed clam digging was her favorite childhood experience. Her dad and I would take her to a favorite beach when the tide cycles were low. Each of us armed with our own bucket and long-handled shovel, we'd slog through the soft sandy mud in our rubber boots out far enough until we could see the clams squirting at us from under the muck.

It generally took little time to fill our quotas, which was whatever we decided was enough to eat for several days. I don't remember ever buying a shellfish permit and the fish cops were never about.

We'd bring home our bounty and soak them overnight in salt water and add a bit of cornmeal to it. This was the best way for the clams to clean themselves before we would cook them. Kashmira's dad had a recipe for fried clams on the half shell that was divine.

Kashmira and Iven were visiting the Northwest from Bangkok with their children and she wanted her young ones to learn of the enchantment of clam digging. So we organized an expedition into the tidal world of bivalves. I contacted the Washington State Department of Wildlife's Bivalve Specialist, Camille Speck (aka Clamzilla) for tips and pointers. Then we armed ourselves with everything we could have possibly needed as per Clamzilla's suggestions, forgetting to bring along the common sense.

Within one minute of gaining the beach and without (intelligent) adult supervision, four of the six children had been sucked into the mud and fallen face down. We lost one shoe. It will never be found. There was a gravel path next to us that everyone else on the beach walked on, which we ignored. Pulling out the children from the strong suck of the beach, we continued through the sticky muck. Kashmira was pushing the one year-old in a stroller, off-roading in the "Bob." When her boots stuck, she also fell forward into the miasma of mud.

What was I supposed to do? She being my daughter and I being her mother, I just burst out laughing til my sides hurt. Covered in the muck, she dissolved into laughter too. The children stood silently, looking confused and wondered why they had been brought there.

Rinnan found a clam

Believing myself to be such a great Nana, I picked up the almost-three-year old and gingerly tried to make forward movement, protecting her with my warm embrace. My boots stuck, and down I went. I gently landed Tirzah in and up to her neck in mud. She roared, but it wasn't laughter. This was not funny to the almost-three-year old.

My son-in-law Iven was the only person on the beach with an

ounce of sense that day. I handed Tirzah off to him. They went back to the truck to clean up.

Kashmira was undaunted. With determination, grit, and her intrinsic sense of adventure, she called out to us, "Keep moving forward! WE CAN DO THIS!" As she wrangled the "Bob" out of the mud, passers-by cheered us on and were inclined to point out our mistakes. Kashmira yelled back to them, "Save yourselves!"

We eventually did find "the spot." We dug and measured our quota of clams as our shellfish permit allowed, filling all the buckets. Bespattered with mud, we celebrated over lunch at the Gear Head Deli. Everyone in Quilcene had already heard of us, put their heads together and whispered loud and indelicately about the folks from out of town.

Nothing about this clam digging venture was remotely similar to anything our young family did 35 years before. Her children were still befuddled. But they hadn't tasted clams fried on the half shell yet. What was similar was Kashmira and I sharing an adventurous moment together, and dissolving into laughter til our sides hurt.

KEEP CLAM!

Kashmira and her children stuck in the mud

POLITICAL FORUMS

I have an understanding of how hard running for elective office is and especially how hard the political forums can be on candidates. Running for Port commissioner was a dehumanizing experience for me, even though I surprised myself with thicker skin than I thought I had. In a small town, where most people are neighbors and see each other in the grocery store, when the very best and the very worst human behavior is exhibited, it feels more fierce.

During my "run" and well into the "race," long after the gloves came off between myself and my opponent, one particular forum was notably brutal.

Afterwards, when the microphone was unplugged, he turned to me and asked if I would be interested in another venue where the two of us could speak again. I looked him cold in the eyes and simply said "I'd rather have a colonoscopy."

"WHAT?" said he.

I had to repeat myself, but he finally got my message.

THE BIG FLAT ROCK

"They" say, "*You haven't been places, unless you've gone aground.*"

Approaching my old friend Nanaimo Harbor, I stood at the helm with both large-scale and small-scale charts spread in the cockpit. I'd read the sailing directions. Being possibly dehydrated or perhaps I had to pee, or just bone tired from the day's run, I was anxious to set the hook. So, blisteringly over-confident and running full speed is how we hit that big flat rock. No amount of rpm in reverse could free us.

Rick (my Rock), eased himself down below, pulled up the floor-boards and inspected our still bone dry bilges. I grabbed the VHF radio, our communication to the outside world. "May Day, May Day, May Day!"

"Diana, don't do that. You've always wanted to do that, haven't you?" Sadly, it was the truth.

The local marine safety patrol motored up alongside within seven minutes. The lowest tide of the year was to peak in seven minutes more. He took our halyard and powered his launch to heel us to starboard from heeling to port to ease our escape. I did not like that at all. When the boat abruptly changed heel to starboard, I let out a proper scream.

That big flat rock is popular amongst cruisers we were told, adorned with multiple bottom paint colors. That knowledge didn't soften the sting of embarrassment as we entered the near full anchorage and noticed every boat had their binoculars trained on us.

But "They" now know, I've been places.

SNOWBIRDS

Snowbirds have arrived in my poplars. What a fracas they put out. I love their tribal mentality, their sound and how they portend the coming of cold weather. When these birds would appear in my yard, fiercely feeding, I noticed a seasonal pattern. Often, snow would fall the next day, hence my nickname, Snowbirds.

I used to be able to identify six bird species. You know them: geese, ducks, seagulls, crows, robins and hummingbirds. Then I met Rick.

We'd drive slowly down Water Street in his big ole Chevy Suburban 454; the engine gargled "Bubbubbubbubbub." Electric and telephone wires crisscrossing the street were chockablock with these birds. Such a charmer, he'd stop the truck and traffic and say, "Watch this." Then he'd honk the horn loud and long and set every bird into cacophonous flight. Not the most virtuous activity of a hardcore bird nerd, but it always made me giggle. I love this time of year when the starlings arrive in my poplars.

TAMANOWAS ROCK

Lunch on the toppa Tamanowas Rock, we shared O-Konomi-Yaki (Japanese pancakes) and a thick slab of apple pie. No one was there except two frisky eagles chirping and circling overhead, ravens clonking as they did fly-bys, an ocean of fir trees, cedars and colorful madrone, the fertile Center and Beaver Valley's farmland, Mount Rainier, the Cascades Range, Mount Baker and our own fair Port Townsend Bay. These were our companions today.

Tank top and rolled up cuffs at the ankles, I exposed my skin for the first time in six months to a fresh warm southerly. Rick said, "Sexy." It was all a balm.

I'd misplaced my memory of early spring in the Great Pacific Northwest; its intoxication and promise of outdoor days, and after such a long cold winter I'm ready for this. The sap is rising.

REGRETS

No doubt about it, I have a few. Like the time I was standing face to face with Bonnie Raitt and Freebo after one of her earliest concert tours and was too starstruck to speak.

More recently, there is one distinct recurring theme.

I've always been strong and direct; some say even pushy. My third grade report card said I was a good pupil, but bossy. In moments of clarity and consciousness, I work at trying not to live up to this attribute. But there are too many times I wish I'd been more true to my nature and went with my gut.

Regarding several dear men in my life, all married or partnered up, they died too soon because someone wasn't able to see the warning signs and intervene medically. But with all due respect, most men I know are proud and continue to embrace their invincibility.

Intervention requires someone who is strong, direct and loving and willing to risk relationship. And yet when I saw the signs, I talked myself into believing it wasn't my responsibility. A wife or girlfriend might take offense or feel I'd overstepped some boundary.

I've struggled with learning what appropriate friendships look like when there is a spouse. Shouldn't they be the ones who make the call? But now I know from living this same situation with Rick, that too often a partner is unable to see what is so obvious to an outside observer.

Make the call. If someone's lips are blue and it's not cold out, take them to a doctor. If someone you know with a heart condition shows up and their face is bloated and all puffed out, take them to the E.R. If someone can't get out of bed for days and is afraid to go to the doctor, scoop them up and go to the hospital with them. Pay the bill. And if someone swears they have food poisoning, and you know what food poisoning is and your gut tells you it's something much worse, call 911.

These are four of my tender regrets.

WHITE WINGS

At the library in Port Hadlock, I spotted an old neighbor of mine from C dock. And Dick is old. Well past 100 now, he uses a walker but appears much younger wearing his full-length raccoon coat. A tall, slender Polish lad and former college professor, his passion was being on the water. *White Wings*, a truly luscious wooden sailboat, was his, always in tip-top shape. He was a consummate sailor.

Maybe 20 years ago or so, Dick decided to motor around Marrowstone Island in his outboard skiff. A circumnavigation. Fifteen miles into the roughly 20-mile trip, his motor died. Having no oars or radio, he drifted off the eastern shore. Well hell, he thinks, I'm a sailor. The only gear he had on board was an umbrella, which he used along with the light southerly to sail downwind all the way to the Boat Haven and back into his slip.

Sometimes you just get lucky.

NEVER ENOUGH

Rick is the first man in my life who has given me flowers, and often, for all the right reasons: just because. It was usually accompanied with a phrase like "I saw these beautiful flowers and it made me think of you." Swoon!

Jim Blaiklock started a tradition for me too long ago to remember: gifts of tulips every spring. For that I would smooch him with my two lips.

And Gordon Neilson used to walk up once in a while for dinner. In the growing season, Maggie Day always had a big bucket of free posies for anyone in want, outside her garden fence. He took a bunch one day and Maggie asked, "Who are they for?" "For Diana." And she would laugh and look at him like he was addled and say, "I think Diana has plenty of flowers in her garden," to which Gordon replied quite wisely, "A girl can never have enough flowers."

PASPA

My neighbor boys in the port, Townsend Bay Marine (TBM), were a "full service shop." Though miraculous with producing a quality paint job, they lacked an in-house varnish department. Paint and varnish are vastly different; paint wants to go on thin and varnish as thick as it can, and still behave. It's a kind of rocket science.

The 65-foot *M/V Paspatoo* (*Paspa*) was a long time client of theirs; she came to them every year and boasted a remarkable amount of glorious teak trim, raised panel doors and majestic cap-rails that wanted to shine with multiple coats of varnish. A Ralph Winslow design, she was built at the Blanchard Boatyard on Lake Union in Seattle and was launched in 1942. Converted to a yacht from a WW II transport boat, her long time owner was a visionary and exacting in obtaining her needs. He loved this boat.

Someone must have looked out their second story windows and noticed me slathering varnish on several of my customer's boats. I never felt like any kind of expert but seemed to be marketable. TBM asked me to consider running a crew to complete their varnish needs on *Paspa*, and I agreed to as an independent contractor. I was given total autonomy but learned a higher level of professionalism working with Daryl Paddock, the project manager. I liked that and him a lot.

The first year, I tried to teach and oversee their in-house paint and finish crew, but honestly found them to be un-teachable. It can be said that varnish is extremely difficult and one must want to walk through fire to learn it. The following year we tried something different.

Paspa's owner was very particular and insisted on certain things. He demanded that his varnish be applied full-strength only; no additives or brush thinners could be used. He could see the difference and had a keen eye. He was wonderful to work for if you followed his instructions. I saw it as a challenge and developed the technique for all my projects. Sometimes kicking and screaming, everyone else on the crew learned full-strength application as well.

Knowing she was coming early in the spring, by October I reached out to a stunning group of individual professional varnishers who agreed to pencil her in as my crew. It can be impossible to find anyone that time of year so I offered them a rate of pay that was enough of an enticement to make them happy and loyal. Over time, the institutional knowledge they brought with them each year saved time and money to the customer.

It always took six weeks and was the best job I ever took on as a boss-lady. I was challenged to learn how to keep a highly skilled, strongly opinionated and valuable-beyond-measure crew, returning and happy enough, more or less throughout the project.

I fired them every Friday night and re-hired them every Monday morning.

Over time, we were able to "get her up," (a varnish term denoting a stable quality of appearance and protection), which would then require only annual maintenance. *Paspa* was happy. We all were; Debi, Dianna, Sonia, Daryl, Korie, M.B., Maggie, Gillian, Julie, Janet,

Gina, Kelley, Molly, Bronwyn, Moriah, Nora and Alicia. Goddesses all!

THE NEW CANADIAN FLAG

I never met a Canadian I didn't like, until that one time. He was a returning customer and though I never knew how he originally found me, through email I agreed to paint his boat. I normally never sought out paint jobs, but the engineering of this one grabbed my imagination. It was the biggest hull I ever attempted, huge actually, and with three excellent finishers (Dianna Denny, Anna Hernandez and Daryl Dietrich) we pulled it off.

Tag-teaming, we had two scaffolding levels set up spanning both the top and bottom sections of the hull. Rolling and tipping together in sync, the four of us blended our paint work up and down as we moved stern to bow, creating a seamless envelope of perfect paint. Saving him roughly $25,000 from the usual big shop "spray job," it looked spectacular and I was proud of the results. He bought me a hummingbird feeder at the end of the job as a tip.

The following year he asked for every-thing inside the bulwarks (everything on deck) to be done. Something about his return visit was different. He openly liked my attractive young crew and did everything possible to advertise his interest. Living aboard on the hard, he routinely jumped on

The New Canadian Flag

his bike each morning to ride to the bathrooms wearing only a "dressing gown" he would loosely tie about himself. The breeze then did what it would. People in the port started to call him "The Dude," referencing "The Big Lebowski," who was decidedly so much cooler.

After his morning ablutions, he would ensconce himself in a deck chair in the shade of Townsend Bay Marine and watch us work. His daily uniform was a well-worn pair of coveralls, opened to his waist to shine a light on his hairy chest. They were missing most of the rear end which exposed his butt. Bob Denny told him to use some duct tape to cover it up.

Hand-washing his Speedo bikini type underwear, he'd hang them to dry at the bottom of the stairway to his boat, the stairway everyone went up and down all day long. The crew called it, "The New Canadian Flag."

Rick was gone to New England during the entire job. It was the first time I noticed that without his silent, strong presence, I was treated differently by my foreign customer. A hint that the respect I was used to being shown may not have been mine alone to claim.

PAM

I couldn't be more proud of my friend and what she's done for our community. Busting through the normal, she was elected Port commissioner, garnering 73% of the county vote. Pam brought a mighty change and breath of fresh air.

We share many similarities. Both of us are strong, independent, courageous, bold and fearless and we mostly agree on politics.

Pam Petranek - photo courtesy of Richard Oltman

RicknI rented the Hama Hama cabin and invited PamnRick to join us. We shared a great meal of salmon and oysters, wine and Jack Daniels. The men retired to the living room to sit and watch the fireplace while Pam and I chit chatted and cleaned up in the kitchen.

The log cabin is modest but wonderfully charming. Built in 1937 by the Civilian Conservation Corps, much remains original. Dimly lit with propane lights and no running water, it still felt majestic to us. We often came here as a total reset from everything boats. Set in the woods close to the Hama Hama River, everything outside is wet. We are experiencing dramatic rainfall and the river is flooding its banks on overdrive. The developed campgrounds just downhill are partially washed away. The sound is deafening.

Rummaging around in search of cleaning supplies, we opened the doors under the sink. To our horror, two tiny dead mice lay in sprung traps. Screaming bloody murder, we both started doing the "dead mice at your feet prance," very much like the scene in "Flash-dance" when Jennifer Beals is working out. The next part was automatic. We both yelled, "RICK!"

SHOP GUURL

There was a guy who had a shop in the port. Actually, I guess he still has a shop in the port.

One day he told Rick how lucky he was to have a girlfriend who worked with him, so she could sweep up the shop.

Rick didn't like that.

DICK

So many Super Bowl games, Thanksgivings, Christmases, family moments spent with

Dick and Linda. One particular Easter, I made a feast and invited them. Leaving the house, he commented it was the best Easter dinner he'd ever had. "Really?" That left me feeling mighty smug.

Then he said, "Diana, I'm Jewish. I've never had an Easter dinner before."

We first started working together cutting and splitting cordwood decades ago, realizing it's so much easier with a friend. He taught me how to properly start a chainsaw, letting the weight of the saw do the work for me when pulling the cord. Later he helped me understand how to build my first Gloucester Gull dory and lent me the jig. It was such an easy kind of construction; it boosted my self confidence in my beginning years and was a worthy first project. We learned together the mechanics and chemistry to do a fiberglass lay-up on a bathtub I'd designed for *Ocean*. When I needed to repair my Kettenburg 38 racing sloop by sistering new frames, he taught me how to steam-bend oak, to slather the wood with linseed oil and move quickly.

Me n Dick Golden

Dick held a doctorate and was some kind of physicist but left that all to be a sailor-boy and raise a family aboard. He developed arguably the highest-quality blocks available for maritime use — Golden Dove Blocks — made of Lignum Vitae, the hardest wood known. The bronze sheaves he turned in his shop on the lathe. When he retired from block making, I learned that art from him too and was gifted his jigs and special tools. Some people call him Doctor Blocks. I call him a good friend.

INGENUITY

Driving through the port in no particular hurry, I stop to gaze and swoon over a very handsome boat in for repair. A steam box is cooking. I turn off the truck in the middle of the road to observe.

A fella grabs a hot juicy piece of wood and runs the 30 feet to the hull. Seconds later, he runs back and props the wood up, just so. His buddy jumps into a pickup truck and carefully drives up on the wood with one tire.

I watch the shape change, from flat to a large curve instantly. Together, they both run back to the hull with this curvaceous aid to boat building. It must have worked, because I never saw them again. Sweet boatyard ingenuity.

RUSSELL BROWN-THE EPOXY COP

I'd seen a particular piece of stunning boatbuilding and then ran smack dab into the guy responsible, Russell Brown.

"Russell, very good job."

"Thanks Diana. I didn't use a single hand tool."

Russell cracks that myth from here in Port Townsend that all work worth mentioning is born of traditional techniques. He is in fact, known as the "Epoxy Cop" for his proficiency with the science and art of epoxy, but he's so much more.

His designs are superb and known for speed on the water, whether sailing, rowing or motor vessels. Everything is built light and strong. Watching him tear up the bay in his *"Grasshopper"* can't help but bring anybody a smile. Combining a pale green 50's style runabout perched over two streamlined catamaran hulls, and driven by a long-shaft 15 hp outboard motor, she looks like a grasshopper. It's clear he brings humor to his passion of perfor-

Ashlyn and Russell Brown in *Grasshopper* - photo by Jan's Marine Photography

mance on the water. Single handing to Alaska in the R2AK race aboard his 32' *PT Watercraft* made this town proud. Watching him smoke the other boats that carried ample crews was thrilling.

I needed help one day in the shop. Completely frustrated with my lack of abilities, I screamed Uncle. Actually, I called Russell. "I can't get the epoxy to lay down. It's a thick mess of attitude. What am I doing wrong?" "You need to read my book, *Epoxy Basics*." "Oh, don't make me read, Russell. Just tell me what to do." "No Diana, I'll be right down."

Thirteen minutes later, he arrived on his bicycle, book of *Epoxy Basics* in hand. He gave me his book and insisted I read it. "Aaagh!" said I. "Such a taskmaster." Thirteen minutes later, before he and his bike had probably left the port, I'd finished reading his chapter on how to make it flow. And flow, it did.

PENANCE

Four decades ago I witnessed a 90-year-old Mrs. Lundgren require young Uncle Jim's attention. He wasn't having it. So she walked up and grabbed the front of his jeans. That did the trick. I decided to extrapolate on her theme and ever since, my standard signature handshake has almost always been pinching someone's butt.

It has never occurred to me in all these years that this was inappropriate in any way as my intent was never sexual. And (like Governor Cuomo) I don't remember ever being directly told by anyone to stop it and that it made them uncomfortable.

Dear friends told me they were shopping at QFC one day and had noticed me in the store. Separated, she gets to the checkout first. Her husband comes up behind and pinches her butt. She never flinches, turns around or acknowledges it. He finally asks why she didn't respond. "Oh, I just thought it was Diana."

Recent counsel from women so much brighter than myself has allowed me to see that this just isn't cool. I sincerely ask forgiveness from everyone whose butt I've ever grabbed.

MY GIRLFRIEND PHIL

Phil was on a first boat project I worked on when I came to town. It was a big job with a large crew of sub-contractors. He was the marine electrician. Never the first person to show up each morning, but the only one to address which radio station we would listen to each day. The crew had a running bet, the minutes it would take for him to step aboard and change the channel. It never took minutes, only seconds.

I used to listen to him DJ on KRAB in Seattle in the 70's. Now I can hear him on Port Townsend's own KPTZ. Radio has always been a large part of his life.

Phil is a gift. Our local anchor DJ, he's offered to the listening public everything concerning Jefferson County in depth since the radio station's inception. His boundless curiosity and fine mind have transported us through music, politics, poetry, storytelling, education, environmental news, sports, maritime, art, culture, history, current affairs, perspectives from all

Phil Andrus and Emmy Lou Stein - photo courtesy Phil Andrus

angles and points of view, health and public safety, agriculture, business, non-profits, youth, festivals, live performances and fascinating interviews. He has brought all this into our homes and workplaces. All local, because our local is captivating.

Phil is more than just my favorite DJ. He's been the rare kind of

237

friend that is always solid and available whenever I might need that kind of friend. So easy to be around, I feel safe with him. He is one of my very few spiritual girlfriends.

AN UNEXPECTED BONUS

This parental voyeurism, watching my daughter being a mother, just keeps getting better and better. I always understood that having children was a gift and opportunity to experience growing up all over again, fresh but with attitude. I neglected to expect how when grandchildren come along, it starts all over; different this time but deeply entertaining.

Every text, phone call or FaceTime brings me right back to my own young motherhood, a tug on my heart or a strongly visceral expression of emotion. Lately the emotion has been boundless laughter.

A welcome phone call from 8,000 miles away asking for help. "Mom, it's time for bed and I don't have a heat lamp for the new ducklings. I can't let them die on their first night."

"Kashmira, I don't remember ever having a heat lamp for ours," I answered.

"Google just said in lieu of heat, give them a feather duster. They seem really happy with this."

This reminds me of placing nursing pads and my Timex wrist watch in her crib next to her head as a newborn baby, to imitate my heartbeat and smell of mother's milk lying next to her, so I could then sleep in my own bed.

Kashmira got up twice that first night to check on the new ducklings, terrified of having to explain mortality to her young children the next morning. Every time she approached the box there was total silence. "Great, just great, I've killed them," she thought. Reaching in and touching each one, the peep peep peep choir started. She could go back to sleep for another three hours before the peep show started all over again.

SANDBAGGED

Rick and Gordon went for a hike in the Olympics one hot summer day. Roots and Rocks, the trail was steep and arduous.

Since Rick is rather tall and athletically competitive, it was always very difficult to even try and keep his pace. Gordon huffed and puffed until at last, he too, was at the summit. Together they sat to drink in the vista. Gordon was parched but it was worth the effort.

Rick asked him if he'd like an ice-cold ginger beer. Wow, thought Gordon, Rick is amazing. He's thought of everything. And indeed he had, because earlier in the day at the bottom of the hill when Gordon's eyes were averted, Rick had secreted 2 bottles, individually wrapped in bags of ice cubes into Gordon's pack.

MAINE ARTIST'S TOUR

Rick's parents were both very ill with devastating cancer. He knew they needed his help and so flew to Massachusetts to do what he could. It didn't take long. Rita's colon cancer progressed so rapidly, they barely had time for all the laughs and deep conversations still wanting to be shared. Rick almost never left her side.

After she died, he came home for a respite of sorts. We went backpacking to Mount St. Helens. Five days later, as we re-entered our home, the phone rang. Dick, Rick's father, was in critical condition, so he flew back the following day. Less than three months later, Dick was dead of liver cancer. Rick called to tell me he was an orphan. I flew to Boston two days later.

Charged with wrapping up his parent's affairs and cleaning out the three-story home filled with 50 years of stuff was daunting. Rick was an emotional wreck and I had to buck up. But in the middle of this hardship, we started to fray. What we needed was one last New England "Surfin Safari."

We instinctively knew we would never visit New England

together again. Holding a deeply sentimental staff meeting, we devised the "Artists of Maine Tour," of which there are a lot! Driving until we could drive no further, we billeted in Rockland. Somehow, we had never stopped here in our original foray into Maine. Small tourist towns like Camden, Rockport and Bar Harbor were shinier at the time.

Rockland was our kind of place. A proud working town filled with a generous population of mini tour guides. We learned about the historic lime quarrying industry by simply asking a local on the side of the road, "What are those funny looking things?" An hour later, we knew all about it.

We spread out from there to every gallery, museum, small harbor, and historic home of the well-known, celebrated artists of the area like Edward Hopper and the Wyeth boys. Seeing the landscape, topography and vistas meant more to our understanding of their work than viewing any painting hanging on a wall, though we saw plenty of them too. It was all a thrill.

Ambling south, we made it to Prouts Neck where Winslow Homer's home stands as a modest museum of his remarkable body of work. Walking along that shoreline, we could see it all.

I shared a cross continent cultural exchange at our last art exhibit, as an appreciative nod to all Yankee-Men. As Rick and I were leaving the Portland Museum of Art, the well dressed, older, stoic docent asked if we had left behind an umbrella. I laughed large and said, "We're from Seattle. We don't need no stinkin umbrella." I caught him off guard and he laughed large too.

TED HUGS

It was a hot August and Ted Pike had just died unexpectedly. Everyone in town was immobilized by grief. We were all in shock.

Ted had a unifying ability to make everyone he was with feel seen, heard and important. He was beloved in our sailing community; his handshakes were legendary, as were his hugs. He would always look you in the eyes and hold your hand firmly, never letting go until he knew you felt truly connected to him. His hugs were precious, warm and freely given.

I woke early that next morning to the thought that his boat was broiling in the summer sun out back behind my shop on the asphalt. We enjoyed working together and he had brought *Annie Too* in for some loving care. Wooden boats don't do well on land and I knew it had to get back in the water quickly. I took it upon myself to make that happen, knowing Kate, his wife, had more important things to deal with.

Ted Pike, Jim Ferris and Lucky Me - photo by Elizabeth Thomson Becker

Rushing to the port, numbed by sadness, I mixed up the topside paint and grabbed my painting kit. The hull was prepped and I was on autopilot. As I'm climbing up to the scaffolding, a place where Ted and I had been laughing together just days before, Kaci Cronkhite drove by. I might have screamed something like, "We gotta get it launched!"

Without hesitation, she parked her truck and climbed up to join me. Together we rolled and tipped the hull, a caring team of *Annie Too* fans, finishing up with a well-learned Ted Hug.

A LORDLY CEDAR

Paul and Lorraine brought one of their boats to our shop in Port Townsend for a major shampoo and set. Dave Ullin came also, worked on it and lived in the shop for the duration of the haul-out. Like old times when he lived at Raven Marine's shop 25 years earlier, it was good to have him around.

Dave Ullin and Lorraine Svornich

Towards the end of the project, Rick and I asked everyone up for dinner. I went to Dave to be sure he would eat black cod and his face lit up. It looked like it was a go, but anyone who knew Dave well understood that his uncompromising choice of fare was simple, basic, possibly uncooked. But never hot, nothing fancy, elaborate or artificially sweet.

As a hostess I have always tried to accommodate any dietary restrictions a guest might have; vegetarian, vegan, dairy and gluten intolerant... and make it enjoyable. But Dave's normal cuisine did not register with me as a dietary restriction. So I just built a meal that was fit for a king.

It was at least four courses: black cod smothered in rich Sake Kasu sauce, a huge salad with dressing, rice and vegetables. We were celebrating a job well done so I am positive I also served a rich gooey

THE CENTER OF BUOYANCY

dessert, laced with sugar and plenty-o-fruit. All of us being big eaters, except for Lorraine, I made what I thought was more than plenty. But as the evening sped by, Dave went back for seconds, thirds, and I ran out of food. At the risk of making Dave seem indelicate, I believe he licked his plate.

This was such a delight. After dinner, Paul leaned in privately and said, "I can't believe he ate your food! He won't eat anybody's food."

"I'm a good cook," said I. But of course it was much more than that. We five old friends shared an evening of laughter, memories, light and deep conversation and the simple pleasure of sharing a meal together. Dave's desire was to live life purposefully. What could possibly be more purposeful, especially since it has left me with this lovely memory of my dear friend?

I never told Dave I loved him or how lucky and grateful I was to have him in my life. But I'm sure he knew.

Shortly after Dave died, George Buehler lovingly sent me this remnant of a poem by Edwin Markham. Written for Abe Lincoln, I'm sure Abe doesn't mind sharing this tribute with Dave.

"...he went down
As when a lordly cedar, green with boughs,
Goes down with a great shout upon the hills,
And leaves a lonesome place against the sky."

GEORGE BEUHLER

Thanks to all the people who aren't afraid to do or think things for themselves, and thereby keep this world from becoming too boring. That was George. He had many gifts – his world view, intellect, pragmatism, sense of fun and of course his boat designing and no-nonsense/can-do kind of boat building. Able to reach so many people, he no doubt launched a thousand ships. But the genius I knew and loved him for, was his kindness and depth.

I first met George more than 40 years ago when we both owned boats at the same marina. It is not overstating the fact to say that George liked women. Since I am a woman, he wanted to like me. He would come by my boat often, asking me to go sailing with him. "I'm busy George!" "Ah come on, it's just a day sail." "I'm not interested George!" "Come on, come on, come on..." He was singularly relentless.

"FINE! I'll go sailing with you." And so we did. I was without a doubt the most boring decorette any boat ever sailed with. Even the food I brought was boring. He never asked me to go sailing with him again and so we could just get down to becoming friends. And George became a great friend to me. We had the kind of relationship where we could just truly be ourselves with no tension or expectations.

Some 30 years ago, he came to visit at a time when I looked my absolute worst. I was embarrassed and told him so. Holding me with his eyes, he shared that he would always only see me the way I looked the first day we met. That simple kindness has helped me get up every morning since and helped me realize I look at all my friends that way too.

More recently we've spent time together whenever he passed through Port Townsend. He'd stop by the shop and we'd sit on the bench out front and get it all talked out. Whatever it was: life, happiness, aging, death, illness, marriage, devotion, loyalty, suicide, friendship and never anything about boats. Over the years, his thoughts were so profound, deep and life changing; in many ways, he has helped me become a better person. I'm not sure he ever fully understood what a good man he was, though I told him often. I will miss George terribly and his $7 hugs.

He and Dave Ullin were very close friends. They had drifted apart, as friends sometimes do, but deep love remained.

I took a phone call from George one early morning. He was distraught. A disturbingly real dream had upset him. In it, Dave had come to visit George to tell him he had died; a last visit to his old friend before he passed into a different realm.

I listened well but knew it was only a dream. Only days before I had heard that Dave was at Shilshole, hauled out with his old tugboat *Spruce*, catching up on deferred maintenance. I calmed George down and only said goodbye when I felt he was relieved.

George Beuhler - photo courtesy of Gail Beuhler

Two hours later, Dave was found alone on his tug. He had died the night before.

CHAPTER II
HEAVY WEATHER
2016 - 2020

photo by Kim Carver

"I was amazed that what I needed to survive could be carried on my back, and most surprising of all that I could carry it."

—Cheryl Strayed

JUST SAY NO

There came a time in our partnership when absolutely everything was wrong. Rick and I even went to couples counseling, which impressed the hell out of me, the fact that he agreed to go.

Looking back several years, a progression of subtle, then obvious changes about Rick were undeniable. Things he said or didn't say, what he did or now did not do, were stunning and counter to his nature. His craftsmanship declined, along with his work ethic. He had always been well-liked by his customers, but even they saw a difference and one by one, he was fired from every job. He took to spending his days sitting at his desk, shuffling papers from one pile to the next.

Something had to change. When the counselor took me aside privately and encouraged me to dump him, I knew I had to do just that. It never occurred to me to have a doctor check him out, nor did the professional counselor advise me to do so.

I faced it with resolve, girding myself for it.

We sat together quietly. As I spoke of my frustration and total resignation that our relationship was over. I said, "You absolutely must move out." We sat in our living room, surrounded by the many things we shared together that had made our house a home. Thinking calmly, he offered his response. "I'm not leaving."

This completely took me by surprise. Imagining this whole conversation, I had not considered this outcome. And yet this moment was reminiscent of a similar conversation 20 years prior when he had said, "I feel you slipping away from me." And I had calmly replied, "Don't let it happen!"

I sat with this moment myself for a good long while, mulling every possibility. Then I said, "Okay." It never occurred to me to have a doctor check him out, nor did the professional counselor advise me to do so.

Where did that leave us? It had been a thorough throwing down of the gauntlet on my part and him picking it up and kissing my hand instead, asking for compassion and grace.

SCOTT AND BECCI

Scott stopped by to see me one day when I wasn't home and spoke with Rick instead. There was a message from him that evening:

"CALL ME RIGHT AWAY!" I wondered what in the world I had done now. The conversation went like this: "What's wrong with Rick?"

"What do you mean?"

"Something is seriously wrong with Rick."

I thought Rick was off, but living closely with a deteriorating illness, it's harder to recognize changes as a spouse than what an occasional visitor can see. My talk with Scott was my first indication that something was indeed alarmingly wrong.

Becci Kimball and Scott Walker - photo courtesy of Scott Walker

I love men, but men are weird. It may be just my cultural generation, but guys my age resist showing any sign of weakness. I could not get Rick to go to a doctor or convince him something was wrong. In came Becci.

Scott had the great good fortune to fall in love with Becci and I fell in love with her too. Becci is many things: a deep thinker and communicator, compassionate and patient, but also a true healer. When you tell her that, she simply says, "I just listen well."

Once she heard of Rick's condition, she took me aside, explained to me in ways I could not misunderstand that I had to get Rick to a doctor soon, to secure a diagnosis. She gave me the strong but loving push to get it done, whatever it took.

INTERVENTION

It was impossible to get Rick to see his doctor with any kind of reasonable nudging by me or other caring friends who had made an effort to talk with him. His ears were closed. I had to switch to quiet intervention.

We shared the same primary care physician so I made an appointment. Unsure just how to do this, I was vague about my medical symptoms but they fit me right in. Once there, confessing it was an intervention showed me the tender side of healthcare previously unknown to me. Being unmarried, I learned I could legally discuss medical concerns about anyone with their doctor but Rick's doctor could not share personal information with me.

Our doctor is a kind of superhero, he could not have been more helpful. I explained Rick's symptoms and stark new limitations. Together we developed our plan. The doctor would phone our home to speak to Rick, tell him it had been too long since he'd seen him as a patient and suggest he come in.

The call worked perfectly and Rick was thrilled with this personal attention from a professional. It started us on the next path, a series of neurological specialists that eased us into our new reality.

DIAGNOSIS

We were sent to the Neuropsychology department at Harborview Medical Center in Seattle where most everyone in the Puget Sound region goes to test for brain function. The test can take from 4-6 hours and measures a range of mental acuity – reading, language use, attention, learning, processing, speed, reasoning, remembering, problem solving, mood and behavior. During the first hour, a spouse is meant to attend and the process was astonishing. If I had had any doubts about Rick's cognitive limitations going in, I had none going out.

Sitting in the waiting area, it wasn't even a room, just the hallway close to the elevators. No people bustled around, there were no magazines on end tables to thumb through as a distraction from the enormity of our situation; there wasn't even a window to look out of.

The neuropsychologist invited me into her office to answer any questions I could think of. I started with, "How long do we have of mobility and semblance of quality of life?"

She had answered this question so many times before, "A general rule of thumb is you have as long as it took you to get into this office. That doesn't mean he will die then. He may live 20 more years but probably in a care facility." Doing a quick mental calculation, it hadn't been that long since we began this process. My anxiety grew.

"How do people usually die from this disease?"

"Falling is of concern but generally they die of pneumonia. You should definitely address any bucket list you may have very soon." I didn't remember any bucket list we might have had.

I sat alone the next three hours in the stark, cold, clinical hallway, dumbfounded as to how we got here. Ironically, a close friend had watched his mother suffer and die from Alzheimer's. He had been consumed with panic that his genetic makeup would produce the same illness in him and he spoke of it relentlessly. As his friend I had tried to assuage his fears by continuously encouraging him not to worry, because worry never helps us deal with any unknown fear. Nor would it keep Alzheimer's away. I knew nothing about this illness except for its reputation of being extremely difficult to live with.

Rick pretty much flunked every test. In 95% of them he was found to be so severely limited, any developing medications or clinical trials were unavailable to him due to his advanced diagnosis. I had taken too long to get him there. They wished us well as we left.

Driving home he asked me, "Do people die from Alzheimer's?" I truthfully replied, "I don't know but I think a patient will develop serious mental limitations." Faced with the inevitability that we wouldn't grow old together on the same page, we talked about our future and made a pact to live the rest of our lives the very best we could.

After Rick's diagnosis, I felt the weight of years of penance to make up for when I had unwittingly blamed his behavior on his apparent indolence. I wanted to kneel now before him in supplication, begging for his forgiveness.

Rick had introduced me to hiking and backpacking decades ago. Up front I had been tentative and asked his guidance. Always reticent, he simply said, "Just pick 'em up and put 'em down. In six feet, you'll be an expert."

I sought refuge in this counsel now, not knowing what was ahead.

LEARNING TO LIE

When asked how I came to my choice to care for him, I had no hesitation. I knew in my heart that to help Rick die well was my sacred duty. I never questioned it. Even in hindsight and having lived that relationship, I would not have done it any other way. I'm not overstating in saying it was the hardest thing I've ever done in a very long life. The four years of 24/7 caregiving took its toll. A brief glance at me by an untrained eye, tells the story that I'm "not right." I likely never will be "right." But it has been my choice.

Early on, several of my friends spoke with me privately, told me things like: "No one would do what you're doing," "He wouldn't want you to suffer," " You have your own life to live,"" Institutionalize him and turn the page." These comments weren't helpful as I'd already made my decision. What I needed were supportive friends.

And of course, going into something like an Alzheimer's diagnosis, you can't know what you'll be facing. It is different of course, but isn't marriage or parenting? Isn't life itself a tremendous unknown?

We were fully committed to each other, loyal and true. With decades of friendship to bank on, this large withdrawal of energy we'd need still left our mutual love account full and earning interest. It's a good thing too, for we would need it, the next four years.

So I chose my course and wouldn't you know, it was likely the very best thing I ever did. Marriage, and ours specifically, is never perfect. The final four years we worked together as a cohesive team. We were on the same page – to live well -- and had no other real distractions. We faced every minute, not just the day, head on and present. They were the best years of our life together. I'm so grateful for the gifts we gave each other.

I quickly learned to lie. In my lifetime, I can count on one hand the number of times I've lied. Which is a lie, of course, but you get the idea. I'm honest.

As his dementia progressed I had to evolve to every need instantly. Fighting it, I came to understand that lying helped him and me not get freaked out. He might say, "Someone is stealing my stuff, my wallet, my money." And I found if I said, "Not to worry. We have insurance. We'll get it all back." It soothed him. Or (always at 2 a.m.), "I want to go home. You need to take me home now." If I said, "Of course I'll take you home. But look, it's really late and everyone at home is asleep. You don't want to wake them do you? I'll take you first thing in the morning." He'd smile and go back to sleep. We were sweet with each other.

The very best help I had was to be part of a support group, several women living the same reality. Nothing but trust, truth and understanding. Caregiving is emotionally and physically exhausting. I remember at the group one day saying, "I've finally found something that feeds my soul. Aren't we supposed to feed our soul?" I burst into tears because, "I can't remember what it is."

I remembered later of course: it was when I sat down to write after Rick went to bed at night. Writing! Something I never knew I wanted to do but found it so personal and private, and necessary. If I hadn't found it, I think my heart would have burst.

And that's another huge gift Rick gave me.

DIMMING LIGHT

Our social life began to evaporate. One thing we had enjoyed the entire time we lived together was hosting small and large parties for every possible holiday or spontaneous whim. We shared our home and our fortune with good friends. Almost abruptly I saw a shift after diagnosis and disclosure. People still came to our parties, but we were rarely invited to theirs.

When I told a close friend that Rick was really sick and I needed the support of my girlfriends, she never visited me again. Even now, I only see her in passing. Others confessed they were afraid of Rick, that his "brain damage" made him dangerous and unpredictable. It seemed like some people felt Alzheimer's was catching. But it may have just been the fact that we weren't fun to be around anymore. I was overwrought and grave and Rick's brilliant light was dimming.

As I was always prone to self-doubt, analyzing our changing friendships drove me nuts. Unless someone told me why they pulled away, no amount of wonder would answer my questions of why. It was a supreme waste of time.

One friend told me she could be there for illness but never for the grief of death. This gift of honesty helped me come to understand that everyone has their own unique gifts which may not be the everything you want or need them to be. They also could be carrying invisible trauma and needed to put up boundaries. These changing relationships helped me to stand stronger on my own, eventually without judgment.

As friends faded away, others miraculously stepped up and stood in for us. Cathy, Gordon and Lennea checked in weekly, sat with us and provided normal-like adult conversations those last four years. Catherine and Mark jumped in as well. It kept us from total isolation and was a life-saver.

SMELL THE ROSES

253

When I was in college, my entire math department voted me as the person most likely to stop and smell the roses. Sometimes I forget to.

Cathy Langley said the darndest thing. "Every day is precious." I heard it loud and clear when she said it and my life instantly became so much easier. Such a sweet smell.

TURNING THAT PAGE

Being a sailor-guurl resonated more with me than possibly anything else. It was my chosen identity. Even after retiring from sailing offshore, I had the thirst to keep the wind in my sails inshore.

Working at keeping a boat in the slip in my harbor, well-maintained and provisioned, ready to cast off the lines on a whim, was a lot of work but work I enjoyed. Loving a boat as a family member became a commitment that continuously brought depth and a greater appreciation of the world to my life. Like every relationship should. And as all things undertaken in my youth, I never once looked ahead to the possibility of my sailing ever coming to an end. At the moment of that first kiss, few of us are looking ahead several decades to a time when we may need to be caregivers for each other. It seemed to happen so fast.

Waking one day to our situation that Rick required my attention 24/7, it was so obvious that I could take care of the boat or I could take care of Rick, but I couldn't take care of them both. The slip rent was due in three days and being unable to work now, funds were tight. My choice was clear.

Three days later, we motored to Sea Marine, de-rigged and pulled her mast. We hauled the boat and put her on Gus's boat-moving trailer. Then brought her home to the driveway and shored her up. Quite unceremoniously, my life as a sailor-guurl was over.

As I looked at her poised and ready with her bow facing the road, I instinctively knew I'd never sail again at her helm, nor likely any other helm. Every day that I looked at her out my bedroom window, decades of memories flooded back. Like the first time I sailed was on a wooden boat under the Golden Gate Bridge and felt the ocean swells that would someday be a kind of home to me. I later bought my own first wooden sloop and learned that the wind didn't always come from behind. And jumping aboard *Izzy,* our Caribbean to Puget Sound big mucky muck offshore adventure experience. Or sailing and fishing with our young family in the western Pacific and Alaska aboard *Ocean.* When I finally learned to sail proper aboard my Kettenburg 38, *Scandia,* my definitive nuanced sailing instructor. And cruising Puget Sound and Canada on *Taku,* the orphan we took on that became our wonderfully delightful family member.

I cried and cried and cried for three days until finally woke to a blanket of calm that enveloped me. I wasn't sad anymore and recognized how lucky my sailing life had been. Spectacular, really. Plus, I never had to haul out and maintain another wooden boat ever again. Whoo Hoo!

CLOSING THE SHOP

It was past time to dismantle our shop. Almost 18 years to the day we had enjoyed this slice of creative opportunity and made a living to boot. Our shop was precious to us. Living just a mile up the hill, we would ride our bikes to work, sometimes ride home for lunch, then back down to finish a work day. It kept us healthy and fit. Sometimes we would order a takeout meal from the Blue Moose Café and ride out the Larry Scott Trail to the old wooden picnic table where we would take stock of our empire and smile a lot. But now, we both knew it was time to call it a day.

We built a small shop on our property at home. Anything under 200 square feet could be built without a permit from the city. I turned to the research of how to create a stick structure. There's a lot to know. My design was simple and the few necessary sub-contractors we needed were available. Suddenly I was banging nails for maybe the first time. When I reached the point of needing to stand up the walls, I uncharacteristically cried Uncle and asked for help.

So many friends showed up, it was very touching. Tracy Lee made a crew lunch for us and we all banged more nails and raised the walls. It was still early in the day. Tim Lee softly suggested, "Diana, why don't we build the roof too while we're here?" D'oh! A bonus! With so many hands and such a small space, the shell was completed in no time.

I kicked butt on finishing the rest of the build and hired some friends to help. When it was done, we'd have a place to put the tools we couldn't bear to part with from our shop in the port.

Most everyone could see the writing on the wall, that our days were numbered as tenants down there. Early on, we were approached by two different boat builders wanting their own port footprint. The first had a plan, a partner, customers waiting, tools and experience. Early in the spring we made a gentleman's agreement that he could "buy" the shop and shook on it. Some of our big equipment would go with him too and all of our customers. It felt right.

I approached the Port to negotiate a lease agreement that would satisfy all of us. There was a new E.D. and property manager just getting started. He looked things over, came and measured the space inside and out and spoke about how he understood the pressures of a new entrepreneurial venture. He said he'd make it easy for everyone and sounded so convincing and sincere, I let my guard down. Consumed with the timeline of building a new shop as well as tending to our altered life due to Rick's illness, I left our lease arrangement in his hands.

While I was swamped with multitudes of personal needs, the calendar kept turning pages without my notice. All of a sudden it was the end of summer and I'd not heard a peep from the property manager. When I confronted him face to face in the administration building, he professed embarrassment. He had done nothing in my regard. I went to his boss to complain and she professed greater apologies, claimed she'd moved him away from his job description title to do other things at the port, but would make my needs a top priority. Almost immediately he called to meet with his lease proposal.

After a quick read-through, even for me who had limited experience with Flim Flam men, I knew I was being railroaded. The proposed agreement was a joke, counter to everything he had said up front, and it did not pencil out. Security deposits up front would consist of the total of one year's rent: an initial cash fee of $5,000 along with a surety bond of $15,000. The new lease rate schedule raised the rent yearly at an alarming pace. The price for "land stalls," or space out back for boat storage, was untenable to start with. It was also scheduled to be raised shockingly fast. But the doozy in the deal was that the next tenant would have to pay 2.5% of the business's gross income, (2.5% gross revenue on $0-$500,000 and 5.0% gross revenue on $500,001 or more), audited by and paid to the port quarterly. It was to be a revenue share program for the pleasure of doing business. This, he said, was a new port policy they intended to implement with every tenant. Taku Marine's proposed lease was the acid test. Now I could see the writing on the wall.

I apprised our guy of the port's intent and suggested he negotiate his own deal. Very quickly, he and his business partner decided they did not want the pleasure of working in the port after all. And who could blame them. I turned down the property manager's offer and told him we were just happy to be leaving with our health. A sad irony. It came as no surprise that after all these years of sparring with the port, it would end this way. But this became the beginning of a revolution that swept every entity doing business with them, as they heard of our situation. Though our maritime colleagues were too late to save us, their combined voices eventually brought the administration to its knees.

By now, I could see no other recourse than to just move out. Over time we had amassed a sizable stack of quality boat lumber. We had billions of hand tools and thousands of power tools. Deciding what to take home and what to sell was painful. Friends came and paid top dollar for our stuff. Bit by bit, our pared down equipment and lumber made it up the hill. The rest we gave away. One or two longtime neighbors made an effort to say goodbye.

LIVING WELL

Our days became our own. With no external responsibilities or distractions, every morning would start with, "What shall we do today?" Our fit and healthy bodies allowed us to pursue what had always been our place of well being, exploring our natural world.

Exercise was key to brain health, so if we planned to stay in town, we would walk to the library to read the daily papers and then stop at Pane d'Amore for a snack. Munching it at the Bell Tower, we'd survey our mighty kingdom and languorously share a smoke. Then we'd off to downtown via Haller Fountain to count the quarters in the pool, visit the bank and bookstore, after which we'd walk home. Probably four times a week. It never felt redundant and always made us smile.

Our love of "Surfin Safaris" grew (driving anywhere farther than Chimacum). In the early years we could still hike and backpack and often revisited our catalog of secret stash places. Thursday mornings might find us driving, as Tim Quackenbush would DJ on KPTZ. We loved his choices of music and being stuck in the truck for hours together was sometimes the best. The reception was clear the whole 80 miles to the western shore of Lake Crescent.

We went to new places too. Mount St. Helens was our final high country adventure. Five days in new terrain late in the season, we were practically alone. Heavenly, it was.

Rick had worked there after "the blow," hired as an assistant to a fisheries biologist, who had him jumping between slippery rocks counting fish. He showed me special gems, not in the guidebooks. The very best secret surprise was a huge waterfall a long ways in and known to only a lucky few.

But it was there that I learned his lack of ability to reason could bring dangerous consequences. He had lost his ability to set up a tent and was fiercely resistant to my help. We stayed closer to civilization afterwards.

All this was possible with the help I got from Linda and Carey, our two respite care-givers. Each brought their own unique gifts into our home four hours each week, allowing me some time to get away and recharge my own tattered batteries. The help was immeasurable and kept us going.

Later in our dance together, leaving town became impossible. I'd still wake up each morning and say, "What shall we do today? Oh! I know, I know. Let's go grocery shopping!" He'd smile broadly, get in the truck and off we'd go to shop well together.

Rick at Yoho National Park, B.C.

OUR NEW SHOP DOOR

After weeks of fretting, designing, procuring, measuring, and cutting, (Measure Twice; Cut Once) then muscling into place (it's a big frick'n barn door) and installing, I was giddy with accomplishment. The mechanism was so smooth! Smiling broadly at Rick I declared, "Watch this."

Sliding it open with glee, I watched as it slid right off the track onto the ground. I had forgotten to install the stop. Goll durnit. So we had to muscle it back into place and re-install all over again. (Muscle Into Place Once; Install Once!)

TERI

Because going public with the devastating diagnosis of Alzheimer's opened up so many vulnerabilities, I was slow to be forthcoming. Not truly knowing what we faced compounded my reticence. Any semblance of strength or resolve had left me after the neuro-psych appointment at Harborview. I suddenly felt very small.

Most people don't know what to say, even your closest friends. My early conversations felt forced and inconsequential, or worse: "Are you getting enough help?" "You need help," "No one should do what you're doing," "You should institutionalize him." It made me sad. I longed for someone to step in and tell me how they intended to offer help.

Teri crossed my path one day. True to my nature, I spilled the beans. She thought for a moment and calmly said, "I've heard that's really hard. I'm sorry. You can talk to me anytime, about anything." And true to her nature, she meant what she said. It soothed me.

SUCKER PUNCHED

We walked for miles today beside the crescent lake. Soft blue overhead, steep slopes rich with evergreens, whitecaps on the water. The strong easterly breeze was hot on our smiling faces.

Stopping for lunch, we chose a shady spot. Rick turned away from me to face the turquoise lake to drink in our perfect moment. One minute later when he turned back, I was a malevolent stranger.

His fear and confusion rocketed into an acute rage in him I'd never seen before, and it was directed solely towards me. Moments earlier the two of us were happy-go-lucky. No soft sweet lyrical words or soothing murmurs could alter the wall of ferocity facing me now.

Though he never landed a blow nor even made a fist, his outrage had straight away amputated our deep and tender bond. I felt a phantom limb pain in its place; burning with the cruel reality of this disease and that it was finally in my face like a sucker punch.

Both of us were scared now. Rick walked away quickly back towards the truck. It was clear he needed to get away from me, but I needed to keep an eye on him. A thick lowland evergreen forest ran parallel to our trail, and I worried what would happen if this powerfully athletic man decided to disappear into it. Instead, I was barely able to keep pace with his long strides but he stayed on the gravel path.

Miles later we arrived at the truck. He stood next to it, knowing it was his but unable to negotiate opening the door. He was still enraged. It took a very long time of soothing speech from me to entice him into the passenger seat. Longer still to try to pull the seat belt around him. And in truth instead of succeeding at that, I fastened myself in, locked his door from my side and drove towards home. While driving I was composing explanations to any State Patrol that might pull us over for seatbelt non-compliance.

It was the longest two hour drive I could remember. Terrified that he would open his door and jump out, I was dangerously distracted. Slowing my speed on the highway I was riveted to the position of his hands, watching for movements towards his door handle. But before we reached the city limits to home, Rick's demeanor was calm and back to "normal."

For both of us, it's getting weirder.

THE THING ABOUT DEMENTIA

Most might argue that there's no silver lining, living with dementia. Except of course if you do or say something terribly unfortunate and your partner's short-term memory is really bad. You can pretty much get back to normal in a flash, with almost no scars.

We did share a different kind of miracle some years back that could only have happened because of dementia.

Marriage is hard sometimes. You do your best, give and take and be kind throughout it all. A girlfriend once told me there were things she just chose not to say for forty years. Things best left unsaid.

Rick didn't recognize me, Diana - me - anymore as Diana. I was three separate people to him: the woman he slept with, the woman who walked with him and drove him places, and the woman who took care of his body. None of those three women had names known to him. He talked to me one day, his momentary best friend, to share his deepest thoughts about Diana. Eloquent and thoughtful, he spoke of years of all the good and all the bad; deep, considered observations. I quietly sat and listened.

Hearing it was eye-opening but not surprising. I am fully aware of my imperfections. In a normal situation, I might have wanted to get a baseball bat and crack him over the head with it. But he was lovingly expressing his private feelings, almost for the first time, about his best friend, to his best friend. It was a precious moment.

NINE-ONE-ONE

The first time I called 911, my feelings of dread were based more on the thought I was abusing this service than worrying about sharing our family struggles publicly. The first responders were so compassionate. Sussing out my situation, they made it clear that this was exactly why they were here to help and I should never hesitate to call when I needed it. Thereafter, I trusted my ability to know when 911 was required and used it again.

Rick was struggling. Understanding words or even being able to speak coherently was hit and miss. The language disorder, aphasia, dominated his communication skills.

Early on I'd discovered that the content of what I was saying meant far less than the tone at which it was delivered. I could say "The puppy got smushed by a dump truck," in a lighthearted tone and he would smile and feel at peace. Conversely, when he tried to tell a story, if I could glean the emotion it was centered around, I would respond appropriately. If he was laughing as he spoke, I knew it to be a joke he was offering and I would laugh heartily along with him, never knowing the words he was trying to speak, only knowing he was trying to be funny. Heck, I knew him so well by now that he almost didn't have to speak for me to understand whatever was on his mind.

We got to the stage where our days went like this: After a hearty breakfast, he'd thank me for the food and say, "I have to go." His desire for autonomy was fierce and he didn't want me walking with him anymore. I was operating on autopilot and wasn't ready yet to lock him up in a facility. I let him walk by himself even though it was clear he could no longer find his way home. Waiting the two minutes it would take him to get to the bottom of our hill, I'd watch to see which way he turned, and then jump into the truck to follow him discreetly. Holding back several blocks, I'd pull off to the side, until he turned and was lost from sight. Then I'd advance slowly, keeping my watch. He never looked behind or knew I was there.

So many times he walked past the trails leading into the park at Fort Worden where he could get lost forever; I prayed he'd stay on the road. He did. He generally tired after three or four miles. I'd drive up next to him, lower the window and sweetly say, "Hi Rick. Do you want a ride home?" He'd always smile and say, "Yes. Where have you been?" Back home, I'd fix him a hearty lunch and it would start all over again. Three times a day he'd make a getaway and three times a day, I'd bring him back.

The Covid lockdown had just begun and the whole world was anxious. We were unable to keep our two caregivers, and friends stayed away as well. My fortitude changed with the added responsibilities and lack of sleep. I became vincible. The sheriff's department knew of our struggles, called and had tried to enroll me in a radio tracking system program. Everyone was so helpful and honored my desire to keep him home. But we decided it wouldn't work without Rick's understanding to keep the beacon on him. Everything I'd placed in his pockets to identify him would be gone after every walk.

Then we both caught a debilitating flu. Barely able to care for myself, I let my guard down and he broke out of jail. Rick was stealthy and could away himself from our home invisibly. My sweet neighbor Steph, across the road – an angel — appeared at the door to tell me that Rick was headed downhill. I went looking for him, drove all the usual routes but he slipped through my net. I called 911 again. A kind policeman found him straightaway and drove him home. Rick was so happy. He had made a new friend. I explained our situation to the policeman and asked if he would drive Rick to the hospital. Happy to do so, he also took it upon himself to inform the E.R. doctor of our special need for admittance.

They tested and found we both had a virulent flu. I explained my current physical inability to care for him and shared my helplessness. I asked for compassionate care and told them I had enough money to pay for their services. This was my hospital after all, my last line of defense. I didn't know what else to do. A social worker was called from upstairs to assess our situation. She concentrated on the important questions: where did I live, was it a one story or two, how did I get here, did I own a car, and what kind was it. We could sign up for social service programs for the following month but we sure as heck couldn't expect the hospital to help now. Told I was obviously capable of managing this, they discharged us.

Devastated, I remember wrapping my arms around Rick to protect him from harm. We left as we had come in, in distress.

Early the next morning the phone rang. It was a night nurse from the E.R. She and her crew had listened in to the conversation between the social worker and myself and was calling to make sure we were OK. She deeply apologized for how I was treated. This went a very long way to make me feel better about my hospital.

ADMISSION

Weeks later, he startled me awake needing physical help, which led to a horrifying incident at 2 a.m. When I went to assist him and touched his arm, he exploded with rage and tried to hit me. This symptomatic response to his fear and confusion was shocking to me. If anything, dementia had enhanced Rick's gentle personality. I quickly backed away into the kitchen while he followed me, swinging his fist repeatedly. I kept yelling, "Don't you dare hit me!"

One of the limitations of advanced dementia is an inability to gauge distances, hence when trying to put a cup on a table, it may miss the mark. This is what saved me. Every time he tried to land a punch, he was 6 inches short. I was panic-stricken. Rick was a big, powerful man and intended to hurt me. I kept screaming, "Don't you dare!" He stood between me and the phone. I was unable to call 911. For two hours we stood that way, neither backing down from our position, until we both eventually slinked back to bed.

In my original research of all possible Alzheimer's symptoms, combativeness had been prominently listed. I had made a solemn vow with myself, if Rick ever turned violent, I wouldn't hesitate to have him institutionalized. Here we were at that critical juncture, four years later.

The following morning, we woke to our usual routine. Rick's memory didn't serve, but I couldn't forget last night. After breakfast, I walked him outside, knowing he was about to split. Needing time to myself, I risked not being able to find him later. Standing in our driveway together, he put his arm around my shoulders, looked down deep into my eyes with his bright Irish blues and told me, "You are so beautiful."

I needed to call our doctor, let him know of Rick's change in behavior, and ask for a medication shift. He called right back and told me to get him to the hospital a.s.a.p. I was terrified to be alone with Rick now and requested him to speak to the E.R. doctor on our behalf, to help get Rick admitted to the hospital. He said he'd do his best but offered that the E.R. had complete control over admissions.

I jumped in the truck and went looking for him. Driving his usual loop unsuccessfully, I realized where he would be found. He often got lost, one road north from our house. There he was. Wildly walking down the middle of the road, flailing his arms. I pulled up alongside him and parked. He was indecipherable, yelling only strong emotional sounds. Something was seriously aggravating him and no amount of calm, sweet sounds from me seemed to help. I could not entice him into the truck.

Our next door neighbor was working in his garden. Rick went over to yell and flail at him. This was one time I wished I'd had a cell phone. All I could do was not lose sight of Rick. Scott Swantner came driving down the hill. His truck was undeniably recognizable. I stepped into his path and flailed my own arms, asking him to stop, which he did as quickly as those old brakes would let him. By now Rick was walking downhill in the center of the road still yelling. Scott and Rick were friends. I told him of my situation and asked to use his cell phone. He didn't own one either! So I asked him to drive down to Rick, and invite him to get in, then to take him to the E.R. I felt my moment of grace had expired.

"You want me to take him to the E.R?"

"Yes please Scott. Do you mind? I need some help."

"Okay then Diana, I will!"

Watching from uphill as he pulled alongside and spoke with Rick for a minute, I could see it wasn't going to work. Rick kept walking wildly. Scott waved goodbye so I turned the truck around and drove down to where I could stop, unroll the window and sweetly say, "Hi Rick. Want a ride home?" He smiled widely and calmly got into the truck. We drove to the hospital where the E.R. doctors could assess his condition.

I explained his violence towards me, my terror and need to relocate him immediately. I was told that no other facility would accept him until he was medicated beyond violence, or over-medicated. My regular doctor would have to address that.

And then the E.R. doc looked me in the eyes and assured me that I had everything I needed to handle this situation at home; Rick would be discharged to my care. I was resigned to nothingness.

While Rick was receiving an I.V. bag of fluids, a very nice social worker sat with us and helped make plans for his next residence. It took hours and was clear Rick never understood a word. We both spoke in soft tones of all the pros and cons of every memory care facility in the region. Then he left me promising to make it all happen as soon as possible. All the while, Rick laid on the gurney smiling and looking content. I held his hand throughout.

The nurse came in to help him dress but I was happy to do it. Everything went well until I tried to help him with his t-shirt. Once again, he exploded with rage and tried to hit me. I ran out of the room and yelled, "My husband is messed up." The entire E.R. crew looked up and came running. Rick emerged from the room. Nurses tried to intervene and stand between us. He pushed them out of the way, grabbed me, shoving me towards the exit. Security arrived and everyone pounced on Rick, forcing him back into the room. Staying in the hallway out of sight, I could hear him breaking and smashing equipment, all the while asking for me. A nurse finally injected him with a powerful sedative. That was my last sight of him being conscious. Surprisingly, they admitted him to the hospital.

His affection for me one moment, turning instantly to uncontrolled rage the next, had left me feeling eviscerated. I went home and locked all the doors for the very first time, unreasonably frightened that he would break out of the hospital and find his way home.

But I'll bet he was even more scared than I.

The following morning I met with the attending I.C.U. physician to plan for Rick's treatment. We agreed he should be discharged eventually to a memory care facility after different drug regimens were tried. Every subsequent day was an experiment and the first two, he needed restraints on his arms. He continuously fought to be set free. This was at the peak time of Covid hospital protocols, limiting anyone from visiting the campus. But they invited me to go up and see him. Remarkably, I declined, a first for me to admit I was too fearful to risk another scene of violence.

I sat shell-shocked alone at home for two days, staying in touch with the nurses twice a day by phone.

The mix and amounts of medications didn't make a change until late at the end of the third day. They called to say he was non-speaking but calm, unable to walk but sitting peacefully, looking out at Port Townsend Bay. Angels of the A.C.U. were sitting with him, holding his hands, which were finally unrestrained. Soon he would be able to be discharged. Did I want to see him now? Grateful for his marked improvement, I still declined but agreed to visit first thing in the morning. A major regret.

I slept better than I had in weeks. The phone rang very early the next day. It was the head nurse of the A.C.U. She called to say "Rick had a change last night." "I know," said I. "Isn't it great? He's happy." "No," she countered, "He aspirated in his sleep last night, has pneumonia he won't survive, and so will never be able to be discharged to another care facility. Do you want to come see him now?"

Barely able to speak, "I'll be right there."

A WHISPERED EXHALE

The next three days I stayed by his side in the hospital room.

Never standing vigil before, I was fearful to leave the room and miss this final collaborative moment. The whole first night I sat impotent in the big brown recliner, holding his hand all dutiful-like. It felt so adjacent to the experience. The following morning I knew this was bogus and I needed to do more.

The next few days we often lay together in the single hospital bed; my arms enveloping him, our faces so close, we felt as one. I whispered words of friendship, encouragement and love. Pneumonia had put him in a coma and his breathing came hard. I would say, "Hi Rick," in a lyrical tone and he would stop breathing for a moment and wait for whatever I said next. It soothed me to know he was still able to understand what I was saying.

Not only did the nurses tend to his every need, they wrapped me up in care as well.

Completely out of my realm, I sat muted and numb, forgetting to ask for food, water or extra blankets. They were unobtrusive and compassionate, thoughtful humans with invisible wings. Covid restrictions were softened by them momentarily so Connie and Jeff and Gordon could say goodbye to their good friend.

Shockingly fast but in a long drawn out way, Rick then chose to die. Standing by his bed, holding his cool bare feet, I watch him take his last breath. Puhhhh, Puhhhh, Puhhhh; a whispered exhale. So heartbreaking and poignant, I am devastated and crawl back into bed with him. I whisper more messages of love, knowing somehow he's still listening.

Seeing this coming hasn't helped prepare me for this moment. Prognosis means nothing until I'm faced with the indisputable result of witnessing the end of his life. To say I am destroyed doesn't come close to my heartbreak. I feel like I'm bleeding out.

CHAPTER 12
SCANDALIZING THE YARDS
2020 - 2021

"Paths that cross will cross again." —Patti Smith

MY LOVE LETTER TO RICK

Rick was a thoughtful man, gentle and kind, a deep thinker. "Strong like ox, smart like tractor." Born of his desire for objectivity, clarity and openness to all perspectives, he chose his words carefully. As he was naturally reticent, I would always feel wiser whenever he shared his thoughts. "Think positive and the rest will follow," a common phrase he would offer to nudge me back to a better way forward. Considerate, he was a truly equal partner in everything magnificent and mundane throughout our life together. Gracious and respectful, he silently yet wholly stood with me. He celebrated me, willing to step in and help, but only if I asked. My spiritual bodyguard.

Conscious and attentive, he would give me flowers for no particular reason, tell me I was beautiful. Profoundly connected to the natural world, his enthusiasm for being in it never waned. Soared, in fact. And, he had a wicked funny wit and humor. His rich blue Irish eyes would sparkle and light up the world.

We were able to spend the last few days of his life together at Jefferson Healthcare through their grace and consummate compassion. A tender and horribly beautiful time, while he worked so hard to live, he worked so hard to die. I am immensely thankful for the entire staff who cared for our every need.

Rick loved a good party, surrounded by friends he admired. As a memorial to him, I think he would rather that those who cared for him, simply step outside, smell the rich earth, look to the sky, listen for the birds, feel the wind on your skin, breathe in the power of the waves and salt air, pick up a rock, hike a mountain trail; spend time in nature with a keen eye to all we have to learn from it. Then to hug those whom you love, long and hard and tell them of the joy they bring to you every single day. For he taught me that every single day is precious.

Peace and boundless gratitude to you, my dear sweet man.

SIGNIFICANT MOMENT

For a very long time after Rick died, I was panic-stricken to leave our home. In this small town I was bound to bump into someone I knew and would likely have to mention it. Close friends brought me meals initially when I was in immobilizing grief, but eventually I needed to go shopping for myself.

An old friend stopped to talk in the produce department; the weather, masks, Covid, protests... I stood there waiting, looking deep into his eyes and his heart. Waiting. Finally he took a step closer and said, "I understand you recently lost Rick. We were so sorry to hear it. He was a good man." And then he said what so many friends, old and new have expressed to me. "I didn't know if I should say something. It might make you sad."

I can only speak for myself, but your not saying something to me about Rick when we meet in public makes me sadder. I am fully aware of his death. You mentioning it won't remind me, it will show me that you care about the significance of "our" moment.

Friends can help friends in grief by broaching the subject first. I cannot overstate how painful it is to slip into a normal conversational voice and offer, "Oh by the way, Rick died."

Astonishingly, two months later, this friend's wife died unexpectedly. He reached out to tell me, "Now I know."

LUPINES

I forced myself; I had to force myself to leave my private bubble of home to go for my first hike alone in the mountains. I seem to have to force myself to do everything now. But Deer Park, an old friend, called longingly to me.

Ever since Rick died, whenever I've walked places we used to walk together, my body feels unconnected to the earth. Like my feet aren't really touching the ground, I'm floating. Going up steep inclines seems effortless. Today I swear, I felt Rick's two hands on my butt, softly pushing me uphill, just the slightest help.

Accessing the trailhead, the air was pungent, clearly summer evergreens in the high country. Feeling as if I were 300 years old, I finally came upon the place we had shared our lunch not long ago. A gentle slope mostly denuded of trees but with a smattering of tiny precious wildflowers and lupines. I sat to wonder. A chipmunk scooted by me.

"Hi Rick!"

Opening my pack, I took out the bag. The air was serene. I held the ashes and crushed bones and then randomly spread them, to form a kind of filigree on the subalpine vegetation, a place Rick loved so much.

I heard the human sound of sobbing; moaning and deep throated cries fill the mountain air. It was me! It came so savagely, there was nothing to be done.

Afraid someone would break a leg, running down the trail to save a woman in distress, I finally muted the best I could.

There were way too many people on the trail today. More precisely, the right person wasn't there.

THOUGHTS OF SUICIDE

I'm no expert, never having successfully pulled one off, but my father was and so I know the crushing sadness suicide leaves behind. It is perhaps, the main reason I've stuck around, not wanting to continue that legacy for my family and friends.

Regardless of intent, it often crosses my mind, a lifelong self-indulgence; feelings of isolation, the constant. In the grief of losing Rick, twice this year I found myself in serious discussions about checking out.

My first foray into despondency, my friend Amy noticed some-thing in my physicality; my spirit flagging, my spiraling down. She broke all the rules that suggest only a listening ear with no fix-it solutions offered. Practically yelling, "You need to do something!!! Start doing something!!!" Her strength (and volume) got my attention. The following day I started painting my kitchen. By lunch I was happy again.

MAY 11

Brion Toss - photo courtesy of Christian Gruye

Today is Brion Toss's birthday. I see it coming every year. And here it is and here he isn't. I think of him more than I imagined I would. He was known internationally as a first-rate traditional rigger, educator and raconteur. But many of us knew him to be a very good man!

Doubtful if anyone ever had a nonplussed reaction to meeting him, his spirit so fierce, beautiful and unbridled. You either instantly loved him or you didn't.

He took a strong dislike to me when we first met and I summoned the grace I did not know I had to turn everything around. I shamelessly name-dropped DicknLinda Golden, told him they were my friends. Because of my bragging, immediately we became fast friends also, and stayed that way until he died.

Brion was brilliant. His humor and wit, curiosity and scholarship were so attractive, engaging and joyous. Whenever I heard him speak, I was rapt. It was like listening to powerful music and it made me cry. I had, on occasion, watched some of his instructional videos. You know the ones, "How to Splice 7 x 19 Wire," or some such thing. Normally a big yawn for me. And yet every time I watched it, I cried with emotion, his eloquence and elegance caught in my throat.

We worked together over the years. He would call me up, offer

274

me really cool woodworking jobs, specialty rigging stuff. I always felt noticed by him, supported and appreciated. And this is the gift of his I most admired. Not the jobs he gave me but the way he treated everyone equally with no hint of patriarchy. He was, I'm thinking, the first man I ever knew who was a true feminist. In life — and especially in my line of work — this is a very rare thing.

What a great guy you were, Brion Toss. Happy Birthday Bud.

JULIAN

"Business is booming." —Julian Arthur

Julian was a stellar crane operator, motorcycle racer, artist, community volunteer, and friend, and the best Elvis and Hugh Hefner impersonator ever. He was kind and generous. Outspoken and funny, he never learned the technical terms of the boats he worked on. Instead of bow and stern, his voice would swell when he'd say things like "The pointy end, " the other end," " roundy thing," " the pokey hole," " back there, grab onto the... you almost have it, No, No, NO, NOT YET!"

I learned early, about those hand signals, the unspoken language of crane operators. I had witnessed too many times Julian erupt in loud disdain of someone's ineptitude. I'd think "Oh please, oh please, don't yell at me." Sound travels over water and his voice was booming, just like business. But Julian never even came close to finding fault with me.

There've been a handful of men in my career who have gone out of their way to tell me how much they enjoy working with me. They always treated me with such respect, dignity and appreciation. Julian was one of them. It was like getting a b(l)oomin' medal.

GORDON
"It's all good." — Gordon Neilson

In my heart, I knew for a very long time that the sole reason Gordon was put on this planet was to support Ricknme. He was to be a witness and our closest friend. Gordon participated in our life regularly with meaning and purpose for too many years to remember. No doubt about it, we've shared hundreds of meals. He offered advice and help only when we've asked for it. And boy did we ask for it. I'll wager many other people feel the same about him.

Gordon Neilson

As Rick's illness progressed, being around him became very difficult for everyone. There were times when Rick was confused and afraid. "Call Gordon," he'd say, remembering him to the very end. And I would. Angel that Gordon was, he'd walk up to the house to sit with Rick. He'd talk with him, calm him and be an exceptional friend. He just had that ability; abundant love, generosity and courage. He showed loyalty and kindness for all. A rare and precious human being.

Gordon dealt with his own health and mortality. He truly fought a vicious cancer caused from exposure to Agent Orange during his three voluntary deployments to Vietnam. After Rick died, Gordon and I sometimes continued our routine of lunch on Wednesdays. He would guide me softly if I asked for help. Never being a widow before, I didn't know what to do. Somehow he did.

Our last Wednesday together, he said, "We have to go to the

276

Spruce Goose at the airport." This had been a favorite eatery of all three of us, and he wanted to pay tribute. The mountains were out that warm fall day and we sat outside at the table for two. Without speaking of it, we both knew this was our last lunch together. We spoke instead of every other thing that could possibly be on our hearts. We spoke of dying too, the burden of lovers and friends; watching someone leaving us, dying slowly. A sadness no one should bear, and often overwhelming. But I assured him that I would not have missed the last four years of life with Rick or him. It was a very long executive lunch.

Autumn was his favorite time of year so I drove home slowly and in awe we watched

the maple leaves along the way. Days later, he chose to leave us, to cease to walk upon this Earth, as the leaves were turning.

PONY BRIDGE – THE MIGHTY QUINAULT

It can be said that the year 2020 was punishing. Not only did Covid upend our world, but more than a handful of my dear friends died. Starting with Jim Blaiklock in late 2019, then it was Rick. Five weeks later, Brion left us, and then Julian, Leif Erickson and finally Gordon died; all these beautiful men.

Watching Gordon physically decline was rough. Every visit I shared with him felt precious. I chose not to leave town in case he decided to call for a lunch date. After he died, I realized I could begin to move about the country to spread Rick's ashes everywhere I could still get to, that we ever went.

The East Fork Quinault River Trail is different now than I remember. There's a bridge over Graves Creek. We'd had to ford the river to access the trail in 1995. In late August the flow had been slow and barely over our ankles. Walking barefoot over slippery rocks, our feet dried quickly in the summer heat. Now in late October, I found there were almost no humans, but the wildlife was abundantly present and diverse; birds, deer and coyotes.

Anderson Glacier Tarn

Pony Bridge was one of the first campsites we ever shared, on our way to Enchanted Valley, Anderson Glacier and Honeymoon Meadows. In my bathroom now there's a joyous photograph of me, a remembrance of that trip. With a lupine wedged behind my ear I stand naked in a snow-melt tarn. The water temperature was 33 degrees but I'm smiling. It was there where we encountered our first Black Bear. He was a big'n. Sharing our early morning coffee, we heard that sound – the sound only a bear could make in the woods. We watched the forest across the river change dramatically. Ten and fifteen- foot saplings were just going down, right and left. Baboom, baboom, boom. We waited.

When he emerged through the undergrowth, he looked so happy. We too, were thrilled and then managed to do everything wrong. "Hi bear, hi Mr. Bear, bear, bear, bear, hey bear, Heyyyy Bear!"

He looked up at us and his face just fell. MAN! We had completely ruined his morning, so he turned away and lumbered uphill.

Standing on the edge of the near sheer cliff face this time, I peer over to the raging river and the "swimming hole" below. I remember us scrambling down a route only fitting for mountain goats and taking a plunge one hot summer day.

Tarn at Honeymoon Meadows

KACI

We began our time together working on her new, very old boat. I was the hired shipwright and she was the first-time wooden boat owner. Already a circumnavigator, she had massive sailing experi-

278

ence but the wood part was new and different. I can't deny I took great pleasure in acquainting her to this "sickness" of which the learning curve can be steep and slippery. We started with the basics of terminology.

Immediately it became clear that this first of many haulouts to come was more expensive than she'd bargained for. Wanting to save on labor costs and being handy, Kaci asked for a job to do. "Since we're prepping the hull for new steam-bent frames, you could take off the ceiling inside," I suggested. Perceptibly, her lower lip started to quiver as she struggled to say, "But there's nothing wrong with the ceiling. It's just dirty from the wood stove."

I mentally clocked out and touched her arm softly. "Let's go in the boat together. I want to show you something." Once inside I pointed to the Alaska cedar strips of wood on the inside of the hull. "This is the ceiling." And pointing to the dirty "ceiling" above our heads, I said, "This is the overhead. We're keeping the overhead but the ceiling must be removed carefully before we can frame. Do you think you can do that?"

It just got better from there. We worked together on *Pax* for years, deepening our friendship. Once I left "the game," our friend-ship changed. No longer one of commerce, we fell into the equality you never quite have in a working relationship. Better.

Our differences are many and obvious. Where I will choose plain, direct and unvarnished speech, Kaci takes great care with her delivery, leaving the recipient unbruised. I have witnessed her, when she was the Wooden Boat Festival Director, take a full-face-frontal verbal assault from an extremely unhappy attendee and turn it into a mutually acceptable outcome for them both. For the life of me, I cannot understand why she doesn't have any gray hair yet.

After Rick died, I had more time to give and take in deep conver-sations with my friends. Somehow we discovered our staggeringly mutual similarities, and we help each other ponder them. Our inter-ests vary but building community and supporting women is chief among them. Everything else takes off from there and we seem to go everywhere.

The first February after he died, Valentine's hit me so hard, I augered down. When next she sat at my picnic table I confessed, "I think about suicide all the time." Her body straightened and tensed, hearing what I guess now was a cry for help. You could almost see her cogs and synapses snap into shape.

Everything changed after that. She called me frequently, came to visit, made real time for me. This attention denied me any feelings of isolation. The depression, sorrow and despondency I had felt, evaporated.

Kaci's friendship has made all the difference and allowed me to want to live.

Diana and Kaci Cronkhite - photo by Jan Davis

CHAPTER 13
IN IRONS AND ADRIFT
2021 - 2022

"Seeking means having a goal, but finding means being free, being open, having no goal."

—Siddhartha
— Herman Hesse

MONTANA

S
ometimes I just want to move to Montana and change my name to Sally. Get me a job in a diner off Highway 15, call everyone Hunny. Everyone! Dye my hair red, let the roots grow long. Wear a pink uniform with a lacy handkerchief in the pocket. Top two buttons, always undone. Brassiere and straps showing some. Primary colors. I'd wear sensible shoes and take up smoking again. Camel straights. Again! Finally learn to drink beer, but not lite. Cuss even more. It might be possible.

There once was a flirtatious gal,

Who went by the nickname of Sal,

Her spring rolls, unique,

Décolleté gave a peek,

But her pies really made her yer pal.

HYDROLOGY

I made sweet time today for a renewing walk by the Dungeness River, my old friend. Starting high in the Olympics at Mount Deception and Mount Constance, this 32-mile river drains a watershed that covers 215 square miles.

While not at peak flood, it was nonetheless a sensory overload experience. All the recent rain and subsequent melting snow were sluicing down the channels at breakneck speed and power.

Walking up to it, my whole body tensed with a kind of joy. First the thunderous sound, then the visual sight of tumult, chaos and free for all. The smell in the air was decidedly winter-freshwater-pungent and my face felt the thick wetness I was entering.

Several large uprooted trees had traveled downstream, collected together as a sort of dam where the traditional deep channel always was. This river wasn't having any detriment to free flow and so carved a different route, now the main one.

Think I'll try and be more like a river.

THE PINK MAN

I was given a balloon for Mother's Day by a sweet friend to spread some joy, now that I live alone. My new roommate, it hung out at ceiling height for days. Slowly as the helium lost its umph, it lowered down to eye level.

Groceries in hand, I pushed open the door. A slight breeze entered and the balloon started bobbing up and down in my face, startling me.

I screamed bloody murder, a volume that surprised even me.

Well hell, checking my fear at the door, what did I think? A pink man was lying in wait, bobbing in anticipation, ready to pounce and steal my bananas? Horrors!

OUR LIBRARY

I didn't realize how emotional and powerful the simple event of walking into the library would be. I mean, it's the library. But of course almost every time I've been here the past five years, I've been with Rick. The power of this grief thing still surprises me. My heart can catch in my throat or tears can burst out from the dam, without warning. Onlookers are kind.

A lifelong student and scholar, Rick was so comfortable surrounded by books and people of learning, even as he struggled so much in the final months. The library was a balm for him and the librarians were all his advocates and angels.

ASKEW

Something was wrong. The world felt tilted. Walking around this morning, I couldn't shake the feeling that something was askew. Only to realize that for the first time ever,

I'd put my underwear on 90 degrees to the left. Is this the beginning, or am I well into it?

RICK'S GARDEN

It is Rick's Garden, for he was the architect of its form and function. When new to us, the yard was barely more than several dying fruit trees and a kind of lawn, a palette to build on.

He started with a rockery to define my flower beds. A Yankee boy, along with most of the young men of New England, he had learned to build rock walls, rocks being as plentiful there as lobsters and haddock.

Rick and Stitch

Next we built raised beds for our vegetables. We argued about it, as I was more familiar with unrestrained rows of compost and dirt. He was right, of course.

I planted dahlias, tulips, daffodils, lilies and other stink pretty loud, colorful flowers. He chose a wide selection of native plants and bushes, and propagated a small forest of baby trees. Together we dug the hole, dug the hole, dug the hole. He taught me how to make my own dirt/compost, when and how to prune.

When things started to heat up at home in his early teens, as a healthy distraction, he volunteered his time to the Endicott Wildlife Sanctuary, a 40-acre Audubon site. Several times a week, Rick would ride his bicycle from Beverly to Wenham, an eight mile round trip, where he would do whatever was required, trail maintenance and such. In the years he was there, he became a world class bird nerd. He took me to visit his childhood second home several times. We walked the grounds together and always got lost.

Rick loved birds. Planting native plant species attracted so many, better than a bird feeder would. The bees loved them too. When he died, I lost the heart to grow vegetables anymore. I dedicated our two largest raised beds to a chaos of wildflowers. Our yard is now a mini kind of sanctuary, thanks to my architect of form and function, the gardener who propagated our friendship into this sweet love.

THE HIPSTERS
AMY, ELIZABETH, KACI AND SONIA

Grief took its toll on my body as well as my heart. Everything stopped for me after Rick died. I felt eviscerated. All the things we used to do together felt wrong to do without him. Things like cooking and eating real food. I couldn't read anymore or listen to music. My bike sat idle and I never walked. I just sat and felt I could do no more. For months I did this.

Some time later my sedentary life caught up with me. Pain from arthritis had always been mitigated with regular exercise. Sitting exacerbated my deteriorating hip joint and the bone-on-bone pain drove me to a hip replacement. It was a horribly painful experience and terrified me.

I came face to face with the undeniable fact that I lived alone now, my daughter lived 8,000 miles away. A surgery like this absolutely required someone to physically help me for a while. Aside from being legally restricted from driving for six weeks after the operation, my hip joint could not break 90 degrees when I sat. I was unable to shower for weeks and had to wear hip-high compression socks to reduce the threat of blood clots. Those socks were almost impossible to put on if I could reach my feet. I could not reach my feet.

I'm a supremely proud and independent, autonomous in-charge, boss-lady. Or I wanted to be. Friends with experience, love and great courage stepped in to help. Knowing me as well as they did, each one could look me in the eye and say, "I know you want to do it that way, but we're gonna do it this way instead." Each friend had some special gift they foisted on me and I begrudgingly, though gratefully, accepted their gifts. I was driven to the hospital and they made sure I didn't ditch out the back door before surgery. Someone sat with me as I woke from anesthesia and tried to navigate medications and instructions. I was too stoned to understand the O.T. and P.T. when they lined off my next steps after release from the hospital. Someone showed up to meet with them and downloaded it to me later. And I was picked up when the hospital unceremoniously kicked me out with 20 minutes notice. A nurse had wheeled me into the corridor while I waited for my friends. I sat in that chair sobbing like a dam burst. My friends took me home and gently put me in my bed whilst I continued sobbing uncontrollably.

Food was delivered, shopping was done, and I was driven back to the hospital when my dressing blew out. Tenderly, my compression socks were changed out. My feet were washed! They communicated with each other to be sure all bases were covered and compassionately stayed in touch with Kashmira so she wouldn't fret. Each one was a team captain of tenderness, care and good humor.

This was totally humbling for me to watch myself go through. It felt long past due as suddenly I was on the receiving end of unconditional care. And I realized that I, like everyone, need help sometimes. It was also a gift to my friends that I trusted them enough to ask.

I believe I will ask for help more often.

SEEING BEYOND MYSELF

Walking at Chinese Gardens next to Fort Worden State Park an early morning Saturday, it is surprisingly empty of people. Everything about the day seems right.

Just before entering the forest, I'm enveloped in today's hatch – millions of tiny insects. Disturbing my serenity, they are bugging me.

Unable to run away, I just cover my nose and stay still.

Seeing beyond myself, the sky grabs my attention. There are thousands of birds, swooping and harvesting. I'm not sure I've ever seen a sky so littered.

DELICIOUS AUTUMN

I must go to the high country often, where Rick and I could find such peace, or else I fear I shall expire.

The delicious spicy scent of this verdant evergreen forest. It's abundantly healthy, even though the mountain rooftops are practically naked of snow. I see every possible shade of green, from almost golden yellow to probably quite blue. There is an occasional swath of primary and secondary colors in a vein of deciduous bushes, singing loudly their song of autumn.

Large sleek ravens flying high overhead are laughing at my pace. A hawk is hunting low, searching for the ubiquitous chipmunks which move with chaotic purpose, because that's who they are.

The only other sounds: a warm breeze that rustles and then it's gone. The distant river deep in the valley, thousands of feet below, is a mere whisper. If you try very hard, you can hear it.

A feast for my senses, this place. Which by the way reminds me, I'll most likely be sore tomorrow, but today was so good, I shan't expire.

UNFETTERED

Me on an Elwha trail pony - 1963

In the early 1960s after the Hood Canal bridge was finished, sometimes my family would load up the dusty blue Pontiac and head for the woods. Usually it was the mighty Elwha that called us. We'd car-camp in the developed sites up by the natural hot springs. Sometimes we'd even hire a guided horse tour, which I loved. Good times I remember well.

I evacuated Port Townsend and headed west one morning. Turning onto the Elwha road, I remember too all the dozens of times

I've been there. Every one good except the backpacking trip Kashmira and I took where I chose a place named Happy Lake as our first night's encampment. Happy Lake turned out to be a five-inch-deep mosquito breeding ground; billions and billions of mosquitoes. We evacuated there too, at first light.

Today I find the river calm and fairly docile. Bluebird skies. A light dusting of powdered sugar on the foothills. The scant west wind is very cold in the shadows of the evergreens but the truly fierce early spring sun surprisingly gets me to shed down to my tank top. This place is almost empty of people and the sounds of the river, frolicking down to the Straits, feeds me. She's different now and boasts her change.

In the very early 1970s, I ceremoniously burned my brassiere, a clarion call and metaphor for me to choose my own path, to not be fettered by the inflexible rules of the men in my life then. When the two Elwha dams came down in 2014, it was like she was burning her

Diana and Kashmira - 1996

brassiere too, free at last to choose for herself – and it shows. The road has been washed out so many times; the Park is letting nature take its course, not bending to the wants of car-campers.

I walked today to the first washout, sat in the sun for a good long time. Three years ago, almost to the day, Ricky and I last sat there together, so in love. I remember it well.

~

CHAPTER 14
MAKING WAY
2022 - 2023

photo by Kaci Cronkhite

"...Love is touching souls, surely you've touched mine..."—Joni Mitchell

YOUNG FOLK

I nvited to a sweet barbecue in the port with mostly young folk; they are the next generation of marine trades. I am incredibly interested in what they're doing. This was a kind of re-introduction for me, going back to my familiar place, but seeing it with new eyes. I fell into a conversation with a young, new business owner. We hardly knew each other.

After a casual exchange, he leans in and asks, "What have you been doing?" This stops me cold. I can see deep into his eyes, he honestly wants to know. No one ever asks this of me. They all say, "How are you doing?" To which there is no answer.

I take a breath and tell him what I've been doing this past year, trying to build up my strength, my stability and my emotional health. I lean in closer and quietly say, "I miss Rick every day."

He and his friend listening both proclaim, "I think about you a lot and can't imagine how hard it must be for you."

I'm deeply touched; these young men whom I hardly know are openly able to ask, listen and express concern. This is so refreshing and hopeful.

WOMEN OF OUR WORKING WATERFRONT PROJECT

photo by Ashlyn Brown

I used to feel uncommon, a woman working on, living in, owning and sailing boats. Starting to emerge from my coma of grief and looking around, I could see women are everywhere on the waterfront now. Impatiently waiting for decades, the change seemed to happen overnight. There is a new kind of support, even celebration of the growing percentages of women in the trades.

Port Townsend is arguably known as the center of the universe regarding wooden boat restoration and repair. Few places can boast the depth and breadth of services available, all within walking distance of each other. This is why I moved here, that and its stunning visual beauty. Our diverse, collaborative maritime industry has been fed a precious workforce since 1981 from graduates of the Northwest School of Wooden Boatbuilding. And since 1978, wooden boats repaired and restored by our marine trades have been showcased every year by the Wooden Boat Festival.

Ann, Nicki, A.J., Kat, Diana, Maya, and Sue. - photo by Elizabeth Thomson Becker

Culturally accepting, Port Townsend has also been known anecdotally for decades as a place with more women captains per capita than anywhere else. Naturally, over time, women's boat ownership has helped encourage and support women entering the marine trades. We're making a good life for ourselves and helping to shine an international spotlight on Port Townsend. Moms are teaching their children the joys of this natural feast, leading the next generation of sailors refreshing our waterfront. It's a joy to be part of such a diverse, engaged and matchless community, but I wanted to do more than just observe it.

Creating my WOMEN OF THE WORKING WATERFRONT

PROJECT, I was inspired to compile a spreadsheet with every woman's name and maritime attribution I had ever known or heard of from Port Townsend. It is shockingly huge. Building on this record, my friend Becci suggested I organize a gathering and collect a group photo with every local woman I could reach.

When we met downtown on City Dock, an even more dynamic document was created. Women wrote their origin stories, lending their collective voices to show their contributions and also how we have helped build our waterfront into the priceless place it is.

We stood together and looked around. We are so much.

WOWW - March 2022 - photo by Jeremy Johnson

LUNCH

Kashmira and her family have made the enormous decision to leave their beloved Bangkok and move to Washington State. After careful consideration they choose a small northwest town to grow American roots in, not far from Port Townsend. It's been 15 years since Iven and Kashmira have lived stateside. All their children were born in Bangkok. This is a big deal!

I see them much more often now. We generally plan a good-weather outing doing something we all enjoy. But this particular visit came with mobility limitations.

It was one of those silly accidents that made no sense. Playing soccer with her children, Kashmira kicked the ball and broke her foot. Besides the pain, she was relegated to a wheelchair for several weeks while the bad break healed. Routine life in her home came to a halt and I was pleased to witness her taking care of herself first and foremost, as moms rarely do.

She invited me over for a family outing and suggested we make time to go shopping for brassieres. Covid travel restrictions had kept us apart for so long, our foundation garments were sad.

I followed behind their family van loaded with the kids in my truck to Padilla Bay Shore Trail. Since it was ADA accessible, her wheelchair could travel it while the children spread out running and curious. This park was new to me. They came here often.Without thinking, I started pushing the wheelchair which felt surprisingly like pushing her in a stroller 40 years before.

We went past the fields of agriculture along the tidal canals of the Skagit Valley. Rusted industry, half submerged in gooey black mud, boasted of a different time when the boat houses next to them were daily used. We peeked through gaps in the ancient wood siding of those buildings to see what goes on inside now. It just looked like a lot of empty history.

After our stroll, Kashmira and I peeled off from the rest of the gang. Driving past Edison and Bow, we serpentined up Chuckanut Drive. The venerable maple trees lining the road were green this time. Not like the autumn colors we drove up to see so long ago; during a "surfin safari" in the "No Work Car" with Jessie, the duck.

Our mission today was shopping for underwear. But we rearranged our usual routine and went to lunch first. Lucking into a phenomenal Asian restaurant, we sat on the sunny deck and made the place our own. Falling into a dreamy conversation, we sat together for hours and got it all talked out, everything that was on our hearts and minds. Only when the dinner hour loomed on the clock, did we break the lunchtime spell and go searching for new brassieres in the malls of Bellingham.

I was well into my 50s before I ever took my own mother out to lunch. We're winning already.

A PICNIC TABLE

Rick died at the very beginning of the Covid pandemic. Everyone I knew was afraid to get together in a crowd so a memorial was out of the question. In all honesty, I couldn't face the idea of any public gathering immediately after his death nor any time later. This surprised me since I have attended many memorials which left me feeling better about losing a loved one. But this was the loss of more than a loved one. This was the loss of Rick, my Rick. I was crushed by his death.

Scattering his ashes in all our old haunts provided me a private connection with him almost as a new lifestyle. It invited me to leave our home, get out in nature and try and re-engage with it. It never felt like a happy thing. I always cried buckets. But it felt like a necessary thing.

To honor him more publicly, I donated money to nonprofits that he felt deep connections with. This didn't make me feel happy either, though I was glad to do it.

Rick was unpretentious, resisted shining a light on himself. Bronze plaques or marble headstones would not interest him. Something practical and beautiful and built of wood was a more desirable choice for his tribute. A picnic table to replace the one we had sat at for lunch on the Larry Scott Trail so many times. It had eventually rotted away and been replaced with a cold cement one. This seemed a perfect idea and made me happy.

Long after he died, I was afraid to cut wood, knowing my attention to safety with power tools wasn't back yet. I found a young woman who would take on the build. A.J. did a stunning job. We loaded it up on Mark Stout's forklift and delivered it to the spot of the original table on a rainy Sunday morning. Many questionable activities go on then. Choosing to not ask permission from the city, we took our chances not to get in trouble.

She sits there now, on picnic table point, well used by anyone who cares to enjoy a lunch while taking stock of their empire. Eventually she too will rot and be discarded, but not in my lifetime.

BUILDING KASHMIRA A TABLE

Being me has never felt so difficult since Rick's death. Building and delivering pies to friends is about the only remnant of myself I still enjoy doing. Everything else is a struggle, something I must force myself to do: reading, riding my bike, listening to music or even stepping aboard a boat. My life feels monotone, singularly depressive and valueless. Oh dear.

Iven, Kashmira, Tirzah, Elian, Tovah, Kyin, Rinnan and Izayla

Kashmira and her family moved back to the northwest after 15 years living in Bangkok. Having family nearby is a huge change; there are eight of them. As they set up their new home, a few essentials are missing. "Mom, we need a dining table large enough for 12. Would you like to make one for us?"

When Kashmira left home and attended university, I was bored with the usual gifts I had given her for Christmas: socks and pajamas. She needed some essentials then too and so I began a tradition of building furniture with some stunning Pennsylvania Cherry we had; a coffee table, bookshelf and blanket chest. I even created a signature shape I incorporated into every piece, a kind of Momdom attribution of my work for posterity.

Right now my dance card was empty and the idea of building a piece of furniture at her request seemed a delightful invitation. Without thinking about the process, I "just said yes."

Our shop had sat fallow for a long time, with cobwebs the only structures being built in it. The workbench was used for small household repairs only. I had not used the table saw in over 4 years. Walking in with renewed purpose, I was honestly nervous to fire it all up again. I began with the easy stuff, tool maintenance. Changing blades, checking for square, oiling everything, moisturizing the steel surfaces, pulling out specialty tools hidden from my memory. Slowly I regained my place here; I am a wood butcher.

We had kept our favored boat lumber moved up from the port in a shed out back. I remembered that Howdy Springer had given me four, 16-foot-long, 15-inch-wide planks of old growth Philippine mahogany 20 years prior. He had had them since the 1960s when he ran a boat shop in Seattle on Lake Union. They sang out to me and asked to be used. Stored on the very tippy top, this mahogany would be challenging as all get out to move. So I recruited a large crew of strong, willing helpers: my six grandchildren and their father and mother. But first we had to move the skiff out back on the industrial saw horses to other horses in the way out back to make a place for the wood. This, I was reminded is why boatbuilding sometimes goes over budget, the unforeseen obstacles.

Kashmira, Iven and I designed an agreed upon shape after considerable discussion. It would be 30" wide by 8 feet long with removable legs to allow ease of moving in and out of their small home. I was to build two long benches that would fit five adults per side. With room for a diner at each end, 12 could be accommodated for the large dinner parties they enjoyed.

They behaved like customers so I treated it like a job. There was nothing about marketability in the time it took to complete, but complete it I did. It took so long, in fact I was reminded of my nascent years as a woodworker, when I equated my efforts to a monkey given a typewriter. If given enough time, eventually it will type the Encyclopedia.

Once the construction was done, it had to be finished with something waterproof and shiny. That process took longer than the build, reminding myself again how valuable professional finishers are. When completely "cured," I loaded each piece in my pickup truck, tightly wedged with every pillow and blanket I owned, and delivered it to them, a two-hour drive away. Once again, all the grandchildren jumped to it and after a half hour, the legs were re-assembled and we all sat down for lunch. They sit there now, every day. That brings me joy.

After reacquainting myself with my shop out back, successfully designing a challenging piece and turning on the table saw and keeping all my fingers, it felt like starting all over again. Only this time I knew what I didn't know; so much math that used to be readily available in my neocortex seemed to be on vacation.

Kashmira and Her Table

Turning another page of living in the grief, I got dirty and made noise and found joy in it. I let old customers I loved know, that I was available to help with their boats or their houses. "I don't sand" was the only caveat, despite my two PhDs in sanding. Now that an hourly rate wasn't part of the equation, it was especially gratifying to teach these former customers how to care for their boats. Several friends signed up. More joy.

My girl has a degree in Social Work. She's wise beyond measure. I wonder if she knew that to nudge me back into my shop was the very best medicine for a broken heart.

ASTERIX

Rick acquired a 14-foot rowboat from the Northwest School of Wooden Boatbuilding when he was a student there. He named her *Asterix*. Known as the "One Day Skiff," it was a popular design to teach in the early years. Dozens were built. Bob Prothero, the school's founder, knew from watching generations of other boat builders that pretty much everywhere there was water, people build near-identical boats. Astute, he had simplified the design and methods used to build it; fastenings were galvanized nails, so it could be banged together quickly. In his youth, Bob and a friend would build the skiff in one day and then sell them for $14.00. This was nearly pure profit because wood costs then were somewhere between 1 ½ and 3 cents per board foot. Fourteen dollars split between two young guys back then was darn good money. The joke at the school was, it was a One Day Skiff that took a quarter of the year to build.

We towed her everywhere we went regionally, behind whatever sailboat we were traveling in. Flat bottomed, with four seats and two rowing stations, she could pack a load; her full keel helped her track and was stable and trustworthy in a chop. She wasn't slow either and I loved her.

In our beginning, we had three sailboats and three rowboats. One by one, we pared down our fleet. When Rick sold his 26-foot pocket cruiser *Kah Tai*, he sold *Asterix* along with her for an additional $75. I about killed him. But even I knew three rowboats was two too many.

Twenty years later, I took a call from Don, who had bought Rick's boat; "Would we like to have *Asterix* back?" He wasn't going to use her anymore. No hesitation before I said, "Yes Please!"

Rick and I made a journey down to Anderson Island, the southernmost island in Puget Sound. We'd never been there. A tiny car ferry from Steilacoom takes 20 minutes and scoots past McNeil Island, our state's former penitentiary, another place we'd never been. Don and Julie had kept the rowboat in covered storage for quite a while. She looked like an old wooden boat just itch'n to see salt water again.

Back home and excited to have our old family member back, I immediately jumped into the minor repairs she asked for. Simple stuff really. My hope was to put her in the water and take Rick out for a paddle as often as we could go. It didn't work out that way. By then, Rick's illness had so progressed, I couldn't find time to finish the repairs. So *Asterix* went to the way out back amongst the flowering currants, under the Deodar Cedar, to sit on horses and dream of saltier times.

Years went by. Rick died and more years went by. Boats under blue tarps, if they are far enough away from your eyes, can wither alone, unrequited.

The Wooden Boat Festival was coming up as it does every year in September. Local sailor-guurls, also from Momdom, Ashlyn Brown, Sarah Kolbeck and I, fell into a scheme to promote a new on-the-water festivity. The "Row Row Row Your Boat Rally" would be wrapped into festival Sunday. Ostensibly to encourage children into rowboats, their parents could join too. In conversation, the idea to promote it was to use the phrase "Pull your boats out of the blackberries and take them for a row." I offered that I could literally be that poster child and was inspired to do just that.

By now, the poor old wooden boat was even dryer and more opened up. When I took the tarp off, she exhaled audibly. "She'll be right," I told her.

So long since doing the work of restoration and repair, my sense of confidence was dull. I sought advice from my friend Ray Speck, who offered this: "Stop manipulating the wood now until you put her in the water for a minimum of two weeks. Let her sink and swell up. Only then will the wood be pliable enough to move back into place." I'd forgotten all this knowledge about lovely wood.

I negotiated a deal with the port. They gave me a slip next to the launch ramp for two weeks free. In exchange, they required I post an explanation of the science and tradition of the process, to save them hearing that a boat had sunk. But mainly to celebrate the history of our industry. This simple gesture went a long ways to soften my heart towards the port.

Tools Come Out For *Asterix* - photo by Kaci Cronkhite

Several of us muscled her into the water, including my oldest granddaughter. Wearing a lifejacket, she threw a long mooring line across the expanse between floating docks. We taught her how to use a cleat, then watched *Asterix* go glug, glug, glug.

Two weeks later, hauling her back home, the seams were almost tight. Only a bit of cotton did she need. I rolled it in with Moose's brass pizza cutter. Moose sold Rick the 26' *Kah Tai* and they had been close friends. Something felt very full circle.

Daryl Dietrich and I

Slathering her inside and out with boat sauce, some sun to drive it in, two coats of bottom paint and then Vaseline in the oar locks to lubricate the metal to metal; she was ready to get wet.

I launched her on a snotty southerly cold afternoon. Hardly like a pro had I struggled to keep her off the cement ramp while searching for my rowing chops. Bit by bit, old habits returned. Sitting in that dear old rowboat, I felt connected

300

to everything and everyone who also was connected to this saltwater life.

Daryl Dietrich asked to row with me, to learn and be my partner for the Row, Row, Row Your Boat Rally. There's a wondrous world outside the breakwater we explored together while she learned to feather her oars.

The Rally was wildly successful on that warm blue-sky day early Sunday morning, with a zero on the Beaufort scale. The large flotilla of every kind of human powered vessel made their way from the Boat Haven to Point Hudson, en masse. Children rowing prams by themselves, their parents close behind in stand-up paddleboards, kayaks, canoes, dories and skiffs. There was even an electric assist vessel with a dad and young child that we organizers happily gave a wink to participate. Neither a race nor smattering of competition, everyone won first prize that day, just by being there.

AND IN THE END

The Wooden Boat Foundation bestows a lifetime achievement award each year to honor contributions of individuals in the wooden boat industry. It has always been my favorite event of the Wooden Boat Festival. Colleagues and friends join together to witness this joyous celebration.

Many life experiences catch my heart in my throat but when they chose me it also left me speechless. Being a part of this wondrous world is honor enough. Truly! But I wrote a speech to share that honor.

I used to believe that I was surely born in the wrong century. When I happened upon the waterfront and began immersing myself in everything boats, my personal choices always seemed to lead me to the technology of the way back when – rowboats, skiffs, sailboats, all engineless, building boats with a brace... My desire was shaped by a lack of education or experience, or was it a touch of the armchair romantic?

When I first came to Port Townsend with my Kettenburg 38, it needed a bit of work; Jim and Daubie Daubenberger made my acquaintance and could not have been more supportive of my project. They had both sailed extensively on K 38s and had a love of them, which I too eventually came to. But I remember feeling so proud, so with it, when I said to Daubie, "I'm really excited, I finally have a modern rig."

Daubie laughed and said, "Diana, this boat was built in 1949. It is not a modern rig." But it was the first boat I'd owned equipped with winches.

As I discovered things like engines, electricity, plumbing, power tools, even epoxy, I realized I had been born in the perfect time; long enough ago to have cut my teeth on the traditional arts of the sailor/boat builder, but also to be in a place and time where innovations were everywhere.

My first teachers were almost all older men, many who had lived their youth embracing those traditions. My great fortune was that I was geographically and culturally placed, where I was able to meet so many of the Northwest's designers, sailors and boat builders. And they all recognized my genuine curiosity, and desire to learn. I found that most people are just thrilled when you ask them, "How do you do that?" and are happy to share their unique knowledge. It's a gift to ask and a gift to tell. My education was an unexpected gift from all of these people.

I moved to Port Townsend on the invitation of a boat shop owner. He had told me, "We have a ton of work going on and could use another shipwright. It's all work-boats. You can name your own wage and work for yourself outta the shop."

I said "YES!" But there was the issue of affordable housing. **"It _don't_ come easy"** - Ringo Starr.

With two canvas bags of hand tools and nothing more, I was penniless. Ricky Oltman let me stay on board his fish boat until I found other digs. Don Fauth and Jack Finney, new friends, were both merchant seamen. They had opposing schedules, six weeks on, six weeks off. They also had beautiful sailboats moored across the dock from each other on C Dock, the cool dock. They let me live aboard while they were out at sea. When one came back I would move across the dock to the other boat. I *built a dock box between them and had a phone installed with an answer machine in it, just to stay in touch. Neither one ever asked for money.*

Rob Iverson at the Landfall Restaurant took a chance on me too. A girl's gotta eat but I was seriously living in poverty. I'd eat a short stack every day and that's what I lived on. Between paychecks, Rob carried a tab for me. I was so thin! Ed Louchard made room for me in his very crowded shop so I could rebuild my mast and then there was Brion Toss. The first autumn I was here, isolated from family, he made sure I had a Thanksgiving dinner to attend, friends around the table, understanding how such a small gesture can make or break someone. These people didn't know me at all. But they were showing me great kindness. I paid attention.

Moving to Port Townsend taught me a life lesson I had not noticed before – that life and especially life here – will be as much or as little as you invest in it. Paul McCartney had said, **_"And in the end, the love you take is equal to the love you make."_**

Ray Speck and I - 2023 - photo by Nate Rooks

Probably 20 years ago I was working a job in my shop with a lovely young woman named Kelley. I happened to say to her, **"All things must pass."** *She looked at me quizzically so I said, "George Harrison." She replied, "Who's George Harrison?" 20 years ago and my first indication that I might already have been past my pull date.*

Anyone who knows me well understands a few things about me: I love people, I love building community and I love big dinner parties. All three of those things combine into one tasty dish. My friends know how I feel about them because it's important to me to tell the people you love, you love them. So many have helped me live well, especially these past several years when my world became impossible to understand. John Lennon said it best, **"All you need is love, love. Love is all you need."**

But there is one person, one man who I must call out, for I have blessed or cursed him every working day of my life, depending on the job at hand. And that of course is Ray Speck, who providentially inspired me to this life.

And we've still never worked together!

LOVE

I walk slow now, like every step means something and should be noticed. I feel light and very free.

Ending up in the port today on some monkey business, I flirted happily with a passel of beautiful men, stopping to chat on a beach log or slowing the traffic flow. I love the Boat Haven. It was here I found a connection strong enough to want to stay and make a life.

The sun came out in force. This slowed me down more.

At the head of C dock, I leaned up against the environmental center, opened my coat, let my black tank top suck in the unseasonal warmth. I stayed there some good time.

This is where Rick and I first kissed. He had waited his whole life for it and could wait no longer.

Neither could I.

Rick, my Rick and I - photo by Joni Blanchard

EPILOGUE

Kashmira's High School Graduation

"You can have the other words - chance, luck, coincidence
serendipity. I'll take grace. I don't know what it is
exactly, but I'll take it."
—Mary Oliver

GRACE

Paul and I never really talked about why I left the life we'd built together, our home, our boat, our family. Everything we shared had been hard-won. Why couldn't I fight for our marriage? The choice was not frivolous but came only after years of failed efforts on my part to feel an equal partner in the decisions of how we lived our life. It seemed a simple need but it went beyond our established relationship roles and no amount of discussions moved either of us towards a compromise. It was killing me.

At the end, we shared words about who gets what, but never another proper sit down for a horribly uncomfortable conversation that addressed why I was leaving. The step I was taking was cavernous and it fractured our young family. My memory is that the space between us was so deep and painful, the loss so dear, that I just had to go and couldn't risk additional hurt.

Even though I moved one hour away, we still shared parenting of our young daughter, Kashmira. It was she who suffered the most from our divorce. A great sadness to me, and yet, I knew it was the only choice I could make and still stay true to myself. Knowing this, we tried to mitigate her fears and confusion with as few changes as possible while we found our new way.

Kashmira was eight and enrolled in third grade when I left the family home in January of 1990. Her Nana was her best chum and lived just down the street. They saw each other every day. All things comforting to her were on Bainbridge Island, so we modeled our break-up to her needs. Both our careers were seasonal; Paul went fishing after school let out and repairs in the boatyard on fish boats evaporated at the same time. The decision was made to share parenting seasonally. Our boat *Ocean* came to the Boat Haven in October after the albacore season for me to live on. Kashmira lived at the barn, had her Nan down the street and stayed in school. I visited her there most weekends, that first year. When the seasons changed,

I moved back to the barn while Paul went fishing. It seemed a reasonable compromise we both could accommodate.

Eventually, Paul and I built separate lives. Paul met and married Lorraine and I met Rick and moved in with him. The first 10 years were the most difficult. After Paul's new marriage, my moving back to the barn seasonally just wouldn't work anymore. By then I had established my own home so Kashmira came to Port Townsend, enrolled in school here and lived with me full time on my 38' sailboat. She and her Dad saw each other when they could but everything changed, of course. We weren't a couple anymore, making decisions together. Both of us were angry about the failure of our marriage and none of us handled the change in relationship well. Divorce is hard.

Once our daughter graduated high school and left home, our need to talk dwindled, along with any perceived requirement to argue. We didn't stop being angry with each other, we just saw each other less. Rick and Lorraine formed an important friendship, sharing a unique view into our family dynamics. Slowly, things improved.

Twenty years after our break-up, Paul would bring *Ocean* to our shop for yearly maintenance. If he hired me to do repairs, I noticed I treated him much nicer as a paying customer than as an ex-husband. I leveraged those new feelings into a kinder friendship.

We'd spend time together during holidays and shared vacations, especially after the grandchildren came along. We were an unusual modern nuclear family and appeared to enjoy spending time together. Kashmira had two moms and two dads. Her kids were understandably confused. I was their Nana and lived with their Guji. Lorraine was their Oma and lived with their Opa. When they were little-little, their faces would screw up in a question mark if I shared a story of their mother as a young girl. "How could Nana know these things when Oma was her mom?"

Between Paul and me, though our outward demeanor got more and more familial, there was always a dry powder keg just below the surface. And boy, could it blow! In a moment of unrestraint, he might share my laundry list of imperfections. My triggers could be tender. Perhaps just another design flaw.

Things changed dramatically after Rick's Alzheimer's diagnosis. We all gained compassion. Kindness started to permeate our time together. It was comforting when the four of us would sit around a table sharing stories while also vividly aware of our impermanence. Rick's illness distilled in us the knowledge of what really matters. Love really matters.

Trust replaced old wounds. Paul and Lorraine's support for us was real and they helped through his death and beyond. I was reminded of the reasons why I love Paul.

Before publicly sharing our story, I wanted Paul to read everything I had written about him. No surprises. Most of the stories I wanted to tell are harmless enough, but there were a few I felt could make him uncomfortable. Back and forth I went, deciding to include them or not, but I knew these hard stories taught me lessons that guided my life. They are a big part of who I am. I invited Paul to come to Port Townsend to read them with me in person.

Three days later, when the weather changed to an indoor kind of day, he made the trip up. Serving copious amounts of tap water, my signature cocktail, and chips and guacamole for sustenance, we sat across from one another at my old oak table. We took turns reading out loud. I remembered that we used to read to each other 45 years ago.

From time to time, he'd correct a mis-stated fact of something I'd forgotten. He would say, "What about the time..." and I'd realize another story should be included.

His edits were deeply valuable. We laughed a lot and cried a bit too. It was a long afternoon of connecting with my dear old friend.

This moment was completely accidental and yet somehow we got here together. Anger, resentment, pain and powder kegs were gone now, replaced with a healing dose of gratitude and a lot of happiness.

When he got to the stories that gave him pause, he looked down silently and reflected on the words he now held in his hands; the conversation we never had 34 years ago. He took his time before telling me, "I never knew I did this to you. I am so sorry."

I told him, "When we broke up, I promised myself I would never partner up again with a man who took over and didn't treat me as an equal."

To which he acknowledged, "You never did, because you found Rick."

Acknowledgments

SHIP'S COMPANY

Thank you to the gang who stood watch with me and helped steer my course as a Shipwright -Sailor Guurl. Your time given, understanding, inspiration and encouragement helped me want to face every day.

Ray Speck – The Sausalito Shipwright's Co-Op – Paul Svornich – Nils Johnson – Dave Ullin – Linda Golden – Phil Shiveley – Bruce MacLay – Cathy Nickum – Charlie Bodony – Kurt Ashford – Jim Ferris – Dick Golden – George Beuhler – Andy Goodwin – Mark Julian – Doug Hatfield – Dale Nordland – Jan Watson – Steve Langhorst – David Vohs – Van Hope – Doug Humes – Rob Iverson – Richard Oltman – Ben Tyler – David Langley – Don Fauth – Jack Finney — Juanitta Lang – Mark Stout – Randy Purdue – Jon Gaedke – Dave Thompson – Bob Secard – Ed Louchard – Jim Sr. and Daubie Daubenberger – Claus Dietrich – Paul Kettenburg – Arthur Franklin – Alan Preston – Stan Siver – Nancy Bishop – Bill Sperry – Doug Lockhart and every Yard Boy-Lorraina Julian – Shannon Counselor Meehan – Ted Pike – Eric Toews - Larry Aase and his Maintenance Crew at the port – Al Cairns – Sue Nelson – Eric (Moose) Wilson – Tim Nolan – Phil Andrus – Mark Jochems – Sachiko Scott – Walt Sonen – Mac McKay – Noel Rockwell – Howdy and Jeannie Springer – Kaci Cronkhite – Scott Walker – Johnny Adams – John Zimmer – Brion Toss – Margie Abraham – Adam Henley – Antonio Salguero – Tom and Guch – Jack Landwerkamp – Steve Chapin – Bene Hoffmann – Bill Eppick –

Shawn Ajax – Mark Lindeman – Rita Mandoli – Carlyn Stark – Leif Ericson – David Jackson – Artemis Celt – Daryl Paddock – The extraordinary women on the varnish crew of *Paspatoo*: Debi Saxton, Maggie Day, Gillian Ehrlich, M.B. Armstrong, Julie Anderson, Janet Millar, Sonia Frojen, Dianna Denny, Gina Bonneau, Nora Cosbey, Kelley Watson, Daryl Dietrich, Molly Morrisey, Bronwyn Hughes, Korie Griffith, Alicia Dominguez and Moriah Dailer – Les Schnick – Melissa Carlson Michaels – Ann Welch – Jim Blaiklock – Tim Lee – David King – Julian Arthur – Gus Sebastian – Libby Schnick – Russell Brown – Tyler Thompson – Brian Barger – Pete Langley – Mike Galmukoff – Sheila Murphy – Damon Barlow – Pete Gillis – Cooper Lee – Tallulah Sebastian – Tracy Lee – Beth Robbins – Walt Trisdale -- Lennea Wolfe – Cathy Langley – Elizabeth Becker – Stephen Gale –Townsend Bay Marine – Josh Greene – Barry Stephens – Tom Winkler – David Pratt – Gordon Neilson – Kashmira Svornich and Rick Petrykowski

Special thanks to Jeff Hammond, Amy Schaub, Todd Flye, Julie Hayes, Bev Moore, Ray Speck, Paul Svornich, Tim Nolan and Steve Langhorst who helped fill in these stories with actual facts! John Speck, Kathy Pool, Pam Gray, Teri Nomura and Al Bergstein; who convinced me not to throw these stories in the rubbish. Especially John Speck, whose soft insistence I heard. Jenn Hager, my editor, helped me all along the way to finish it. Robin Dudley and her elegant edits. Marian Roh worked her magic both artistically and through gentle persuasion. Elizabeth Thomson Becker, Sandy Lam and all the other remarkable photographers who graciously shared their work. Thank you!

Xtra-tuff thanks to Kaci Cronkhite, Jan Halliday, and Molly Tyson; my associate editors who were sublimely kind when I needed what they always gave me: a soft kick in the butt while also wrapping their arms around me with grace — you guurls buoyed me up!

And to Rick, my Rick and my Dad. Thanks for the love you gave me. I use it every day.

GLOSSARY OF MY TERMS

ADRIFT - to float without being moored or steered – sometimes called "rudderless"

BALLAST - weight inside or outside of the bottom of a boat to keep it upright

BAND SAW - a stationary saw with a circular blade- a boat builder's friend

BEACH SEINE - a seine net just like the big boys use only smaller, operated from the shore

BEAUFORT SCALE - a scale of wind speed based on visual effects (whitecaps and such) from force 0 (less than 1 knot) to force 12 (hurricane)

BETWEEN WIND AND WAVE - the part of a hull by the waterline that is sometimes submerged and sometimes above water depending on the rolling of the vessel

BLOCKS - a single or multiple pulley with sheaves that line (rope) is pulled through. This rigging system helps control the load on lines from wind and sails.

BOAT SAUCE - a traditional penetrating preservative that smells so good, sometimes made of equal parts boiled linseed oil and turpentine with a dollop of pine tar

BOBSTAY - rigging of line, rod or wire, connected from the bowsprit down to the stem to counteract the upward tension of the forestay

BOLTROPE - a strong rope stitched to the edges of a sail to strengthen it

BOS'N CHAIR - (Bosun) - a wood or canvas seat rigged to a suspended line to aid working from aloft – padded ones are best!

BOW PULPIT - a raised safety rail at the front of the boat to lend a kind of security when working on the forward deck

BOWDITCH - Nathaniel Bowditch wrote "THE NEW AMERICAN PRACTICAL NAVIGATOR" in 1802 - still known as a mariner's "bible" for everything useful at sea - commonly just called "Bowditch"

BOWLINE - "bo-lin" - a simple, elegant knot, referred to as the king of the knots for its importance – mainly that it can be undone after a load is placed on it

BROAD REACH - a point of sail when the wind blows over a boat's quarter - between the beam (the widest part) and the stern (back) – my favorite point of sail

BROADSIDE – the whole side of a ship above the water line

BULKHEAD - a load-bearing wall inside the hull to help stiffen the boat or keep it watertight

BULWARKS - The extension of a ship's side above the level of the weather deck

CAMBER - the curved convex shape of the deck or house tops, side to side, to allow water to drain overboard

CAUL - The amniotic sac that encloses a fetus in the womb, to be "born in a caul" is rare – 1 in less than 80,000 births- or, the water never broke

CAY - "Key" A sand island on the surface of a coral reef

CENTER OF BUOYANCY - see LAUNCH DAY - page 74

CHAIN LOCKER - an enclosed space, generally low and forward in a boat to store anchor chain

CLUB - or "club jib"- a jib sail bent (lashed) to a boom, hinged at the stem head – a super clever way to tend a sail

COAMINGS - part of a boat above the deck to deflect water - i.e. cockpit or hatch.

COLORANT - additive in polyester resin layups – (so many whites)

CORK - properly spelled "CAULK" - to watertight a hull or deck by driving cotton or oakum into seams - some of us prefer to say cork

CUTTER - sailing rig with more than one headsail (jib or staysail)

DAMN THE TORPEDOES - phrase used to express disregard for danger

DEAD RECKONING - navigating by guesswork when sure-fire aids to navigation aren't available, based on presumed location, speed and current drift

DECOLLETE – French word "day-colle-tay" - a low neckline on a woman's garment

DISPLACEMENT - the volume of the hull of a boat which would otherwise be occupied by water

DOLDRUMS - part of the ocean near the equator known for calms where sailing ships can get stuck – it can be a real bummer

DRAW/DREW - or DRAUGHT of a boat - how deep the hull is in the water

DUMB END - the person holding the end opposite from the part being cut or fit. The dumb end wants a smart person

FALLING OFF - to change direction of sailing to point more downwind

FEATHERING OARS - turning the blade of the oars horizontal when leaving the water, which offers the least resistance to air while reaching for the next stroke while rowing

FETCH - the distance over which wave generating winds blow unimpeded by land -- big fetch can build big waves

FINISHING - the art of paint or varnish that "shines" a spotlight on the work done and grabs the eye. Finishers are goddesses and gods

FO'C'SLE - "fohk suhl" short for forecastle - the forward part of a ship below deck, traditionally used as crew's quarters

FORESTAY - rigging, wire or line – connected from the top of the mast leading forward and down to the bow, to support a boat's foremast

FLOTSAM - floating debris after a shipwreck

FREEBOARD - the distance between the waterline and the deck of a boat

GALE - wind that blows from 28 - 55 knots per hour or force 7 - 10 on the Beaufort scale. Don't leave port in one

GANGPLANK - a movable bridge used in boarding or leaving a boat or pier

GANTLINE - a line rove (passed through) a block hung from a mast, used to help raise rigging or workers in a padded seat bosun's chair

GEL COAT - the smooth, hard outside surface layer of a polyester resin structure

GHOSTING - sailing along on barely a zephyr

GILLNETTER - fish boat that set a vertically hung net from a buoy to the stern of the boat and traps migrating fish by their gills

GRID - a tidal grid is a framework that a boat hull accesses at high tide and sits upon securely for underwater work when the tide goes out. Generally next to a dock or pier to lean against. Mustn't tarry though, no time for popcorn. Tides wait for no one

GUDGEON - rudder fittings that attach to the transom, the half of a hinge with the hole, that the pintle fits into

GUNG HO - enthusiastic and eager to work together cooperatively

HARDTACK - a hard, long lasting dry biscuit used as food on long journeys

HEAVY WEATHER - a combination of high winds and rough seas which sometimes requires changes in passage plans to survival mode

HEAVING TO - slowing the boat's forward motion and fixing the helm and sails so no one has to steer

HEEL - the lean of a sailboat caused by the wind's force on the sails

HELM - to take over the steering of a vessel

HIGHLINER - a boat or commercial fisherman that brings in significant numbers of fish. Hanging a broom in the rigging of a fishboat indicates you've caught 100,000 fish so far for the season. So far! More brooms to come

HO249 TABLES - sight reduction tables used by sailors and pilots for finding latitudes with celestial navigation. Knowing math helps

HOMEWARD BOUNDER STITCH - a herringbone style sail repair done in a hurry

HORSESHOE STERN - stern of a boat shaped like a horseshoe as opposed to a transom. Built by stacking staggered timbers. Very attractive traditional fish boat design

HUZZAH - Olde English, said to express approval

JETSAM - floating debris purposely thrown overboard

IN IRONS or IN STAYS - when a sailboat has lost forward momentum while heading into the wind, unable to steer

JIBE, GYBE or GIBE - to swing a sail or boom across a following wind from one side of the boat to the other. Can be dangerous if unplanned

JIG - The structure that defines the shape that a boat is built over but not integral to

JOINERY - collective wooden components of a build – pieces of wood joined together to form complex items. i.e. doors, ladders, cabinets, fine wood-working...

KERF - the slit made by cutting with a saw

KNOCK DOWN - when a boat is knocked on its side 90 degrees, the mast may touch the water. A most unfortunate occurrence

LAMINATE - the building-block process of layering various-weight material, mixed with resin or glue to produce things like fiberglass boats or bathtubs

LAPSTRAKE or CLINKER - where the top and bottom edges of hull planks overlap each other in boat construction

LARGE SCALE CHART - a chart that covers a small area with a lot of detail

LASHING - using small line or wire to fasten something securely

LATITUDE - the distance of a place north or south of the equator expressed in degrees and minutes - the lines on the chart that go back and forth, not up and down

LAZARETTE - a small compartment below deck in the aft end of a boat, used for storage. Sometimes called "the Laz"

LAZY JACKS - a network of lines rigged on both sides of the mainsail, which holds it on top of the boom when the sail is lowered. Like having several extra hands onboard

LEE - or LEEWARD - on the side of the boat sheltered from the wind (downwind)

LIMBER HOLES - a hole through a timber to allow water to drain, especially used in bilges

LINES OF POSITION - a line on a chart that can be translated to a position on the earth. The intersection of two lines of position is called a "fix" and used to identify location when navigating

LOFTING - a drafting technique to generate the curved lines of a boat design into a three dimensional full size pattern for boat building. Knowing math helps here too

LONGITUDE - the distance of a place on the earth, east or west of Greenwich, England, expressed in degrees and minutes, the lines on the chart that go up and down, not back and forth

LUFF - the forward edge of the fore-n-aft sail next to the mast or stay

MAKING WAY - to move forward, make progress

MAL DE MER - French word for sea sickness – Try drinking ginger beer

MAT - light non-woven material of chopped strand glass fibers, starched together, used in fiberglass builds in combination with gel coat and in binding layers between roving

MAY DAY - implies a serious and life threatening emergency

MID-SHIPS - the middle part of the boat

MOLD - an opposite shaped structure that mirrors the finished shape of a glue up or laminated build

MOMDOM - the place where I and all moms reign

MOUSE - to wrap small wire or line around hardware or rigging to prevent loosening or accidental disconnection

NORTH PACIFIC HIGH - large high pressure area of the NE portion of the Pacific Ocean that is often calm and catches sailboats until it decides to let them go

NORTHER - a strong cold north wind.

NORTHING - distance sailing northward

O.G. - original – not old girl

OAKUM - traditional boat building material driven into seams to prevent water intrusion

ON THE HARD - when a boat is hauled out of the water and set up for work, generally in a boat yard

OVER-CANVASED - too much sail is set aloft for the wind conditions, a boat will feel unstable and can become dangerous

PAY OUT - letting out line or rope to slacken it

PEAK - the upper aftermost corner of a fore-n-aft sail

PELAGIC - living in the open ocean rather than coastal or inland waters

PILOT CHARTS - a chart showing compiled historical wind strengths and directions, temperatures, storm paths and information to aid the navigator

PINCHING - when a boat is steered too close to the direction of the wind, the sails will luff and forward motion is slowed. Falling off will help

PINTLE - the pin part that fits into the hole of the gudgeon, the hinge type hardware that connects the rudder to the transom

PIZZA CUTTER - traditional "corking" tool that looks like a pizza cutter and delivers cotton into very small seams when driving with a mallet would be overkill

POLYESTER - a type of resin used to laminate fiberglass boats and such

PORT TACK - historically called LARBOARD - wind blows from the port side of the boat (left, looking forward) – Port has four letters. Left has four letters. Port wine is red. Port running lights are red

PURSE SEINER - large fishing boat (58') that deploys a vertical wall of net between a powerful seine skiff and the stern of the boat. The bottom of the net is held down with lead-line, the top floated with corks, and looks like a purse when circled around a school of fish

RABBET - groove or notch in wood shaped to interlock with another piece of wood for strong joints

RIGHTING MOMENT - the force (of good) that restores a boat to upright equilibrium after a heel to the hull has altered the relationship between the vessel's center of buoyancy and center of gravity in an unstable way. Time to exhale

ROLL AND TIP - A method of painting by using a roller to slather on the product first then using a brush to smooth out lines and bubbles that the roller creates

ROVING - long strands of fiberglass woven material used in polyester layups. The building block that produces the strength of the structure

RUB RAILS - sacrificial hardwood mounted at the hull/deck joint, sometimes over a softwood sponson, to protect the hull and absorb impact from naughty objects

RUNNING - sailing in the same or nearly the same direction of the wind. Must stay awake for this one. One false move or inattention can jibe the main boom. Very bad

RUNNING BACKSTAYS - wire or line rigging mounted on the aft side of the mast at the forestay position mount. They are temporarily and individually attached to the windward side aft deck cleat and changed out as the tack and wind direction changes

SALT SORES - painful sores on skin from too much exposure to salt water and not enough fresh water baths – they really hurt, especially where you sit on them.

SCANDALIZING THE YARDS - To reduce the efficiency of a sail to slow the boat's speed. It is also a sign of mourning for a death aboard a ship

SCANTLING - dimensions of a piece of wood in boat building

SEMI-DIESEL - Pre-diesel - generally low speed 1 or 2 cylinder internal combustion engines that need hot metal to ignite the fuel and are fed by compressed air from a piston, driven by a kinda huge flywheel

SEXTANT - traditional navigational instrument used for measuring angular distances and altitudes from the deck of a moving boat to celestial bodies in our solar system, to establish your location on the big wild wonderful ocean

SHEETS - a line (or rope) used to trim a sail

SHIP'S COMPANY - the crew of a ship

SHIPWRIGHT - they build and repair every kind of boat in all kinds of weather. Bless 'em every one

SHOAL - shallow water

SHROUDS - A rope or metal cable that serves to support a mast from either side

SISTER FRAMES - new frames added side by side to original ones to strengthen or repair a boat. They can be steam bent or sawn

SKEG - can be the keel of a small boat, but generally an addition to the keel in the aft section, used to additionally support the rudder post or stern post

SLACK WATER - the period between an incoming and outgoing tide when there is no tidal-induced current

SLINGS OF A TRAVELIFT - industrial straps that raise and lower from a travelift machine that cradles a hull going in or out of the water

SMACKS - traditional sailing fishing boat that often contains a well to keep fish alive

SMALL SCALE CHART - a chart featuring a very large area with few details

SPONSON - a permanent piece of generally soft wood to mount a sacrificial hardwood guard to, on the hull

SPRING BACK - after unclamping wood that has been steam-bent on a frame, sometimes the shape will soften, so a slightly over-bent piece can be helpful

SQUARED AWAY - all difficulties have been resolved and the person is performing well and is mentally and physically prepared

STARBOARD TACK - wind blows from the starboard side of the boat (right, looking forward). Starboard running lights are green

STEAMBOX - a container that steam is piped into to "cook" wood prior to bending into shape. General rule of thumb is 1 hour per inch of thickness of wood

STEMHEAD - the top of the stem which is the forward most structural piece of a hull

S/V - sailing vessel

TACK, or COME ABOUT - changing course by bringing the vessel's head into and through the wind which puts the wind on the opposite side

THE BAY - San Francisco Bay. She blows like clockwork and the currents are fierce

TIDAL RAPIDS - when saltwater tidal currents are pushed through a narrow or shallow passage, creating waves, whirlpools and water speeds as high as 17 knots

TOE RAILS - wood trim on the outside of the deck, about very big, Paul Bunyan fat toe size

TOPSIDES - just the hull above the waterline – only the hull - not structures on deck - got it?

TRADE WINDS - two belts of winds that encircle the earth above and below the equator, the NE and SE trades generally, reliably blow and meet at the Doldrums

TRANSITING - to pass or cross through an area

TROLLER - a boat that catches fish one at a time by dragging lines with individual hooks. Generally thought of as the highest quality catch. Sometimes called a gentlemen's fishery

TURNBUCKLE - rigging hardware with screw threads, used to adjust shrouds, stays and rods that support the mast or bowsprit. Replaced traditional dead-eyes

WATER MAKER - a device that uses reverse osmosis of seawater to obtain potable water

WATERMAN - someone who lives and works on the water and is proficient in multiple fields of expertise; fishing, rowing, sailing, navigating...

WAYS, or SLIPWAY or MARINE RAILWAY - a structure, generally in a shipyard that hauls and launches a boat for repairs on a boat ramp with various kinds of engineering

WHITEHALL - a 19th century NewYork-designed lap-strake rowboat of 14 - 22 feet, with a wine-glass shaped transom, so beautiful and fast, the darling of any fleet

WINCH - A mechanical device for pulling lines (sheets or halyards) that make the mariner many times stronger than pulling without one

WING OUT - booming out the sails as far as they will go, perpendicular to the boat

YAWED - a side to side erratic movement of the bow and stern because of wave or wind strength. Sometimes when too much sail is aloft, a simple reduction – mo betta